God's World Science Series

# God's Inhabited World

## Grade 6

with special reference
to the
Book of Isaiah

**Rod and Staff Publishers, Inc.**
**P.O. Box 3, Hwy. 172**
**Crockett, Kentucky 41413**
Telephone: (606) 522-4348

**Rod and Staff Publishers, Inc.**

**Crockett, Kentucky 41413**

Printed in U.S.A.

ISBN 0-7399-0617-8

Catalog no. 14601

2 3 4 5 — 15 14 13 12 11 10 09 08 07

# In Appreciation

For the greatness of God and His wonderful world, we give thanks and praise. From the biggest galaxy to the smallest atom, we see the power and wisdom of God. To inspire our children with these wonders, that they might love and fear God, is a sacred privilege and responsibility. We are thankful for the freedom, ability, and resources to have Christian schools. We are thankful for the vision to publish textbooks that exalt God and are based on the truth of His Word. We are thankful for the church to whom God has given gifts to produce this science textbook, *God's Inhabited World.*

We are grateful to God for enabling Brother Lester Showalter to do the original writing. Many were involved in reviewing, classroom testing, and revising. Brother Seth Rudolph and Brother Marvin Eicher were the editors. As each did his part in response to the Lord of the church, there was a blending of efforts, for which we are thankful.

The publishing of this text does not yet meet its objective. These pages have not served their purpose until they become a tool for increasing knowledge about God's created world and, with that knowledge, inspiring the rising generation to worship and serve their Creator. As God has blessed the efforts to produce this textbook, may He further bless the teachers and students who use it.

*—The Publishers*

**Cover photo:** Pittsburgh at dusk. How does this picture show inhabitation by man? What kinds of energy are being harnessed?

# Contents

# Introduction

What is science? It is the study of God's created world. This study will teach you many things that are helpful in using God's creation. As you understand how something is made and how it works, you are better able to put it to good use.

By far the most important lessons you will learn are about God Himself. What good would it be to daily use the things God has created but not know about Him? The Israelite nation of the Old Testament should have known God, but they turned away from Him. "The ox knoweth his owner, and the ass his master's crib: but Israel doth not know, my people doth not consider" (Isaiah 1:3). That was part of the message God gave the prophet Isaiah to tell this wayward nation. God wanted Israel to consider who He was and to return to Him. One way He did this was to call their attention to the created world.

Over and over again, Isaiah reminded Israel of the created world, in verses such as this one: "I have made the earth, and created man upon it: I, even my hands, have stretched out the heavens, and all their host have I commanded" (Isaiah 45:12). What is so special about man being created upon the earth? The temperature, the air, and the other resources on the earth make it a suitable place for man to live. In contrast, the moon has no air for man to breathe. On Venus, man would die from the high temperature. Only on the earth are conditions right for man to live.

"For thus saith the LORD that created the heavens; God himself that formed the earth and made it; he hath established it, he created it not in vain, **he formed it to be inhabited:** I am the LORD; and there is none else" (Isaiah 45:18). That verse is the theme of this textbook. You will learn about many special features of the earth that make it a place to be inhabited. Was it an accident or the result of chance that the earth became suitable for living things? No; God planned it to be that way.

Many passages in the Book of Isaiah call our attention to Creation. You will notice that each lesson in this textbook begins with a verse from Isaiah. God desires that our minds be drawn to Him as we study the inhabited world He created.

God formed the earth to be inhabited.

The study exercises for each lesson are divided into two parts: "Study the Lesson" and "Apply the Lesson." "Study the Lesson" is a study guide for the lesson itself. Usually the questions in this section follow the text in order so that you can find the answers one after another as you read the lesson. Do not guess about an answer; search until you find the answer that you know is correct.

"Apply the Lesson" is a set of challenging questions, projects, and suggestions for further study related to the lesson. Your teacher may assign some of these items for homework. But more often you may want to do these exercises and activities on your own. No textbook can teach everything there is to know about God's world. One very impressive fact about the creation is that there is no end to what can be studied. Some of the projects involve actual investigation of the real earth and are not just a book study. You are encouraged to do these "Apply the Lesson" exercises as you are able.

The review lesson at the end of each unit is divided into three parts: Vocabulary, Facts, and Concepts. The Vocabulary section reviews the vocabulary words in that unit, which are found at the beginning of each lesson and also in the glossary at the back of the book. The Facts section reviews the basic facts that you should have learned in that unit.

In your study of God's world, you should go further than the memorization of meanings and facts. You should learn the lesson concepts as well. Facts answer the questions *what, when,* and *where.* Concepts answer the questions *how* and *why.* Vocabulary and facts involve *knowing* the lesson. Concepts involve *understanding* the lesson.

Beyond knowing and understanding, God wants us to gain something else from a study of His world. He wants us to believe in Him as the Creator. "That ye may **know** and **believe** me, and **understand** that I am he: before me there was no God formed, neither shall there be after me" (Isaiah 43:10).

## Creation Verses From Isaiah

"But they regard not the work of the LORD, neither consider the operation of his hands" (5:12).

"At that day shall a man look to his Maker, and his eyes shall have respect to the Holy One of Israel" (17:7).

"Shall the work say of him that made it, He made me not? or shall the thing framed say of him that framed it, He had no understanding? (29:16).

"O LORD of hosts, God of Israel, that dwellest between the cherubims, thou art the God, even thou alone, of all the kingdoms of the earth: thou hast made heaven and earth" (37:16).

"Hast thou not heard long ago, how I have done it; and of ancient times, that I have formed it? (37:26).

"Have ye not known? have ye not heard? hath it not been told you from the beginning? have ye not understood from the foundations of the earth? It is he that sitteth upon the circle of the earth, and the inhabitants thereof are as grasshoppers; that stretcheth out the heavens as a curtain, and spreadeth them out as a tent to dwell in" (40:21, 22).

"To whom then will ye liken me, or shall I be equal? saith the Holy One. Lift up your eyes on high, and behold who hath created these things, that bringeth out their host by number: he calleth them all by names by the greatness of his might, for that he is strong in power; not one faileth" (40:25, 26).

"Hast thou not known? hast thou not heard, that the everlasting God, the LORD, the Creator of the ends of the earth, fainteth not, neither is weary? there is no searching of his understanding" (40:28).

"That they may see, and know, and consider, and understand together, that the hand of the LORD hath done this, and the Holy One of Israel hath created it" (41:20).

"Thus saith God the LORD, he that created the heavens, and stretched them out; he that spread forth the earth, and that which cometh out of it; he that giveth breath unto the people upon it, and spirit to them that walk therein" (42:5).

"But now thus saith the LORD that created thee, O Jacob, and he that formed thee, O Israel, Fear not: for I have redeemed thee, I have called thee by thy name; thou art mine" (43:1).

"Bring my sons from far, and my daughters from the ends of the earth; even every one that is called by my name: for I have created him for my glory, I have formed him; yea, I have made him" (43:6, 7).

"I am the LORD, your Holy One, the creator of Israel, your King" (43:15).

"This people have I formed for myself; they shall shew forth my praise" (43:21).

"Thus saith the LORD that made thee, and formed thee from the womb" (44:2).

"Remember these, O Jacob and Israel; for thou art my servant: I have formed thee; thou art my servant: O Israel, thou shalt not be forgotten of me" (44:21).

"Thus saith the LORD, thy redeemer, and he that formed thee from the womb, I am the LORD that maketh all things; that stretcheth forth the heavens alone; that spreadeth abroad the earth by myself" (44:24).

"That they may know from the rising of the sun, and from the west, that there is none beside me.... I form the light, and create darkness: I make peace, and create evil: I the LORD do all these things" (45:6, 7).

"Drop down, ye heavens, from above, and let the skies pour down righteousness: let the earth open, and let them bring forth salvation, and let righteousness spring up together; I the LORD have created it. Woe unto him that striveth with his Maker!" (45:8, 9).

"I have made the earth, and created man upon it: I, even my hands, have stretched out the heavens, and all their host have I commanded" (45:12).

"For thus saith the LORD that created the heavens; God himself that formed the earth and made it; he hath established it, he created it not in vain, **he formed it to be inhabited:** I am the LORD; and there is none else" (45:18).

"And even to your old age I am he; and even to hoar hairs will I carry you: I have made, and I will bear; even I will carry, and will deliver you" (46:4).

"Hearken unto me, O Jacob and Israel, my called; I am he; I am the first, I also am the last. Mine hand also hath laid the foundation of the earth, and my right hand hath spanned the heavens: when I call unto them, they stand up together" (48:12, 13).

"Who art thou, that thou shouldest be afraid of a man that shall die, and of the son of man which shall be made as grass; and forgettest the LORD thy maker, that hath stretched forth the heavens, and laid the foundations of the earth" (51:12, 13).

"But I am the LORD thy God, that divided the sea, whose waves roared: The LORD of hosts is his name. And I have put my words in thy mouth, and I have covered thee in the shadow of mine hand, that I may plant the heavens, and lay the foundations of the earth, and say unto Zion, Thou art my people" (51:15, 16).

"For thy Maker is thine husband; the LORD of hosts is his name; and thy Redeemer the Holy One of Israel; The God of the whole earth shall he be called" (54:5).

"Behold, I have created the smith that bloweth the coals in the fire, and that bringeth forth an instrument for his work; and I have created the waster to destroy" (54:16).

"Thus saith the LORD, The heaven is my throne, and the earth is my footstool: where is the house that ye build unto me? and where is the place of my rest? For all those things hath mine hand made, and all those things have been, saith the LORD" (66:1, 2).

# Unit 1

# The Sun and Moon to Rule the Day and Night

"And God made two great lights; the greater light to rule the day, and the lesser light to rule the night" (Genesis 1:16).

Your life is strongly affected by the sun and somewhat by the moon. You work when the sun is in the sky. The moon shines at night, but it gives much less light. That is a convenient time to get your needed sleep.

The length of the year is controlled by the seasonal cycles, which in turn are controlled by the sun. The long days of summer and the shorter days of winter have much to do with your activities.

How is your life ruled by the moon? Even with the electric lights of modern times, you appreciate the soft light of the moon if you need to go outside at night. Those who live close to the ocean know that the moon causes the tides.

The sun and the moon are part of God's wise plan for life on the earth. God created the earth to be inhabited by living things. That is the theme of this science textbook. In this unit you will be considering how the sun and moon fit into this great theme.

## Lesson 1

# The Sun, Our Source of Energy

"That they may know from the rising of the sun, and from the west, that there is none beside me. . . . I form the light, and create darkness" (Isaiah 45:6, 7).

### Vocabulary

**solar** (sō′·lər), of the sun.

**solar system,** the sun and all the heavenly bodies in orbit around it.

**variable star,** a star that changes in brightness.

Every day we see the sun rise in the east, travel slowly across the sky, and set in the west. The sun is so familiar to us, and its journey is so regular, that we may not consider what a wonderful gift from God it is to us.

**The sun supports life on the earth.** The sun provides the right amount of heat and light for living things to survive. By God's command, the sun also holds the earth in place.

The earth is just one of nine planets revolving around the special star that we call the sun. The huge system including the sun and all the heavenly bodies traveling around it is called the ***solar system.*** The word *solar* is an adjective, meaning "of the sun." Not just any star would be suitable to serve as our sun.

**The sun is the right size.** The sun is not a little star, but neither is it the largest star in our sky. Some stars are about 1,000 times bigger than the sun—so huge that if one of those giant stars were put in place

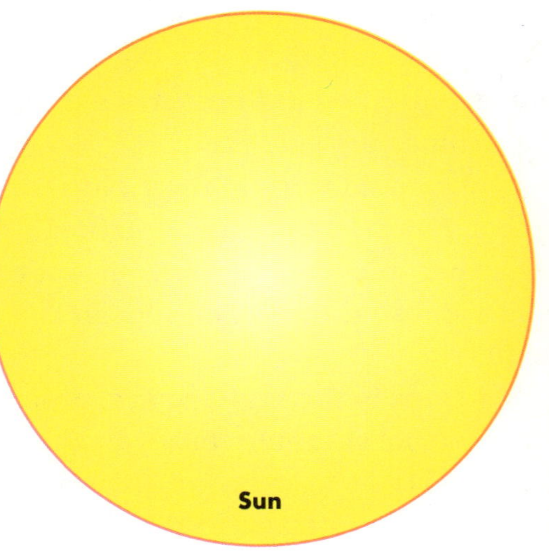


**White dwarf**

A white dwarf is a faint star about the size of the earth. It would take about 100 white dwarfs laid side by side to equal the distance through the sun. And it would take about 1000 suns laid side by side to equal the distance through a supergiant.

On this page, only a tiny part of the supergiant is shown. To show the entire model, the circle would cover a sheet of paper at least 217 feet across!

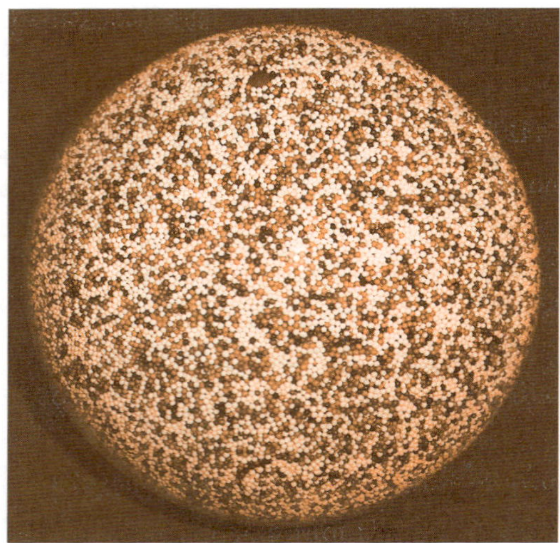

This model of the sun contains nonpareils (sugar pellets) to represent earths. How many earths could fit inside the sun?

of our sun, its edges would reach out past the earth!

Many stars are much smaller than the sun. Such stars would not have enough gravity to hold the earth in orbit. We can best understand the size of the sun by comparing it with the earth. It would take 109 earths laid side by side to equal the distance through the sun. If the sun were a big hollow ball, it would take more than one million earths to fill it!

God created the sun the right size so that its gravity holds the earth and the other planets in their proper orbits and so that we can live on the earth.

**The sun is the right brightness.** On a warm summer day, you may wish that the sun were not so bright. In fact, the sun is so bright that its rays can permanently damage your eyes if you look directly at it. Yet the sun is not too bright. The earth needs all this energy so that it will stay warm enough for us to live. The earth absorbs enough heat during the day to keep us warm through the night when the sun is not shining on our side of the earth.

Some stars give off much more light than the sun. If one of them were our sun, we would die from too much heat. But some stars are very dim or dark. If one of these dim stars were our sun, the earth would be freezing cold all the time. Nothing could live here. God made the sun neither too bright nor too dim. He made it just right.

**The sun is the right distance from the earth.** The amount of light and heat that the earth receives from the sun depends on two things: the brightness of the sun, and the distance of the earth from the sun. God established both of these to provide for life on the earth. The earth is 93 million miles (150 million km) away from the sun. That is far enough so that the earth is not too hot, and it is close enough so that the earth is not too cold.

What temperatures would be too hot and too cold? Your body must have water to live, and the same is true of plants and animals. You need water in the liquid state, not as ice or steam. If the earth were much closer to the sun, it would become so hot that the waters of the ocean would boil away. If the earth were much farther away, the oceans would freeze into solid ice. Then there could be no rain and no creeks or rivers to support life.

So you see that in many ways the earth is suited for man and other living things. The sun is the right size, the right brightness, and the right distance from the earth. Did all of this just happen by chance? We know better! God created everything just right so that there could be life on the earth.

## Study the Lesson

1. What three important things does the sun do for the earth?
2. The sun and all the heavenly bodies traveling around it are called the ——— system.
3. How many diameters of the earth would make the diameter of the sun?
4. The sun needs to be the right size so that
   a. we can weigh the right amount.
   b. the sun can be a steady star.
   c. its gravity will keep the earth in the proper orbit.
   d. the planets can revolve around the sun.
5. What two things determine the amount of heat and light the earth receives from the sun?
6. For life to exist, water must be in the ——— state.

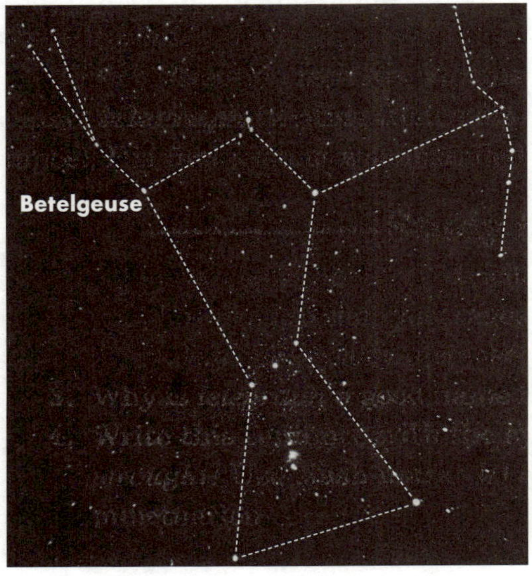


**The sun is a steady star.** Not all stars are as steady as the sun. One "unsteady" star that you have seen already is Betelgeuse on the right shoulder of Orion.

Another very "unsteady" star is in the constellation Cetus, which is just coming up over the eastern horizon in the evening skies of September. Cetus is thought to look like a sea dragon. About halfway up its neck is an interesting star called Mira. Sometimes this star is the brightest star in the constellation of Cetus. Then in about half

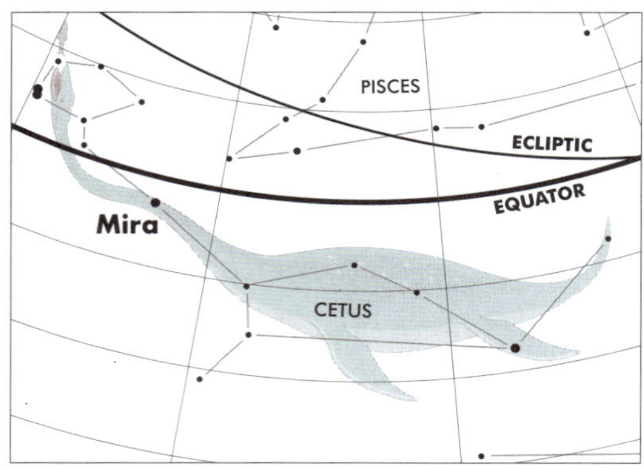


a year, it becomes so dim that it cannot be seen without a binocular. Such a star that changes in brightness is called a ***variable star.*** Some variable stars change from bright to dim and back again in a few hours. Others, like Mira, take many days to go through these changes.

Suppose a variable star like Mira were our sun. As the star grew brighter, the temperature on earth would climb higher and higher until all the water would boil. Then as the star grew dim, the earth would become so cold that all the plants would freeze. Life would be very miserable; in fact, there probably could be no life on the earth at all.

But the sun is not a variable star. The sun is a very steady star. Careful measurements from spacecraft have shown that the sun's brightness changes less than 1 percent. Because there is hardly any change, living things can continue to live on the earth.

As we have seen, many things are just right so that the earth has the right temperature range for living things. This was not an accident or the result of chance. According to Isaiah 45:18, God formed the earth "to be inhabited." In your study of science this year, you will learn many ways in which God made the earth especially for living things. Already in this lesson, you have seen the wonderful way He provided the right amount of heat and light for the earth.

### Facts About the Sun

(All numbers are approximate.)

Diameter: 865,000 miles (1,392,000 km). 109 earth diameters equal 1 sun diameter

Distance from the earth: 93,000,000 miles (150,000,000 km)

Time for light to travel from sun to earth: $8\frac{1}{3}$ minutes

Surface temperature: 10,000°F (5,500°C)

Rotation on axis: 27 days

Composition: hydrogen 75%, helium 25%, at least 70 other elements in small amounts

Surface gravity: 28 times earth gravity

The Fiery Sun

## Study the Lesson

7. Which of the following is a good synonym for *variable*?
   a. controlled c. rising
   b. bright d. changing
8. The sun is a ——— star and not a ——— star like Mira.
9. Who should receive credit for the wise way the solar system is made?
10. Choose the correct words, using the box at the end of the lesson.
    a. The diameter of the sun is about 1 (hundred, thousand, million) times as great as that of the earth.
    b. The sun is about 93 (thousand, million, billion) miles away from the earth.
    c. It takes (more, less) than 10 minutes for light from the sun to reach the earth.
    d. It takes (more, less) than 1 month for the sun to make one rotation on its axis.
    e. If it were possible to stand on the surface of the sun, you would weigh much (more, less) than you weigh on the earth.

## Apply the Lesson

1. The sun is 109 times larger than the earth. If the sun and the earth were reduced until the earth were as small as a softball (3.8 inches in diameter), how large would the sun be?
2. The circumference of the sun is about 2,700,000 miles. If you could travel 100 miles per hour on the surface of the sun, how long would it take you to go around the sun one time?
3. Why would a trip on the surface of the sun be impossible?
4. Fast airplanes can travel at the speed of sound (about 750 miles per hour). At that speed, how long would it take to travel from the earth to the sun?
5. Ask someone who knows the constellations to help you find Cetus. Is Mira visible now? If it is, check on it every week or so to see if it is getting brighter or dimmer. The cycle of Mira is about 330 days, so you cannot expect it to change very fast.
6. If you can borrow a light meter (such as used by photographers), use it with a bright light bulb in a dark room. Notice that the amount of light that falls on the light meter changes rapidly with changes in distance from the light. This will help you understand the great importance of having the earth the right distance from the sun, as planned by God.

## Lesson 2

# The Sun, an Active Star

"That they may see, and know, and consider, and understand together, that the hand of the LORD hath done this, and the Holy One of Israel hath created it" (Isaiah 41:20).

### Vocabulary

**aurora australis** (ə·rôr′·ə ô·strā′·lis), lights in the southern sky produced when the solar wind causes gases in the upper atmosphere to glow; also called *southern lights.*

**aurora borealis** (ə·rôr′·ə bôr′·ē·al′·is), lights in the northern sky produced when the solar wind causes gases in the upper atmosphere to glow; also called *northern lights.*

**helium** (hē′·lē·əm), a very light gas; an element first discovered on the sun.

**radiation,** the transfer of light and heat energy directly through space.

**solar flare,** a bright spot on the sun caused by a storm.

**solar wind,** a stream of fast-moving particles from the sun.

**sunspot,** a dark, round spot on the sun caused by a storm.

From the earth, the sun looks like a quiet, bright light bulb in the sky. Day after day, from 93 million miles away (150 million km), it pours out enough heat energy to keep us warm. The sun not only shines on the earth, but it also sends out its rays in all directions. In comparison to the total space lit by the sun's rays, the earth

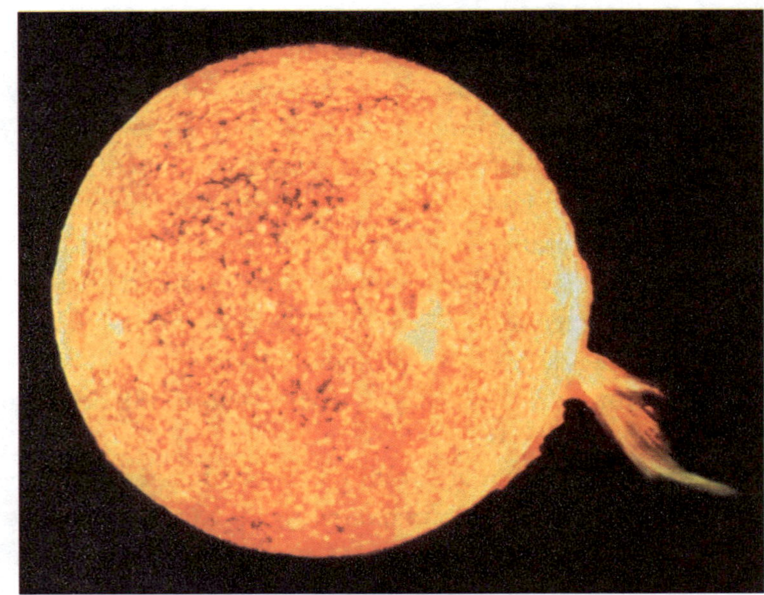

A large solar flare can extend 500,000 miles and release enormous amounts of energy.

is only a tiny spot. Further, the sun is more like a roaring furnace than a glowing light bulb.

**Activity on the sun's surface.** The surface of the sun is far from being a calm, bright sea of light. Rather, it has great flames that leap, fall, and churn in constant activity. Violent activity on the sun's surface is called a sun storm. Such a storm may last from a few days to a few weeks. The number of sun storms increases and decreases in 11-year cycles. In one part of the cycle, there may be more than 100 storms at once. Then 5½ years later, there may be almost none.

Storms cause some areas on the surface of the sun to be cooler and to

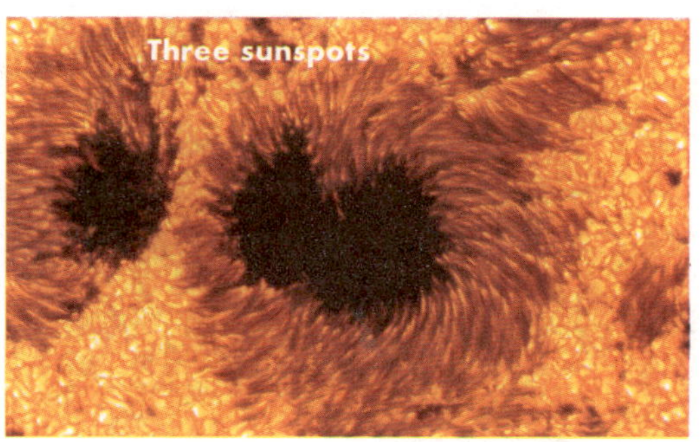


appear darker than the rest of the sun. These are called ***sunspots.*** Some sunspots appear as dots; others are large irregular patches with fuzzy edges. They can change in size and shape from day to day and are often clustered together. Sunspots can easily be seen on projected images of the sun.

Sun storms also cause some areas

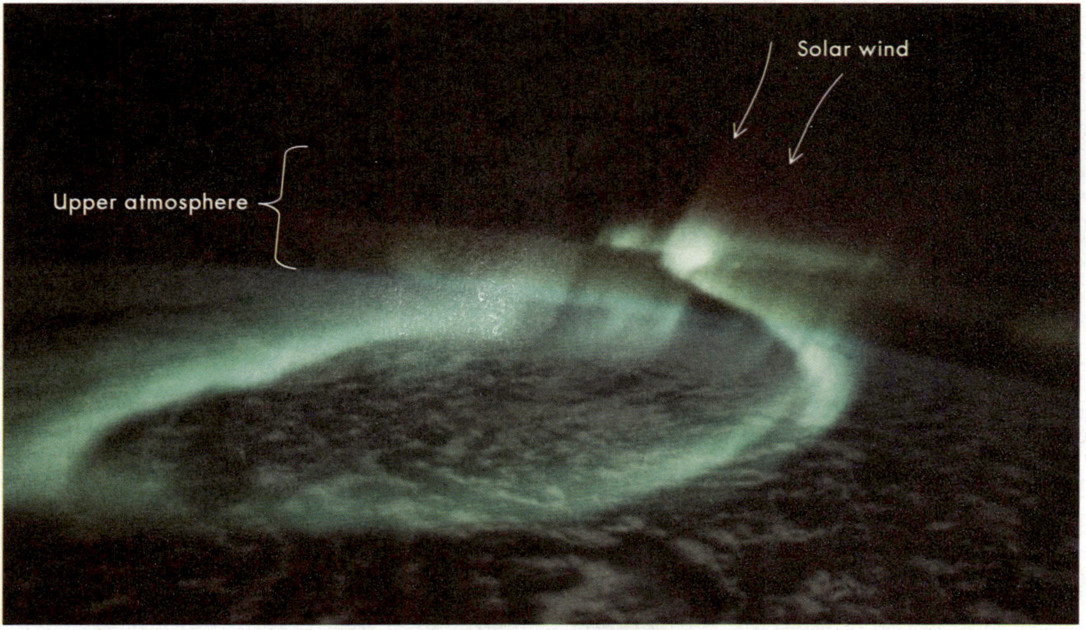


This view of the aurora from outer space shows solar wind colliding with the upper atmosphere and producing light. The gray patches on the earth are clouds in the lower atmosphere.

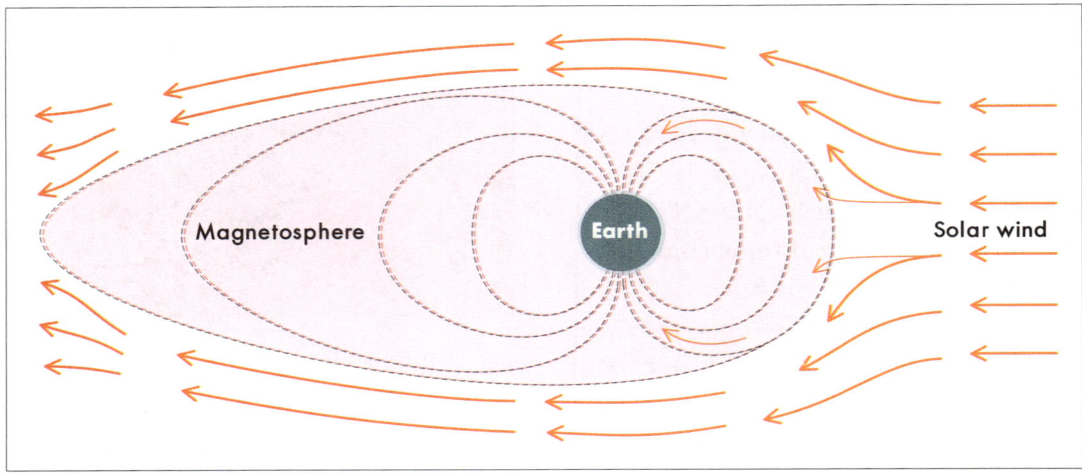


Earth's core generates a large magnetic field. The part above the atmosphere is called the magnetosphere, which pushes aside most of the solar wind. The lee side is not drawn to scale; it is many times longer.

of the sun to appear extra bright. These areas are called ***solar flares.*** A flare may last from 10 minutes to an hour. Rarely are they large enough to be seen with a small telescope, but small flares are common.

Solar flares can also be thought of as explosions or eruptions. Just as a volcano sends off clouds of dust and lava, a solar flare sends off a stream of particles from the sun. This fast-moving stream of particles is called ***solar wind.***

As the earth travels through space, it collides with solar wind. These particles from the sun would be harmful to us if God had not provided two wonderful protections. One protection is the atmosphere. Another important protection is the earth's magnetic field. Men have used the magnetic field of the earth for centuries to guide their ships with compasses. But God has been using it since Creation to protect living things from the solar wind.

The earth's magnetic field attracts some particles of solar wind and draws them into the atmosphere near the North Pole and the South Pole. Here the solar particles collide with air and produce the ***aurora borealis,*** or northern lights, and the ***aurora australis,*** or southern lights. The atmosphere glows much like a fluorescent light. The farther north you live, the more often you will see the aurora borealis. To many people in Canada, they are a common sight. Near the peak of the 11-year cycle of sun storms, there are more northern lights. An especially strong solar wind can cause spectacular displays that can be seen over much of the United States.

**How to Look for Sunspots** (the projection method)

**WARNING: Never look at the sun through a telescope or binocular.** The concentrated rays of the sun can cause instant blindness. A telescope can be used to safely project the image of the sun on a white surface. (If a binocular is used, cover the one lens so that only one side of the binocular will be used.) The telescope should be fastened to a tripod or similar stand so that it will give a steady image. Cut a hole in a large piece of cardboard, and put the eyepiece of the telescope through the hole. The cardboard will act as a sun shield to cast a shadow on the surface where you want to project the sun.

Hold another piece of cardboard (with white paper on it) about 2 feet away from the eyepiece. Adjust the telescope until it is pointed toward the sun. You can tell when it is pointed correctly by watching the shadow of the telescope on the sun shield. By moving the telescope about a bit, you should soon see a bright spot projected on your white paper. By adjusting the eyepiece back and forth, you can make the telescope focus the sun clearly on the white paper. The farther away you hold the paper, the bigger the image of the sun will be.

## Study the Lesson

1. Write a vocabulary word from this lesson for each description.
   a. Transfer of light and heat energy directly through space.
   b. Glow in the upper atmosphere near the North Pole, caused by solar wind.
   c. Brief storm that makes a bright spot on the sun.
   d. Glow in the upper atmosphere near the South Pole, caused by solar wind.
   e. Dark area on the surface of the sun.
2. Why is it dangerous to look at the sun through a telescope?
3. How long is it from one time of many sunspots to the next time?
4. The harmful particles of the solar wind are attracted by the ——— ——— of the earth.
5. The best displays of aurora borealis occur during times of (many, few) sunspots.

**Heat through empty space.** How do light and heat travel from the sun to the earth without wires or pipes to carry them? Light and heat travel by ***radiation.*** Radiation is the transfer of heat and light from one object to another without affecting the space and air between the two. If you point a flashlight into clear air at night, you can hardly tell that the flashlight is turned on. But if you point it at a house, it lights up the outside wall and the surrounding area looks bright. If you hold your hand a few inches in front of a hot electric iron, your hand feels warm, not because hot air is heating it but because heat is radiating directly from the iron to your hand.

Radiation is a very fast way for heat to travel. It carries heat energy from the sun through 93 million miles of empty space to reach the earth. Without radiation, the earth would be cold no matter how hot the sun was.

**How the sun produces energy.** This marvel has puzzled men for many centuries. They knew that burning fuel could not last long enough to make heat for thousands of years. Only recently did men discover what materials or elements the sun is made of and how the sun produces its energy.

Scientists discovered in 1854 that by studying the light from stars, they could tell what elements are on the stars. Each element produces its own special pattern of colors in light. When a prism is used to divide starlight into colors, the elements on that star can be identified.

In 1868, scientists using this method discovered an element on the sun that was not yet known on the earth. They called the element ***helium*** to indicate that it was a sun element. (The Greek word for "sun" is *helios.*) In fact, men learned that nearly one-fourth of the sun is helium. The other three-fourths is mostly hydrogen.

The center of the sun is very hot, possibly about 27,000,000°F (15,000,000°C). At this extreme temperature, small particles of hydrogen unite to form helium. This combining action produces the great amount of energy that we receive as light and heat from the sun. As the hydrogen and helium vapor move out from the core of the sun, their temperature falls to about 10,000°F (5,500°C) near the surface of the sun.

Since its discovery on the sun, men have found helium on the earth. Helium is mixed with natural gas that comes from some gas wells. Maybe you have

A beam of light shining on a house

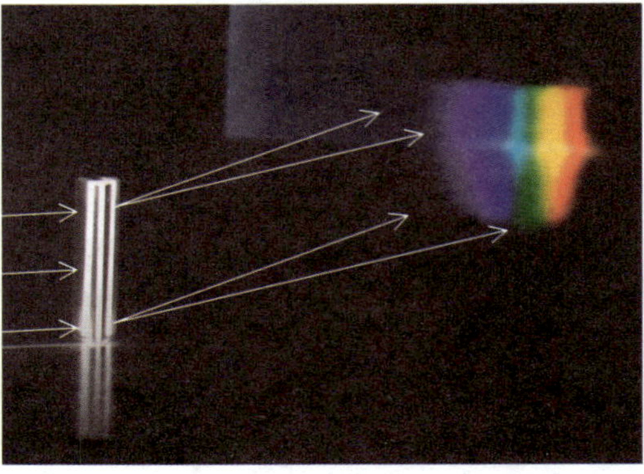

A prism separates sunlight into different colors.

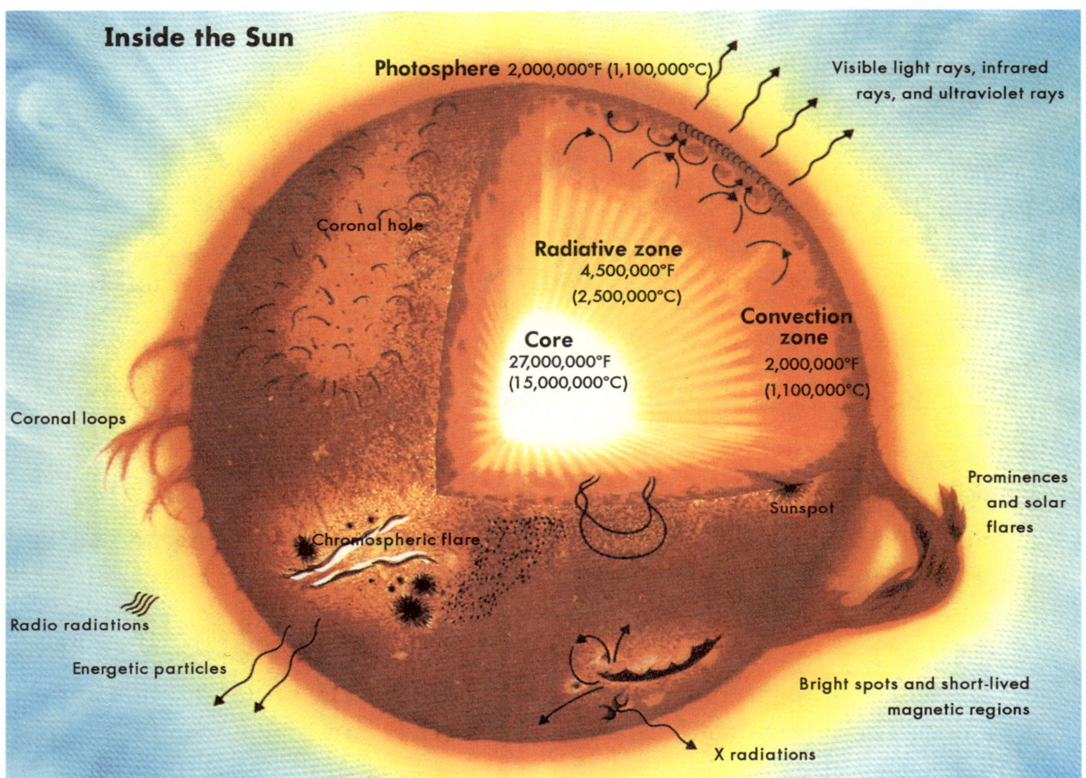


The sun's energy is produced in the core and radiates to the convection zone. Then it flows mostly by convection currents to the photosphere. From there, it radiates into space.

played with a balloon that was filled with helium. Such a balloon will rise in the air because helium is lighter than air. The next time you see a helium balloon, remember that helium was first discovered on the sun and that it is part of the wonderful way God made the sun to produce so much heat and light.

## Study the Lesson

6. Light and heat from the sun reach the earth by ———.
7. Which of the following is similar to the way heat gets to us from the sun?
   a. Cold hands get warm when you hold them a short distance away from a hot stove.
   b. Cold hands get warm when you blow your warm breath on them.
   c. Cold hands get warm when you hold them in the hot air rising from a stove.
   d. Cold hands get warm when you hold them against a warm radiator.
8. How did scientists decide what the materials are on the sun?

9. How did the element helium get its name?
10. The sun is made of about one-fourth ——— and three-fourths ———.
11. In producing the sun's energy, particles of ——— unite to form ———.

## Review Exercises

Turn to the lesson number in brackets if you need help.

1. The sun is a steady star and not a ——— star like Mira. [1]
2. How many earth diameters would it take to equal the diameter of the sun? [1]
3. Water must be in the ——— state for life to exist. [1]
4. The sun is about ——— miles away from the earth. [1]

## Apply the Lesson

1. The sun radiates energy in all directions from its surface. Only an extremely small fraction of the sun's energy reaches the earth. Imagine yourself standing on the surface of the sun and looking at the earth. It would be a very small disk 93 million miles away. By the time the sun's energy reaches the earth, it has spread to a sphere with a surface area of about 110,000,000,000 million square miles (that is, 110 billion million square miles). The tiny disk of the earth has an area of only about 50 million square miles. Calculate the fraction of the sun's energy that the earth receives, by dividing the larger number by the smaller.
2. A peak of sunspot activity occurred in the spring of 2001. Would you expect to find many, some, or few sunspots if you looked today? Would you expect the number of sunspots to be more or less a year from now?
3. Keep a record of sunspots over a period of several weeks. Use the method given on page 21 for viewing the sun with a telescope or binocular. Make several copies of a circle about 6 inches across. Project the image of the sun on the circle, and trace in the spots that can be seen. Date each sheet. Compare the drawings. Can you see evidence that the sunspots change in size, shape, or number? Can you detect the rotation of the sun?
4. The following words from this lesson would make interesting subjects for further study in encyclopedias and books about astronomy.

   aurora borealis    helium    hydrogen    sunspots

   Write a report on one of these things to share with the rest of the class.

## Lesson 3

# The Moon to Rule the Night

"And it shall come to pass, that from one new moon to another, ... shall all flesh come to worship before me, saith the LORD" (Isaiah 66:23).

### Vocabulary

**crater,** a bowl-shaped hole on the surface of the moon.

**phase,** one of the different shapes in the monthly cycle of the moon.

**ray,** one of the lines extending out from a crater.

**satellite,** a heavenly body in orbit around a planet.

**sea,** one of the smooth, dark areas on the surface of the moon.

**tide,** the rise or fall of the ocean surface because of the gravity of the moon.

God created the moon to be "the lesser light to rule the night." He knew we needed the darkness of night for sleep. He made the moon to be just the right night-light so that we can see to walk at night, yet it is not so bright that it disturbs our sleep.

The moon is the only satellite that God made for the earth. A ***satellite*** is a heavenly body that revolves around a planet. Some planets have a number of satellites, but the earth has only one.

**Why does the moon appear as it does?** The moon looks sometimes like a thin, curved slice and sometimes like a half circle. At other times it is a bright, full circle. Do you know what causes these changes?

First of all, the light of the moon is reflected from the sun. The part of the moon where the sun is not shining looks dark. We do not always see the whole side of the moon that is lighted by the sun.

Being a satellite of the earth, the moon travels around the earth. That means we see the moon at different angles as it revolves around the earth. We can see the full circle of the moon when it is on the side of the earth away from the sun. We call this a full moon. The full moon is one of the ***phases,*** or shapes, of the moon.

When the moon is out to the side of the earth, we can see only one quarter of the total moon's surface. That is why this is called the quarter phase. When the moon is on the same side of the earth as the sun, the dark side of the moon is toward the earth. This is called a new moon because the moon is about to start a new cycle of going through

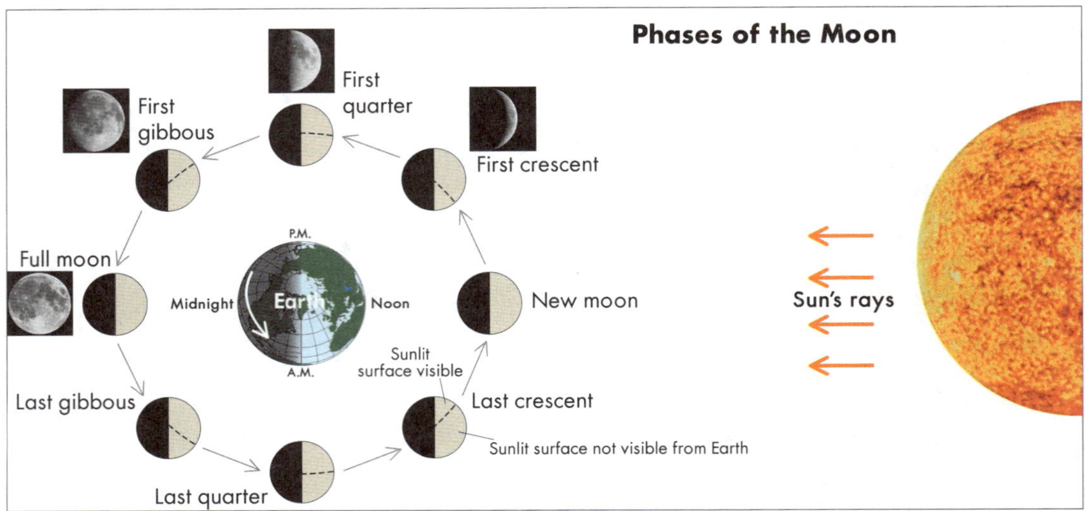


its different phases. The diagram shows the positions of the sun, earth, and moon that make the eight phases of the moon.

Between one new moon and the next there are 29½ days. This is very nearly one month. The word *month* comes from the word *moon*.

Many calendars show the dates for four phases of the moon: new moon, first quarter, full moon, and last quarter. These dates can help you know when to look for the moon, since it is not always visible in the sky. The phases from new moon to full moon are best seen in the evening sky. The phases from full moon to new moon are best seen in the morning sky.

## Study the Lesson

1. The earth has (one, four, seven) satellite(s).
2. First quarter and last crescent are two ——— of the moon.
3. Make a diagram to show the position of the sun, earth, and moon at first quarter. Also make a drawing to show what the first quarter moon looks like.
4. The light of the moon comes from the ——— and is ——— by the moon.
5. Copy the following list, filling in the missing phases.

   new moon, ———, ———, first gibbous, ———, ———, last quarter, ———, new moon

6. From one full moon to the next full moon is ——— days.
7. The first crescent could be seen

   a. at 9:00 P.M. b. at midnight. c. at 3:00 A.M.

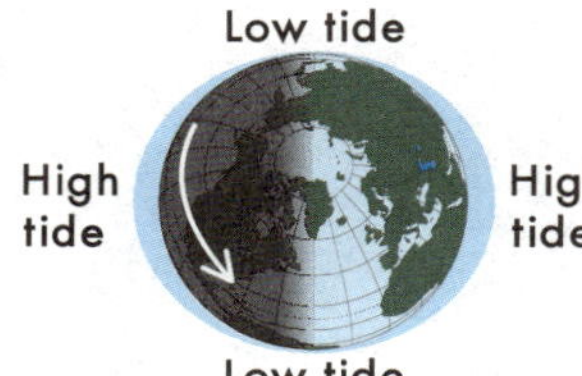


**The moon causes the ocean tides.** The gravity of the earth holds the moon in its orbit. The gravity of the moon also pulls on the earth. It causes the ocean water to bulge outward on the side of the earth toward the moon. This rise of ocean water is a high ***tide.*** There is also a high tide on the opposite side of the earth. Between these high tides, the oceans are lower, making low tides. As the earth rotates on its axis, the tides move westward across the oceans. There are 6 hours between each high tide and low tide. There are two high tides and two low tides each day.

From the moon phases of the calendar, you can predict when the tides will be. At full moon and new moon, high tides will be at midnight and

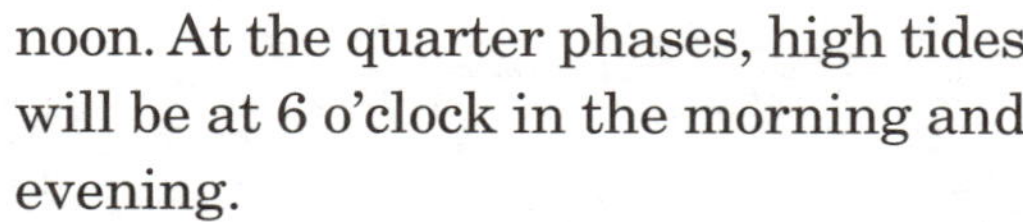

noon. At the quarter phases, high tides will be at 6 o'clock in the morning and evening.

**Interesting features on the moon.** From the earth, the moon looks white and golden. But the surface of the moon is far from white. The moon is covered with dark gray soil and rocks. This gives the moon just the right brightness for our nighttime. If the moon were white, it would shine so brightly that it could disturb our sleep.

The dark areas you can see on the moon are extra smooth and are called ***seas.*** The light areas are covered with mountains and large circular holes called ***craters.*** If you want to look at the mountains and craters with a binocular or telescope, the best time is at the quarter phases when shadows make them very distinct.

Some of the craters have lines extending out from them. These lines are called ***rays.*** At full moon, you can see the long rays of one of the craters called Tycho.

The high tide at the Bay of Fundy, New Brunswick, is nearly 40 feet higher than the low tide.

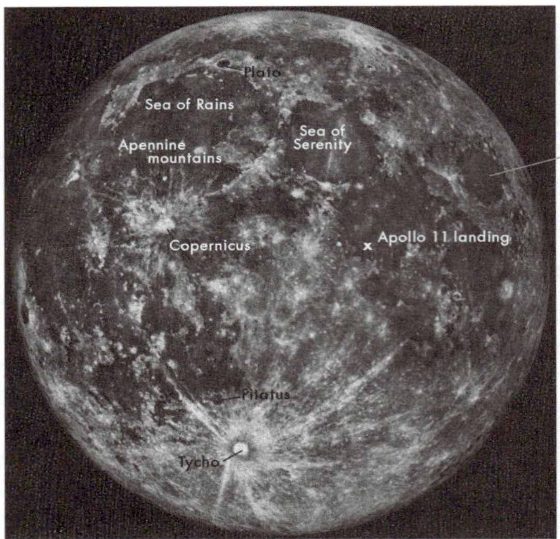

Near side of the moon

Far side of the moon

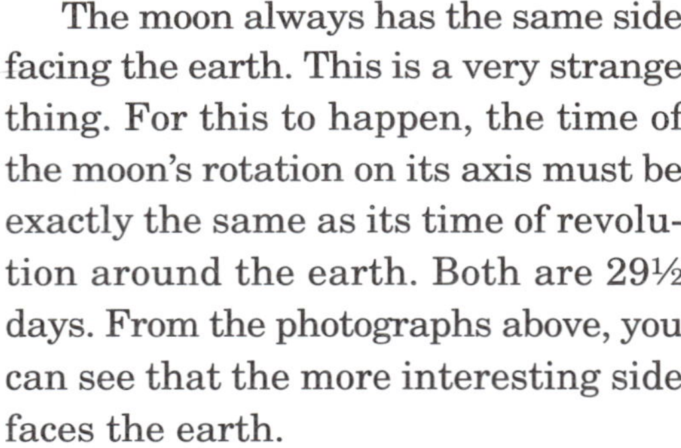

The moon always has the same side facing the earth. This is a very strange thing. For this to happen, the time of the moon's rotation on its axis must be exactly the same as its time of revolution around the earth. Both are 29½ days. From the photographs above, you can see that the more interesting side faces the earth.

**No life on the moon.** The moon is not at all suited for life.

- There is no water on the moon. Living things must have water.
- There is no air on the moon. This means there is no air to breathe, no cool breeze on a hot day, and no air pressure to keep your arms and legs from swelling so much that you could not move.
- When night turns into day on the moon, the temperature changes from being too cold for life to being too hot for life.

The gravity on the moon is only about one-sixth of the earth's gravity. If you can jump a foot high on the earth, you could jump 6 feet high on the moon! This small amount of gravity would make walking more difficult and make it harder to keep things from moving about.

Nothing lives on the moon—no plants, no animals, and no people. When men went to the moon in the late 1960s and early 1970s, they had

An astronaut needs a large, bulky life-support system to stay alive on the moon.

to take along all the food, water, and air that they needed to live. They wore special suits to give their bodies the pressure they needed. God did not create the moon for life. He created it to reflect sunlight so that we have light at night.

The moon is a very interesting satellite. Not only does it give a little light at night, but it also tells us of the glory of the great God who created it. The world God created is orderly, interesting, and beautiful. The moon is part of that marvelous world.

Moon surface

**Facts About the Moon**

(All numbers are approximate.)

Diameter: 2,160 miles (3,480 km). $3\frac{2}{3}$ moon diameters equal 1 earth diameter

Distance from the earth: 239,000 miles (384,000 km)

Period of cycle of phases: 29½ days

Temperature extremes: 260°F (127°C) to −280°F (−173°C)

Atmosphere: none

Surface gravity: about $\frac{1}{6}$ of the earth's gravity

## Study the Lesson

8. There was a high tide at 2:00 P.M.
   a. When will the next low tide be?
   b. When will the next high tide be?
9. Write the term for each of these features of the moon.
   a. darker, smooth areas
   b. circular, dish-shaped holes
   c. lines spreading out from a point
10. What two things does the moon not have, which are needed for life?
11. The temperature on the moon is both too ——— and too ——— for living things.
12. A person who weighs 120 pounds on the earth would weigh ——— pounds on the moon.

## Review Exercises

Turn to the lesson number in brackets if you need help.

1. Heat and light travel through empty space by ———. [2]
2. Dark spots on the sun are called ———, and their number increases and decreases in a cycle of about ——— years. [2]
3. The sun is made mostly of the elements ——— and ———. [2]
4. The sun is about ——— miles away from the earth. [1]

## Apply the Lesson

1. Use a calendar that shows phases of the moon to answer these questions.
   a. Find the day of the month for the new moon in January and in December (of the same year). How do these two days compare?
   b. Does the lunar (moon) month move ahead of the calendar month, or does it fall behind?
2. Follow the moon through its phases. Check a calendar to find what phase the moon is in today. Draw circles with 1-inch diameters for each day of a month. For all the nights you can see the moon, draw in its shape. To see some of the phases, you will need to get up before dawn.

   New moon | First crescent | First quarter | First gibbous | Full moon | Last gibbous | Last quarter | Last crescent

3. The Jews of Bible times used the moon to mark off their months. Write the letters of the following verses that refer to such use of the moon.
   a. Joshua 10:13
   b. 1 Samuel 20:5
   c. 2 Kings 4:23
   d. 2 Kings 23:5
   e. 1 Chronicles 23:31
   f. Job 25:5
   g. Psalm 72:7
   h. Psalm 81:3
   i. Isaiah 1:13
   j. Isaiah 60:19
   k. Ezekiel 46:1
   l. Amos 8:5
4. Go crater hunting. Even a small telescope or pair of binoculars with good lenses will show the biggest craters. On a labeled photograph of the moon in an encyclopedia, find the craters called Copernicus, Eratosthenes, Archimedes, and Tycho; then find them on the evening moon between first quarter and first gibbous. Many telescopes turn the moon upside down when you look at it. Some books print the photograph that way too, so you may need to consider that in trying to find the craters.
5. Set up a tide timetable for your area (even if you do not live near the ocean). The time of the tides moves forward about 50 minutes each day. Suppose the full moon is on September 15. The timetable for three days might look like the one below.

| | High Tide | Low Tide | High Tide | Low Tide |
|---|---|---|---|---|
| September 15 | 1:00 A.M. | 7:00 A.M. | 1:00 P.M. | 7:00 P.M. |
| September 16 | 1:50 A.M. | 7:50 A.M. | 1:50 P.M. | 7:50 P.M. |
| September 17 | 2:40 A.M. | 8:40 A.M. | 2:40 P.M. | 8:40 P.M. |

This chart will be approximate, since it does not take into account everything that affects the exact time of the tides.

## Lesson 4

# Eclipses

"Behold, I will bring again the shadow of the degrees, which is gone down in the sun dial of Ahaz, ten degrees backward. So the sun returned ten degrees, by which degrees it was gone down" (Isaiah 38:8).

### Vocabulary

**lunar** (lo͞o′·nər), of the moon.

**lunar eclipse** (i·klips′), the darkening of the moon by the shadow of the earth.

**solar eclipse,** any darkening of the sun by the moon. A solar eclipse is *partial* if only part of the sun is covered. It is *annular* if all of the sun is covered except a thin ring around the edge. It is *total* if the sun is completely covered.

A source of light will make a shadow when an object comes between the light and the surface where the light falls. That is the principle of the sundial. An upright arm casts a shadow on a dial that is marked off in hours or degrees.

The sun is a very bright source of light. Both the earth and the moon cast a shadow. The moon can cast a shadow on the earth, and the earth can cast a shadow on the moon. This causes the two kinds of eclipses that you will study in this lesson.

**Eclipse of the moon.** When the earth comes between the sun and the moon, it casts a shadow on the moon. Then the moon becomes dark. This is called a ***lunar eclipse.*** The word *lunar* is an adjective, meaning "of the moon." Anyone who faces the moon at the time of the lunar eclipse can see the shadow of the earth passing across the moon. Since the earth must be between the sun and the moon, a lunar eclipse can happen only during a full moon phase.

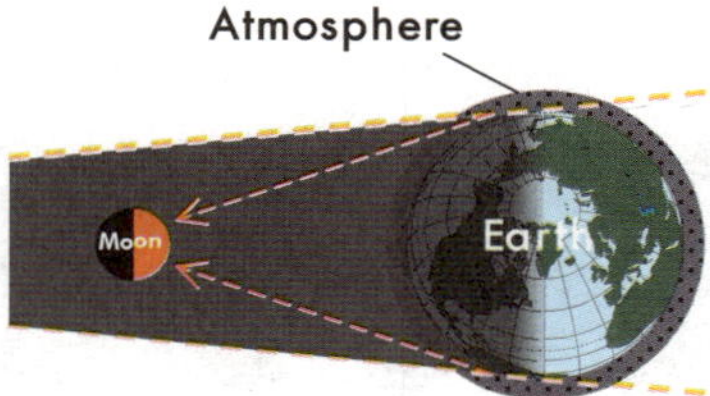


A lunar eclipse. As the sunlight passes through the atmosphere, the light rays bend and cause the moon to receive enough reddish light to be faintly visible.

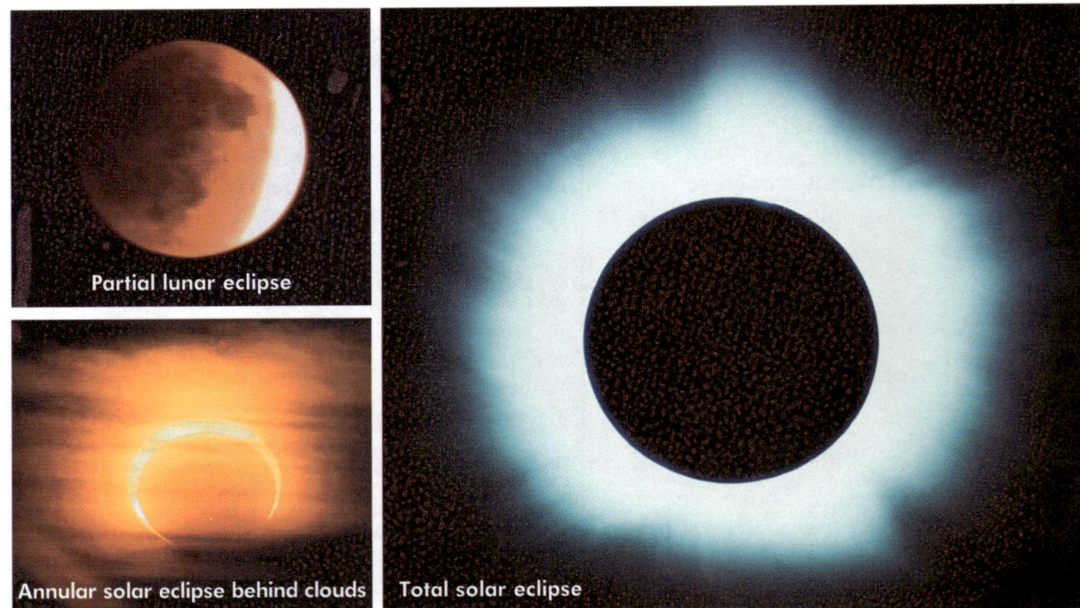

Partial lunar eclipse

Annular solar eclipse behind clouds

Total solar eclipse

What is it like to see a lunar eclipse? As the time of the eclipse approaches, the moon shines full and bright. Then one edge of the moon begins to darken very slowly. As the shadow of the earth progresses across the moon, you can see that the edge of the shadow is curved. The edge is very fuzzy, but there is enough of an outline to see that it is curved. The curve comes from the curved edge of the earth. The curve of this shadow shows how much bigger the earth is than the moon. This was the first visible evidence men had that the earth is a sphere.

In about an hour, the shadow of the earth completely eclipses the moon. The moon is now very dark, yet you can still see a faint copper color on the moon. It is reddish because of the sunset colors of sunlight coming through the earth's atmosphere. What a strange-looking moon!

The moon stays that way for about an hour while the big shadow of the earth passes over it. Then the side of the moon that first became dark

In the solar eclipse shown here, the moon gradually moves from right to left as it covers the sun. At the time of total eclipse, the sun's outer atmosphere flashes into view. The sun reappears as the moon moves on.

begins to brighten a little. The curved shadow of the earth moves slowly off the face of the moon, and finally the moon is again as bright and full as it was before. The whole eclipse may take about three hours from start to finish.

**Eclipse of the sun.** When the moon comes between the sun and the earth, it casts a shadow on the earth. For the people living in the area of this shadow, the sun will be covered by the moon. This is called a ***solar eclipse.*** Remember that *solar* is an adjective, meaning "of the sun."

A solar eclipse can happen only at the new moon phase when the moon passes between the sun and the earth. The shadow of the moon is smaller than the face of the earth, so only a path on the earth will be in the shadow as it sweeps across the surface of the earth. Only people in that path will be able to observe the solar eclipse.

What is it like to see a solar eclipse? There are really three kinds of solar eclipses. During a *partial* solar eclipse, only part of the sun is covered. Very slowly a black disk moves over

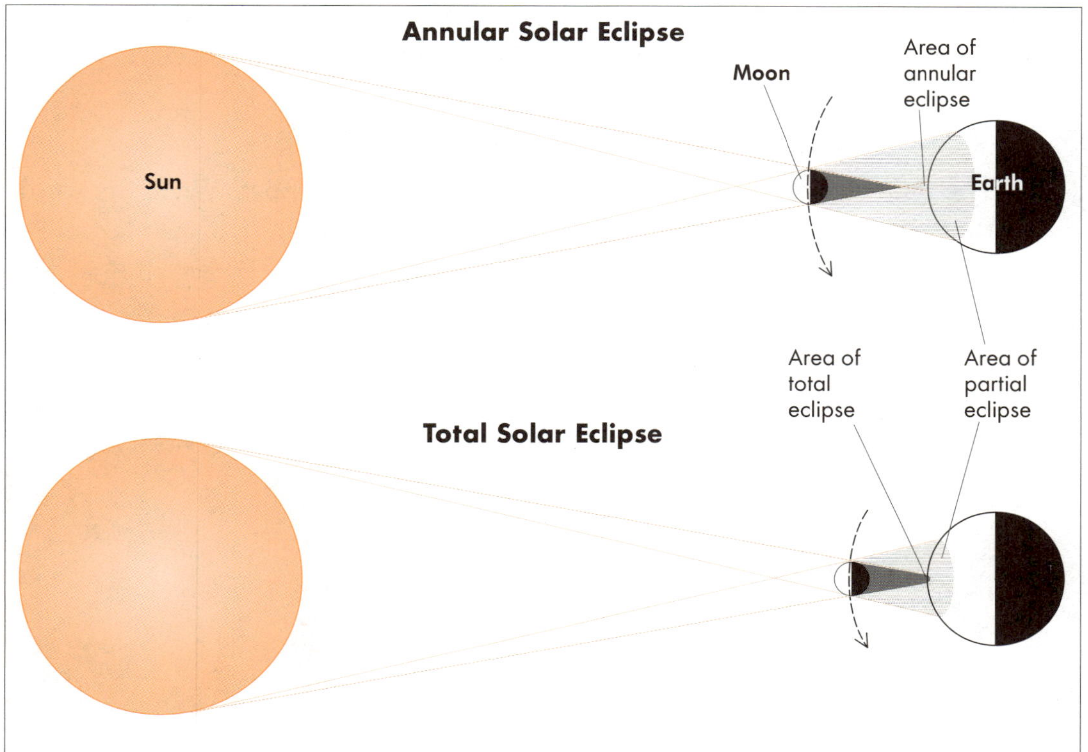


In an annular eclipse, the moon does not completely cover the sun, because it is farther away from the earth. In a total eclipse, the moon is closer to the earth and completely covers the sun.

part of the sun and then off again, without making the entire sun dark. The edge of the shadow is very sharp. There is no fuzziness about it. The curve is much smaller than that of a lunar eclipse, since the moon is much smaller than the earth. As the disk of the moon moves across the sun, it looks as if something is taking a bite out of the sun.

During an *annular* solar eclipse, all of the sun is covered except a thin ring around the edge. *Annular* means "like a ring." The sky becomes very dark during an annular eclipse, but not as dark as night. Yet it is very strange to see the sun as a ring.

The most wonderful eclipse of all is a *total* solar eclipse. During such an eclipse, the moon completely covers the bright face of the sun. Then for about five minutes, it is almost as dark as night. Some of the brightest stars become visible. The animals quiet down, thinking night has come.

Even more interesting is what can be seen around the eclipse itself. Since the bright disk of the sun is blacked out, observers can see huge tongues of glowing gases streaming from the sun far out into space. It is a very special privilege to live in the path of a total solar eclipse. People will travel hundreds or thousands of miles to witness such an extraordinary event.

## Study the Lesson

1. The following chart compares a lunar and a solar eclipse. Write the words that belong in the lettered boxes.

| | Lunar | Solar |
|---|---|---|
| Body that is hidden | a. | b. |
| Body that causes the shadow | c. | d. |
| Body where the shadow falls | e. | f. |
| Which phase of the moon | g. | h. |
| When it occurs (day or night) | i. | j. |
| Size of shadow (large or small) | k. | l. |
| Appearance of shadow's edge | m. | n. |
| Moon's color when total | o. | p. |

2. Write words from the list on the right to match the words on the left.

| | |
|---|---|
| a. lunar | darkening |
| b. solar | ring |
| c. eclipse | sun |
| d. partial | incomplete |
| e. annular | moon |

3. What was the first visible evidence men had that the earth is a sphere?
4. Name the kind of solar eclipse described by each phrase.
   a. A ring of light around a dark center.
   b. Dark as night.
   c. A "bite" out of the sun.

**Total Lunar Eclipses, 2007–2035**

| *Date* | *Length* | *Visible from* |
|---|---|---|
| 03/03/07 | 1 h 10 m | Eastern North America, Asia, Africa, Europe |
| 08/28/07 | 1 h 32 m | Western North America, South America |
| 02/20/08 | 52 m | Europe, Africa, North and South America |
| 12/21/10 | 1 h 14 m | North and South America, Pacific |
| 06/15/11 | 1 h 42 m | Asia, Africa, India |
| 12/10/11 | 56 m | Pacific, Australia, Asia |
| 04/15/14 | 1 h 16 m | North and South America, Pacific |
| 10/08/14 | 1 h 2 m | North America, Pacific, Japan |
| 04/04/15 | 24 m | North America, Pacific, Japan |
| 09/27/15 | 1 h 18 m | Europe, Africa, North and South America |
| 01/31/18 | 1 h 17 m | Pacific, Australia, Japan, China |
| 07/27/18 | 1 h 44 m | India, Middle East, Africa |
| 01/20/19 | 1 h 3 m | North and South America |
| 11/19/21 | 19 m | North and South America, Pacific, Australia |
| 05/15/22 | 1 h 26 m | Europe, Africa, North and South America |
| 11/08/22 | 1 h 26 m | North and South America, Pacific, Australia, Asia |
| 03/14/25 | 1 h 6m | Western Europe and Africa, Atlantic, North and South America |
| 09/07/25 | 1 h 23 m | Asia, Africa, Europe |
| 03/03/26 | 59 m | North and South America, Pacific, Australia, East Asia |
| 12/31/28 | 1 h 12 m | Europe, Africa, Asia, Australia, Pacific |
| 06/25/29 | 1 h 43 m | North and South America, Europe, Africa, Middle East |
| 12/20/29 | 55 m | North and South America, Europe, Africa, Asia |
| 04/25/32 | 1 h 7 m | East Africa, Asia, Australia, Pacific |
| 10/18/32 | 49 m | Europe, Africa, Asia, Australia |
| 04/14/33 | 50 m | Europe, Africa, Asia, Australia |
| 10/08/33 | 1 h 20 m | North and South America, Pacific, Australia, Asia |

The exact day and hour of each eclipse varies depending on the time zone. Check an almanac or a science magazine for details prior to the eclipse.

### Total Solar Eclipses, 2006–2035

| *Date* | *Length* | *Path of total eclipse* |
|---|---|---|
| 03/29/06 | 4 m 27 s | Asia, Southeast Europe, Northern Africa, Eastern South America |
| 08/01/08 | 2 m 27 s | China, Mongolia, Siberia, Nunavut (Canada) |
| 07/22/09 | 6 m 39 s | West Pacific Ocean, India, China |
| 07/11/10 | 5 m 20 s | Central Pacific Ocean, Chile, Argentina |
| 11/13/12 | 4 m 2 s | South Pacific Ocean, Northeast Australia |
| 11/03/13 | 1 m 40 s | Atlantic Ocean, Central Africa |
| 03/20/15 | 2 m 47 s | Scandinavia, Northern Siberia, Arctic Ocean |
| 03/09/16 | 4 m 10 s | Indonesia, Pacific Ocean |
| 08/21/17 | 2 m 40 s | Atlantic and Pacific Oceans, South Carolina to Oregon (U.S.A.) |
| 07/02/19 | 4 m 33 s | South Pacific Ocean, Chile, Argentina |
| 12/14/20 | 2 m 10 s | South Pacific Ocean, Chile, Argentina, South Atlantic Ocean |
| 12/04/21 | 1 m 55 s | Antarctica, South Pacific Ocean |
| 04/20/23 | 1 m 16 s | Indian Ocean, Western Australia, Indonesia, Pacific Ocean |
| 04/08/24 | 4 m 28 s | Atlantic and Pacific Oceans, Southeast Canada, Maine to Texas (U.S.A.) |
| 08/12/26 | 2 m 19 s | Greenland, Iceland, Spain |
| 08/02/27 | 6 m 23 s | East Atlantic Ocean, North Africa, Middle East |
| 07/22/28 | 5 m 10 s | South Indian Ocean, Australia, New Zealand |
| 11/25/30 | 3 m 44 s | South Africa, Indian Ocean, Southeast Australia |
| 11/14/31 | 1 m 8 s | Central Pacific Ocean |
| 03/30/33 | 2 m 37 s | Alaska, Arctic Ocean |
| 03/20/34 | 4 m 10 s | East Atlantic Ocean, North Africa, Middle East, India, China |
| 09/02/35 | 2 m 54 s | China, Korea, Japan, Pacific Ocean |

Check a science news source for the exact location and time prior to each eclipse.

**Never look directly at the sun. Never look at the sun through a binocular or telescope.** The best way to safely view the sun is with the projection method described on page 21.

Or you may wear eclipse shades or use a solar filter to view the sun. Check with an astronomy source. A welding helmet with number 14 shade will also be safe. A total solar eclipse may be viewed without eye protection only while the bright disk of the sun is completely hidden and the corona is visible.

A third way is with a pinhole projection. Cut a 1-inch hole in a large piece of cardboard, and tape a piece of aluminum foil over the hole. Then punch a hole in the aluminum foil with the point of a pencil. Hold a sheet of white paper on the shaded side of the cardboard about 3 feet from the pinhole in such a way that the round disk of the sun's image falls on the paper.

**Eclipses can be predicted.** God made the world very orderly. The moon and earth move so exactly in their orbits that eclipses can be predicted accurately many years in advance. Men predict not only the exact time when an eclipse will begin and end, but also the exact paths of solar eclipses.

They can also predict whether a solar eclipse will be partial, annular, or total. From the earth, the sun and the moon appear about equal in size. But since the orbit of the moon is an oblong curve (an ellipse), the moon is closer to the earth at some times than at other times. When the moon is closest in its orbit, it appears bigger than the sun and causes a total eclipse. When the moon is farther away, it appears smaller than the sun and does not quite cover it. This causes an annular eclipse. By calculating where the moon will be in its orbit, men can tell what kind of eclipse will occur. Such predictions are an outstanding testimony to the perfection of God's creation.

**Why so few eclipses?** Since solar eclipses happen at new moons, you may wonder why a solar eclipse does not happen at every new moon. And since lunar eclipses happen at full moons, why does a lunar eclipse not happen at every full moon?

For an eclipse to occur, the sun, earth, and moon must be in a straight line. But the moon's orbit is slightly slanted in relation to the earth's orbit. This means that the moon's shadow usually misses the earth at new moon, and the earth's shadow usually misses the moon at full moon. Only occasionally will the three bodies line up well enough to cause an eclipse. The really amazing thing is that the times of eclipses can be predicted very accurately.

God deserves the glory for the orderly way He created the movement of the earth and the moon. If you have an opportunity to see an eclipse, remember that God made it possible.

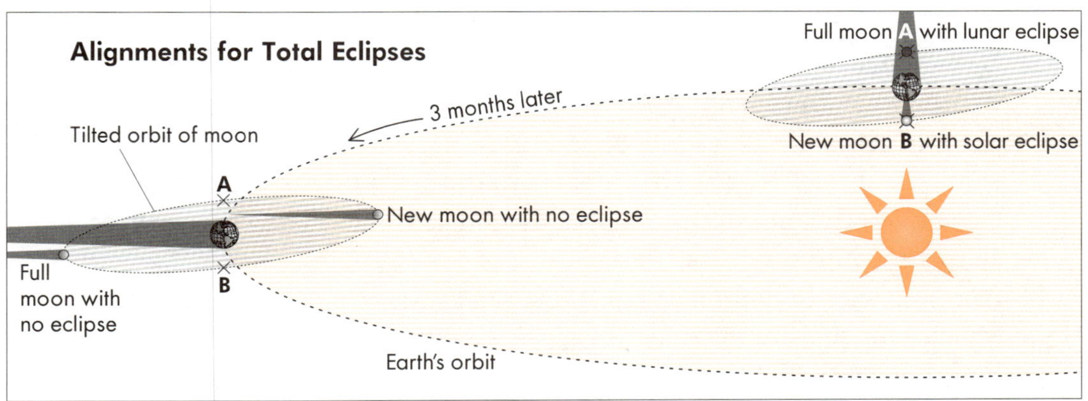


*A* and *B* are the only points level with the earth's orbit. Twice a year, as the earth revolves, these two points are in a straight line with the sun. If a new moon occurs during this alignment, a solar eclipse happens. If a full moon occurs during the alignment, a lunar eclipse happens. All other orbit points are too high or too low for a total eclipse to occur.

## Study the Lesson

5. An annular eclipse occurs if the moon appears (smaller, larger) than the sun.
6. Complete this sentence: A solar eclipse will not occur if the moon's shadow…
7. Eclipses can be predicted accurately. What does this fact tell us about how God created the world?

## Review Exercises

1. The moon goes through one cycle of its ———, or different shapes, in ——— days. [3]
2. The gravity of the moon causes the ——— of the ocean. [3]
3. The sun produces its energy as particles of ——— unite to form ———. [2]
4. The best displays of aurora borealis, also called ——— ———, occur during times of (many, few) sunspots. [2]
5. How many earth diameters would it take to equal the diameter of the sun? [1]
6. Water must be in the ——— state for life to exist. [1]

## Apply the Lesson

1. Demonstrate how eclipses happen. Use a Ping-Pong ball for the earth and a small white marble for the moon. A large, bright flashlight can be your sun. Put the light at one end of a dark room. At the other end of the room, hold the "moon" and "earth" 45 inches apart. Position them until you produce a "lunar eclipse." Then position them to produce a "solar eclipse." You will be surprised at how difficult it is to get the three "heavenly bodies" lined up to produce the eclipses.
2. Demonstrate the three kinds of solar eclipses. Cut out a 2-inch circle of white paper to represent the disk of the sun. To represent the moon, cut out one black circle a little bigger than 2 inches, and one a little smaller than 2 inches. Tape the white circle to the chalkboard. Move the black circles across the face of the "sun" to demonstrate how each of the three solar eclipses would progress.
3. Another way to demonstrate the three kinds of solar eclipses is to use a quarter for the sun and a penny for the moon. Hold the quarter out at arm's length with the left hand. Close one eye, and use your right hand to make an "eclipse" by passing the penny in front of the quarter. If you hold the penny closer and then farther away, you can make a total eclipse and an annular eclipse.
4. Practice the three methods for viewing a solar eclipse before one happens. That way you will not waste time learning how at the time an eclipse occurs.

# Lesson 5

## Unit 1 Review

### A. Vocabulary

Write the letter of the correct word for each meaning.

1. Darkening of one heavenly body by another.
2. Curved phase between new and quarter moon.
3. Of the moon.
4. Phase when the moon is between the sun and the earth.
5. Darkening of the moon by the shadow of the earth.
6. Bowl-shaped hole on the surface of the moon.
7. Darkening of the sun when the moon covers only a portion of it.
8. Phase between quarter and full moon.
9. Darkening of the sun when the moon covers all but a ring of it.
10. Phase showing the entire face of the moon.
11. One of the shapes in the monthly cycle of the moon.
12. Lights in the northern sky caused by glowing gases.
13. Element first discovered on the sun.

a. annular solar eclipse
b. aurora borealis
c. crater
d. crescent
e. eclipse
f. full moon
g. gibbous
h. helium
i. lunar
j. lunar eclipse
k. new moon
l. partial solar eclipse
m. phase

14. Darkening of the entire sun by the moon.
15. Half-circle phase of the moon.
16. Rise or fall of the ocean surface because of the moon's gravity.
17. Dark area on the sun caused by a storm.
18. Star that changes in brightness.
19. Stream of particles coming from the sun.
20. Line extending out from a crater.
21. Smooth, dark area on the surface of the moon.
22. Transfer of light and heat energy directly through space.
23. Of the sun.
24. Sun and all the heavenly bodies in orbit around it.
25. Any darkening of the sun by the moon.
26. Heavenly body in orbit around a planet.

a. quarter
b. radiation
c. ray
d. satellite
e. sea
f. solar
g. solar eclipse
h. solar system
i. solar wind
j. sunspot
k. tide
l. total solar eclipse
m. variable star

## B. Facts

Write the words that belong in the blanks.

1. The diameter of the sun is ——— times the diameter of the earth.
2. The earth is the right distance from the sun so that water can be in the ——— form.
3. Twenty-five percent of the sun is helium; most of the other 75 percent is ———.
4. The earth is kept in its orbit by the ——— of the sun.
5. The number of sunspots increases and decreases in a cycle of about ——— years.
6. During a ——— eclipse, observers can see proof that the earth is round.
7. During a total ——— eclipse, observers see glowing gases stream out from the sun.
8. Scientists discovered ——— on the sun by studying the light from the sun.
9. The earth's one satellite is called the ———.
10. There are ——— days in one complete cycle of the phases of the moon.
11. Six hours after a high tide there will be a ——— tide.
12. A lunar eclipse can occur only during the ——— phase of the moon.
13. The moon is not suited for life because it has no ——— or ———.
14. The earth's diameter is more than 3½ times the diameter of the ———.
15. In a solar eclipse, the black disk that covers the sun is the ———.
16. There is no eclipse at new moon if the moon's shadow ——— the earth.

## C. Concepts

Choose the letter of the best answer in each exercise.

1. If the sun were a variable star,
   a. the length of the year would change.
   b. the earth would be too hot and then too cold for life.
   c. we would sometimes have darkness in the middle of the day.
   d. the distance from the sun to the earth would not stay the same.
2. God formed the earth "to be inhabited." Which of the following things does *not* help to make the earth inhabitable?
   a. The sun shines with steady brightness.
   b. The earth is 93 million miles from the sun.
   c. The magnetic field of the earth stops the solar wind.
   d. The sun has storms that form sunspots.

3. The many things that are just right for life to exist on the earth are a result of
   a. the wisdom of men who have explored the world.
   b. the laws of nature that produced an orderly world.
   c. the wisdom of God who planned it that way.
   d. the chance happenings through many years of slow changes.
4. Which statement best tells how the sun produces its energy?
   a. Hydrogen and helium combine in a violent chemical reaction.
   b. Helium divides in a reaction to make hydrogen.
   c. Particles of hydrogen combine to make helium.
   d. Storms of the hydrogen and helium gas produce heat by friction.
5. The way the aurora borealis is produced shows how God can
   a. produce beauty from the effect of the moon on the earth.
   b. turn what would be harmful to life into something beautiful.
   c. produce beautiful sights that men cannot explain.
   d. produce beauty that is visible only through a telescope.
6. Which group has the phases in the right order?
   a. first quarter, first gibbous, full moon, last gibbous
   b. last quarter, last crescent, last gibbous, new moon
   c. full moon, last quarter, last gibbous, last crescent
   d. last crescent, last quarter, new moon, first crescent
7. Which diagram shows the position of the sun, moon, and earth during a solar eclipse?

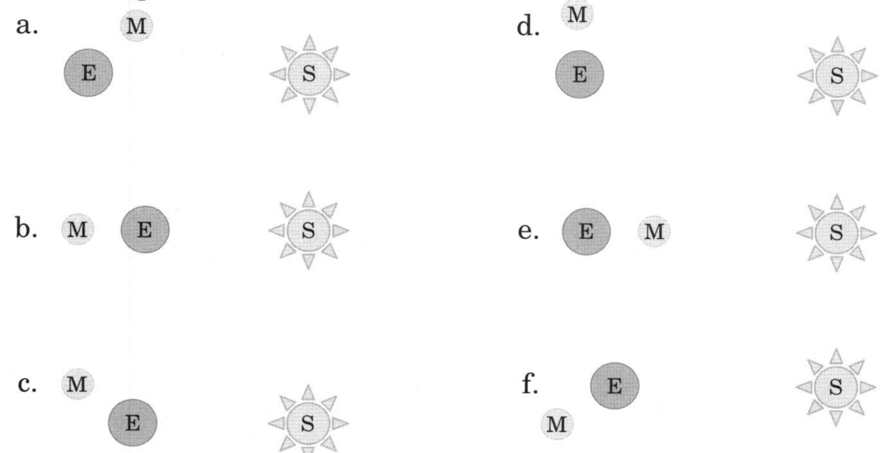


8. Which diagram in number 7 shows the position of the sun, moon, and earth during a crescent phase?

9. You should never look through a telescope to see
   a. rays on the moon.
   b. a lunar eclipse.
   c. aurora borealis.
   d. sunspots.
10. During the total part of a lunar eclipse, the moon is not completely dark because
    a. the moon receives light reflected from the earth.
    b. the moon receives sunlight passing through the earth's atmosphere.
    c. the moon glows by its own light.
    d. starlight reflects from the moon's surface.
11. The fact that eclipses can be predicted many years ahead shows that
    a. there is always the same number of days from one eclipse to the next.
    b. God has told man when the eclipses will occur.
    c. the world was created with order.
    d. men are able to control the movements of the moon.
12. To scientists, a total solar eclipse is of more interest than an annular eclipse because
    a. they can see stars during a total eclipse.
    b. not many people live in the area of a total eclipse.
    c. the total eclipse shows what nighttime is like.
    d. streams of glowing gases are visible during a total eclipse.
13. Compared with the sun, the moon looks
    a. smaller.
    b. about the same size.
    c. closer.
    d. farther away.

14. Which diagram shows the correct arrangement of the sun, moon, and earth?

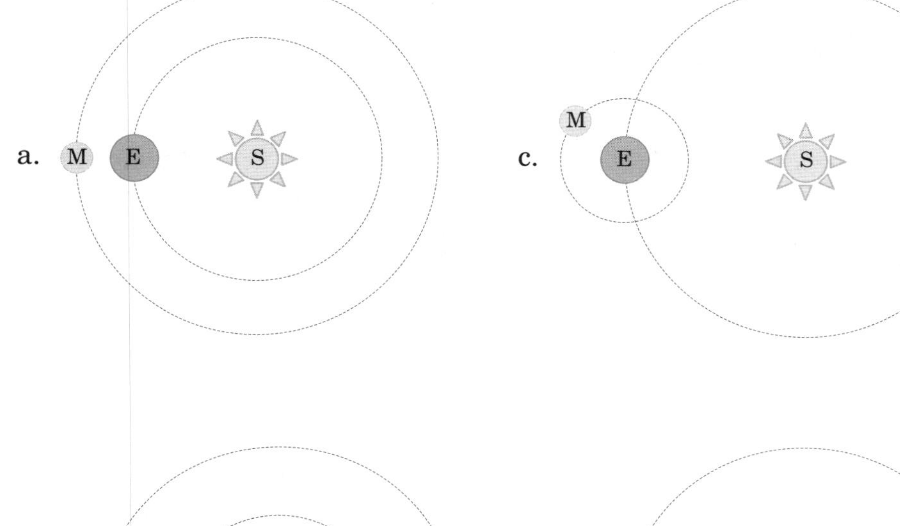


b. S M E

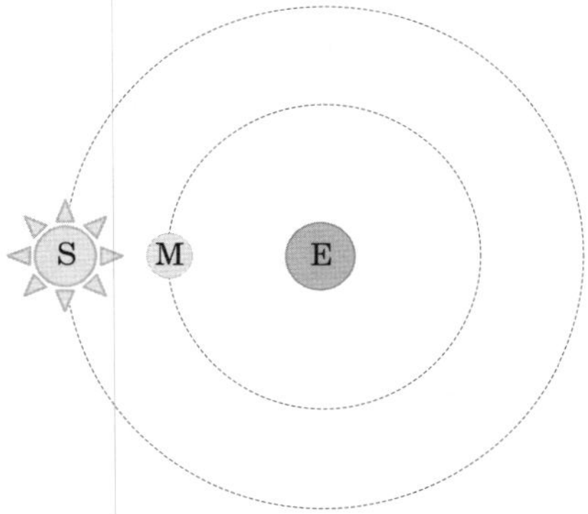

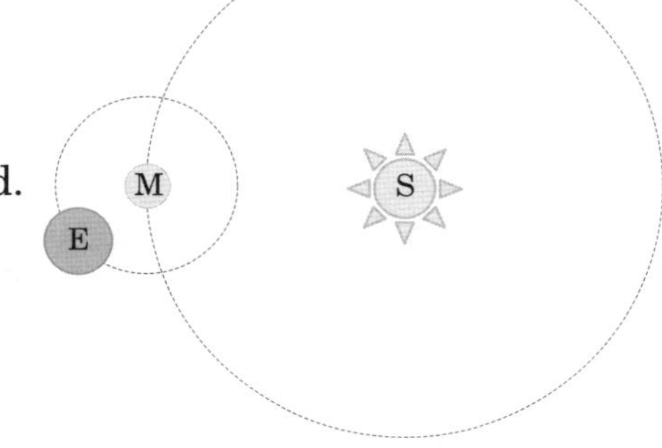

# Unit 2

## The Planets—Beautiful but Lifeless

"Wandering stars, to whom is reserved the blackness of darkness for ever" (Jude 13).

Before telescopes were invented, the planets were thought to be a special kind of star. They shone in the night sky as tiny points of light just like the stars. They changed in brightness, but so did the variable stars.

What appeared strangest about these special heavenly bodies was the way

### Facts Abo

(Measurem

| | Distance From Sun | Diameter | Tilt of Axis | Length of Day | Leng of Ye |
|---|---|---|---|---|---|
| **Mercury** | 36,000,000 mi.<br>58,000,000 km | 3,031 mi.<br>4,878 km | 0° | 176 days | 88 da |
| **Venus** | 67,000,000 mi.<br>108,000,000 km | 7,521 mi.<br>12,104 km | 3° | 117 days<br>(retrograde) | 225 d |
| **Earth** | 93,000,000 mi.<br>150,000,000 km | 7,926 mi.<br>12,756 km | 23½° | 24 hours | 365<br>day |
| **Mars** | 141,000,000 mi.<br>228,000,000 km | 4,223 mi.<br>6,796 km | 24° | 24½ hours | 687 d |
| **Jupiter** | 484,000,000 mi.<br>778,000,000 km | 88,846 mi.<br>142,984 km | 3° | 10 hours | 12 ye |
| **Saturn** | 888,000,000 mi.<br>1,429,000,000 km | 74,898 mi.<br>120,536 km | 27° | 10½ hours | 29 ye |
| **Uranus** | 1,786,000,000 mi.<br>2,875,000,000 km | 31,763 mi.<br>51,118 km | 82° | 17¼ hours<br>(retrograde) | 84 ye |
| **Neptune** | 2,799,000,000 mi.<br>4,504,000,000 km | 30,800 mi.<br>49,500 km | 29° | 16 hours | 165 ye |
| **Pluto** | 3,666,000,000 mi.<br>5,900,000,000 km | 1,430 mi.<br>2,300 km | 81° | 6⅓ days<br>(retrograde) | 249 ye |

they wandered about. Instead of staying at the same place in relation to other stars, the planets moved forward and backward, toward the sun and away from it. "Wandering stars" is a good name for them. It seems that Jude was thinking of planets when he used this expression to describe the lost, aimless condition of evil men.

When the telescope was invented, the planets were among the first things that it was used to look at. Many surprising and interesting features came into view. In this unit you will study the planets and see how they bring glory to the Creator in their own special way.

## Planets

approximate.)

| mber of tellites | Atmosphere (Main Gases) | Temperature | Gravity (Earth = 1) |
|---|---|---|---|
| 0 | almost none | –280° to 800°F<br>–170° to 430°C | 0.4 |
| 0 | carbon dioxide | 860°F<br>460°C | 0.9 |
| 1<br>ne moon) | nitrogen, oxygen | –130° to 140°F<br>–90° to 60°C | 1 |
| 2 | carbon dioxide | –220° to 60°F<br>–140° to 20°C | 0.4 |
| 63<br>4 large) | hydrogen, helium | –220°F<br>–140°C | 2.5 |
| 47<br>1 large) | hydrogen, helium | –290°F<br>–180°C | 1.1 |
| 27 | hydrogen, helium | –360°F<br>–220°C | 0.9 |
| 13 | hydrogen, helium | –350°F<br>–210°C | 1.1 |
| 3 | methane | –390° to –370°F<br>–230° to –220°C | 0.1 |

**Note:**
The length of day and the length of year are measured by Earth days and Earth years.

## Lesson 6

# The Sun Orbiters

"Lift up your eyes on high, and behold who hath created these things, that bringeth out their host by number: he calleth them all by names by the greatness of his might, for that he is strong in power; not one faileth" (Isaiah 40:26).

### Vocabulary

**comet,** a small heavenly body traveling in a very oblong orbit, which forms a tail as it nears the sun.

**ellipse** (i·lips′), the oblong, circular shape of the orbits of planets.

**gravity,** the pull between heavenly bodies.

**inertia,** the force that keeps a moving object traveling in a straight path.

**orbit,** the circular path of a planet or satellite.

**planet,** one of the heavenly bodies that orbit the sun.

The sun is the center of the solar system. Everything else in the solar system goes around the sun. Those two facts were not understood for hundreds of years. If we study the nighttime sky, it surely does look as if everything is going around the earth and that the earth is the center. The moon rises in the east and sets in the west. So do the sun and the stars. And so do the planets.

But the planets do not move across our sky as regularly as the sun, moon, and stars. Mercury and Venus, the two planets inside the earth's orbit, are sometimes in the evening sky and sometimes in the morning sky but never in the midnight sky. The planets outside the earth's orbit sometimes stop and go backward for a while, and then they go forward again. This is especially noticeable with Mars, Jupiter, and Saturn. Even the ancient stargazers could not understand why the planets moved so strangely. How could such a thing be if the earth was the center? We now know that the sun is the center of the solar system.

A ***planet*** is any large heavenly body that revolves around the sun. There are at least nine planets, including the earth. The path of each planet around the sun is called its ***orbit.*** The earth travels around the sun in one orbit, and the other planets move in different orbits. The other planets appear to move strangely because the earth is also moving. The orbits of the planets are so regular that the position of each planet can be calculated for many years in the future.

The orbits of the planets are not exact circles. They are oval or oblong. This shape is called an ***ellipse.*** Because of this shape, each planet comes closer to the sun during one part of its orbit than during another part. The orbits are not exact circles with the sun at the center.

Not all the orbits are flattened or oblong the same amount. The earth's orbit is not very oblong at all. When the earth is closest to the sun, it is 91½ million miles (147 million km) from the sun. When the earth is farthest away, it is 94½ million miles (152 million km) from the sun. In comparison with the distance from the sun, that is just a small difference. (The average of these two distances is 93 million miles or 150 million km. That is why we say the distance from the earth to the sun is 93 million miles.)

It is a good thing that God did not make the earth's orbit very oblong. If it were as oblong as Pluto's orbit, the earth would be only 70 million miles (113 million km) from the sun at one time of the year and 116 million miles (187 million km) at another time. That would make us too hot at one time and then too cold at another time. God wisely gave the earth an orbit that is nearly circular.

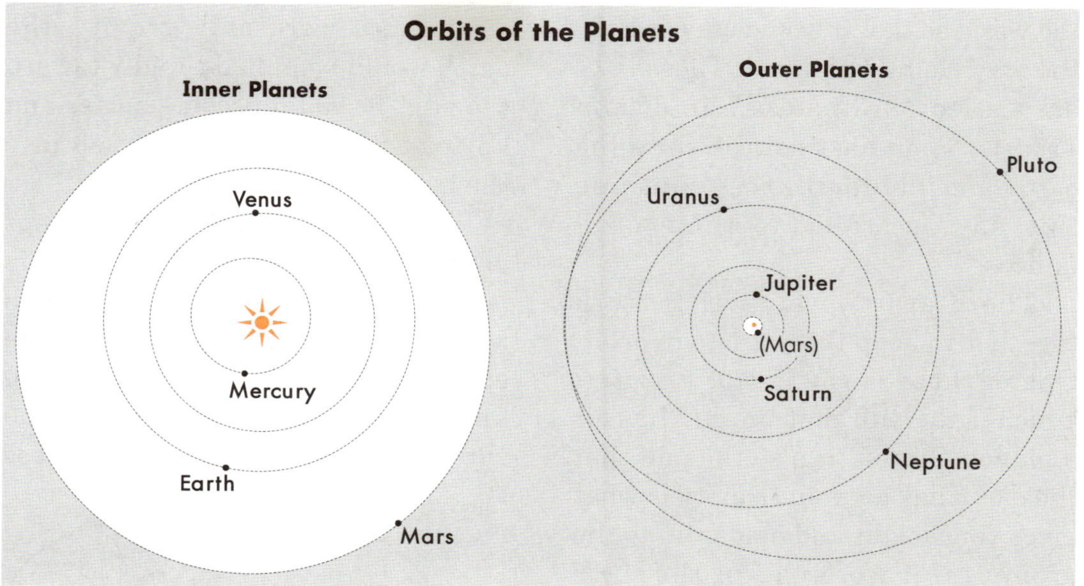


The inner planets are the four planets closest to the sun. Two diagrams are needed because the orbits of the outer planets would not fit on the page if everything were drawn to the scale of the inner planets. In each ellipse, the sun is off-center.

## Study the Lesson

1. Why did many men in the past think the sun went around the earth?
2. The earth is called a ——— because it revolves around the ———.
3. What is the name of the shape of the orbits of planets?
4. Which of these diagrams is most like the orbit of a planet?
   a. b. c. d.
5. Give the earth's distance from the sun at the closest point and at the farthest point.
6. Why is it good that the earth's orbit is not very oblong?
   a. The earth receives nearly the same heat from the sun all year.
   b. The earth travels about the same speed all year.
   c. The gravity of the sun keeps the earth in its orbit.
   d. The earth is a planet and not a comet.
7. Write the names of the nine planets in order, and memorize them.

**What controls the motion of the planets?** God made laws to control the world so that it would stay orderly, the way He had planned. These laws are called "ordinances" in Psalm 119:91. "Thou hast **established** the earth, and it **abideth.** They **continue** this day according to thine ordinances."

There are two laws that work together to keep the planets in orbit. One of these is the law of ***gravity,*** which is the pull that the sun has for a planet. Gravity is also the pull that the earth has for you. Gravity is what gives you weight and holds you to the ground. If it were not for the sun's gravity, the earth would go sailing off into space far away from the warming rays of the sun. Then the earth would soon become too cold for any life.

If there were only gravity, the earth would be pulled rapidly toward the sun. It would become hotter and hotter and would finally crash into the burning surface of the sun.

However, the law of ***inertia*** keeps us from crashing into the sun. Inertia is a force that makes an object try to keep moving in a straight line. As the earth moves forward at 18½ miles (30 km) every second, the gravity of the sun works against inertia and causes

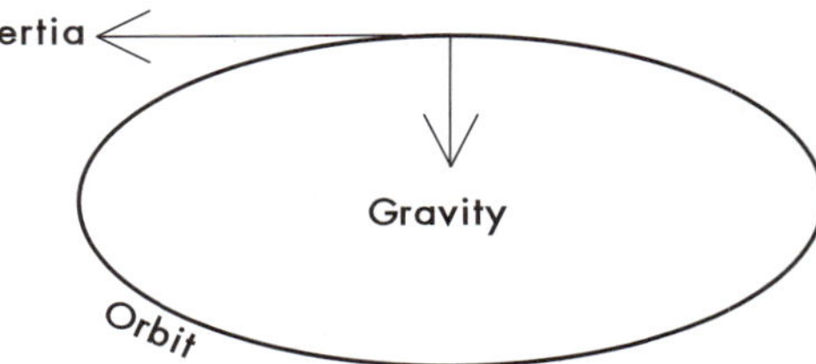

the earth's path to curve. That curve is an ellipse.

The law of inertia would make the earth go away from the sun, and the law of gravity would make the earth go toward the sun—but these forces balance each other. That is how the planets can stay in the same orbit for thousands of years.

The orbits are not perfect circles because during part of the orbit, gravity speeds up the planet. But as the planet speeds up, inertia causes a stronger outward pull that moves the planet farther from the sun. Then gravity slows this outward motion and pulls the planet around in a curve, and gravity again speeds it up as the planet "falls" closer to the sun. This seesaw between gravity and inertia is what makes the ellipse-shaped orbits.

**What are comets?** Occasionally people will become very excited about a special visitor to the night sky. The newspapers will announce when and where the comet will be visible. A ***comet*** is a heavenly body that orbits the sun in an ellipse that is very oblong. During part of the comet's orbit, it comes very close to the sun. That warms the comet and makes some of it "boil" away to make a beautiful tail.

Then as the comet heads back out into cold space, it gradually cools and loses its tail. It also loses speed very slowly as the gravity of the sun slows it down. It may take many years for the comet to stop going outward and start coming back to the sun again. It will take many more years for the comet to gain speed to again zip around the sun. Not all comets have orbits. Some of them approach the sun from outer space and then go back into space seemingly never to return again.

One famous comet that does return is Halley's comet. It last visited the sun in the winter of 1986 and passed the sun on February 9. This comet takes about 76 years to complete one orbit. Comets are the wonderful handiwork of God.

We are amazed at the order and beauty of the solar system. As you look further into the parts of this system, you will be studying what God has made. God wants us to consider His works and worship Him.

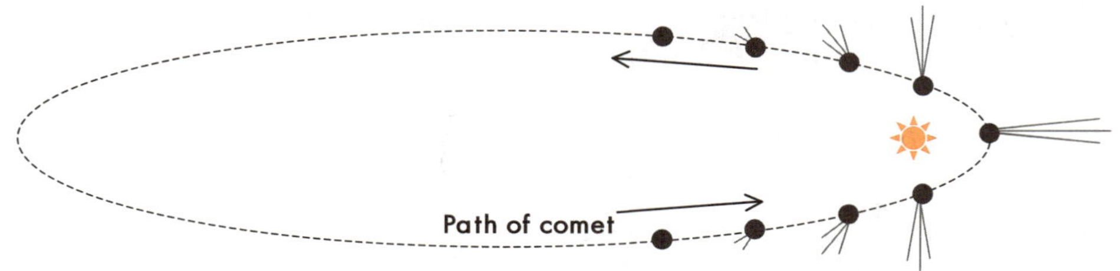

Comets can vary greatly in appearance. The comet on the left is Halley's comet as seen through a telescope.

## Study the Lesson

8. How did God plan for the world He created to be kept in good order?
9. Write *inertia* or *gravity* for each description.
   a. It is the pull that the earth has on your body.
   b. It makes it hard for you to stop when you are running.
   c. It would cause the earth and the sun to move farther apart.
   d. It would cause the earth and the sun to move closer together.
10. What did God do so that the law of gravity would not cause the earth to crash into the sun?
11. Choose all the descriptions that are true for many comets.
   a. Returns after a period of time.
   b. Sometimes called a falling star.
   c. Has a long, sweeping tail as it passes close to the sun.
   d. Orbits the sun in a very oblong ellipse.
   e. Becomes so hot that it burns into dust.
   f. Located between the orbits of Jupiter and Mars.

## Review Exercises

1. The moon goes through one cycle of its ———, or different shapes, in ——— days. [3]
2. The gravity of the moon causes the ——— of the ocean. [3]
3. The sun produces its energy as particles of ——— unite to form ———. [2]

4. The best displays of aurora borealis, also called ——— ———, occur during times of (many, few) sunspots. [2]
5. How many earth diameters would it take to equal the diameter of the sun? [1]
6. Water must be in the ——— state for life to exist. [1]

## Apply the Lesson

1. Draw an ellipse. Tape a piece of paper to a board or heavy cardboard measuring 9 by 12 inches. Space two nails or thumbtacks 6 inches apart near the center of the board. Tie a 14-inch string in a loop. Hook the string over both nails. Use a pen, inside the string, to draw as large an ellipse as the string allows.

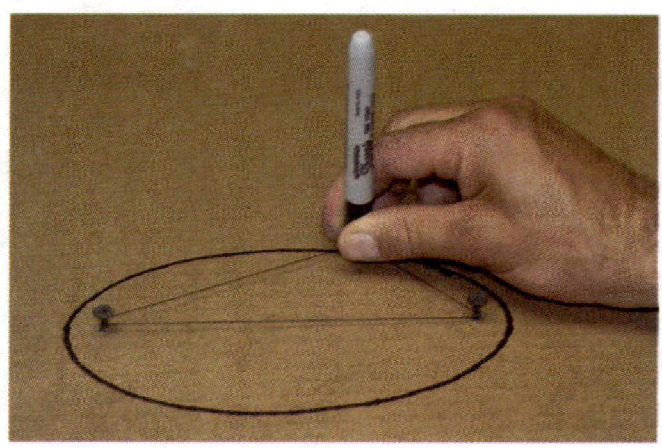

2. Draw the orbits of the earth, Pluto, and Halley's comet. To get the right ellipse for each, use the measurements given below. If you would like to make bigger ellipses, you can multiply all the measurements by 2 or some other number.

| | Length of String in Loop | Distance Between Nails |
|---|---|---|
| Earth | 7⅝ in. (19.4 cm) | ⅛ in. (0.3 cm) |
| Pluto | 9³⁄₁₆ in. (23.3 cm) | 1¹³⁄₁₆ in. (4.6 cm) |
| Halley's Comet | 18 in. (45.7 cm) | 8⅝ in. (21.9 cm) |

3. Were you surprised to learn that the earth travels 18½ miles per second? You can test that number. Calculate the circumference of the earth's orbit by multiplying 3.14 times its diameter of 186,000,000 miles. Divide that number by the number of seconds in a year (31,557,600). This will give you the earth's speed in miles per second.
4. When will Halley's comet return again? How old will you be if you are still living? Look in an encyclopedia to find out when that comet last returned before 1986. What was special about it that time, which was not true of its appearance in 1986?

## Lesson 7

# The Inferior Planets—Mercury and Venus

"I, even my hands, have stretched out the heavens, and all their host have I commanded" (Isaiah 45:12).

### Vocabulary

**inferior planet,** one of the planets (Mercury and Venus) that orbit the sun inside the earth's orbit.

**superior planet,** one of the six planets that orbit the sun outside the earth's orbit.

**transit,** the passing of a planet across the face of the sun.

The planets move at the command of God. All the planets, including the earth, revolve around the sun. So when we watch the movements of other planets, we must remember that the earth we live on is also moving. This makes the planets appear to move in strange and interesting ways. In this lesson you will study the movement of Mercury and Venus, the two planets inside the earth's orbit. You will also learn what it is like on the surface of these planets.

The planets inside the earth's orbit are called ***inferior planets.*** Mercury and Venus are the two inferior planets. Outside the earth's orbit are six ***superior planets:*** Mars, Jupiter, Saturn, Uranus, Neptune, and Pluto.

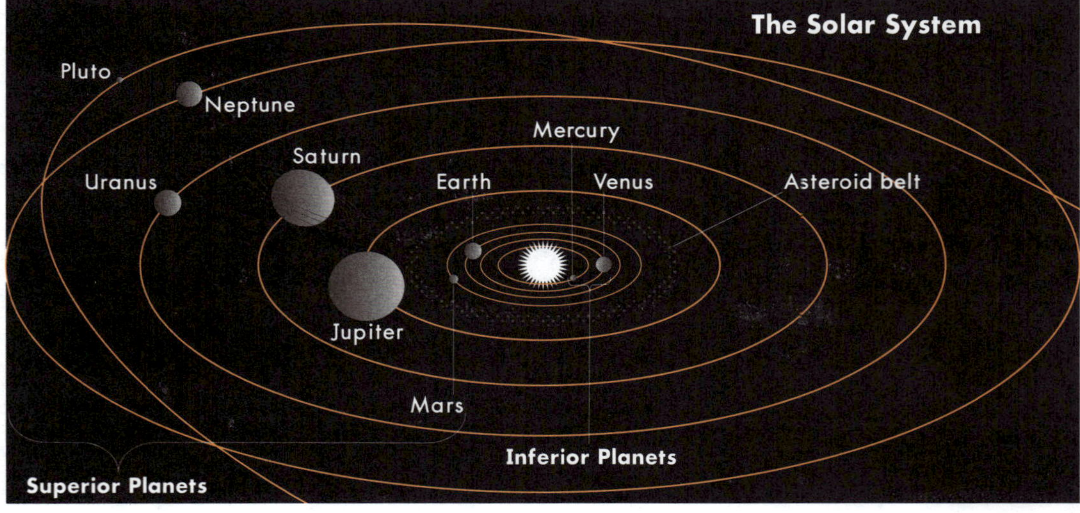

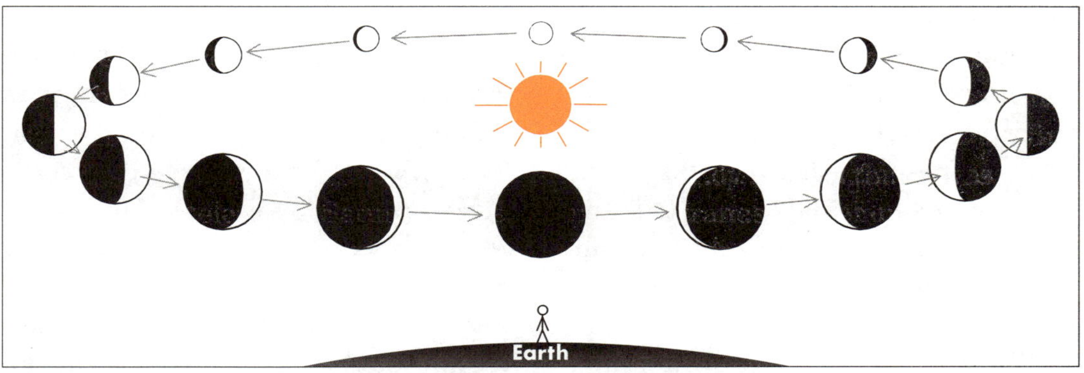

The phases of Venus as seen from Earth

**Phases of inferior planets.** Planets are visible only by the sunlight they reflect. Therefore, Mercury and Venus pass through phases as the moon does. However, both planets are so small in the sky that we must use a telescope to see the phases. Also, Mercury is so close to the sun that its phases are hard to see.

The full face of Venus is turned toward the earth when Venus is on the opposite side of the sun from the earth. For us, it is daytime then, so we cannot see Venus in the full phase. But when Venus is closer to the earth and not in line with the sun, its quarter and crescent phases are visible. These are the times when we can best see Venus.

**Transits of inferior planets.** Sometimes as Mercury passes between the earth and the sun, it crosses directly in front of the sun. This looks like a tiny black dot moving slowly across the face of the sun. Such a crossing of the sun is called a ***transit.*** The transits of Mercury can be viewed in the same way sunspots are viewed, by projecting the image of the sun with a telescope. (See page 21.)

**Transits of Venus**

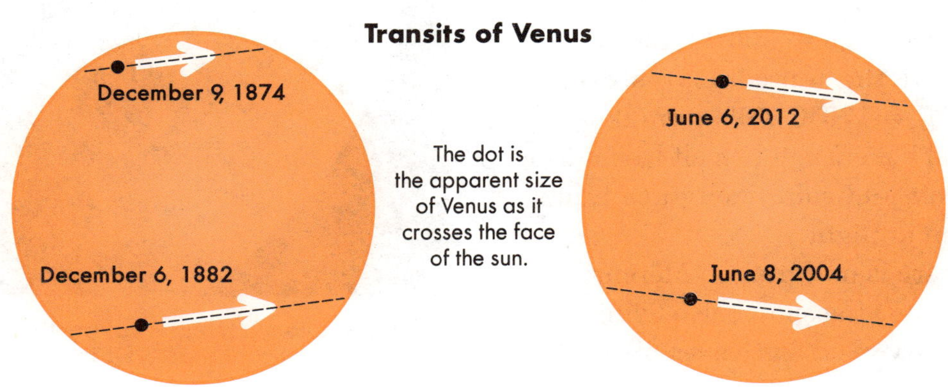

Venus also makes transits, but they are much less frequent than those of Mercury. Transits of Mercury occur every 3 to 13 years. Transits of Venus occur in pairs with over 100 years between one pair and the next. Transits of Venus occurred in 1874 and 1882; the dates for the next pair are 2004 and 2012.

**What is Mercury like?** Mercury is one of the smallest planets, a little more than a third as large as the earth and somewhat larger than the moon. The surface of Mercury has many craters.

Since Mercury is the nearest planet to the sun, it travels faster than any other planet. This is because the closer a planet is to the sun, the faster it moves. Mercury orbits the sun in just 88 days.

The sunlight on Mercury is about seven times brighter than on the earth. This makes Mercury a very hot planet. Mercury has a very slow rotation. One day on Mercury lasts 176 earth days (almost six months). The rotation is so slow that daytime temperatures rise to 800°F (430°C), and at night the temperatures drop to –280°F (–170°C). That makes the ground hot enough to melt lead during the day and cold enough to liquefy oxygen at night.

There is no water on Mercury, and almost no atmosphere. No living thing could survive on this barren planet. God did not make Mercury to be inhabited.

**Appearance of Mercury.** Since Mercury is so close to the sun, it is usually invisible to people on earth. The only time we can see it is right after sunset or just before sunrise. If Mercury is in the right position, it appears in the twilight glow not far above the western horizon. But soon it sinks out of sight. When it is at the opposite side of its orbit, Mercury rises above the eastern horizon just before dawn. But soon the sun rises, and Mercury vanishes in the bright sunshine.

This portion of Mercury was photographed from the *Mariner 10* spacecraft in 1974.

## Study the Lesson

1. The planets located inside the earth's orbit are called ——— planets.
2. Both Mercury and Venus have ——— as the moon does.
3. Both Mercury and Venus make crossings of the sun called ———.
4. If one planet travels slowly around the sun and another planet travels faster, which one is closer to the sun?
5. Give three things about Mercury that make life impossible there.
6. Why is Mercury hard to find in the sky?

**What is Venus like?** Venus is a very hot planet, much like Mercury. But unlike Mercury, Venus has a thick atmosphere. However, you could not live by breathing the air of Venus. It is almost all carbon dioxide. There is none of the oxygen that you need to live.

The sky of Venus is so full of clouds that we cannot see its surface with telescopes. But the clouds do not contain water. They are made of sulfuric acid, a very strong chemical that would burn your eyes and skin. Of course, there is no life on Venus.

On Venus, thick clouds of sulfuric acid prevent views of its surface. The picture on the right was generated from radar scans that penetrated the thick clouds. The color is based on information gathered by probes that landed on the surface.

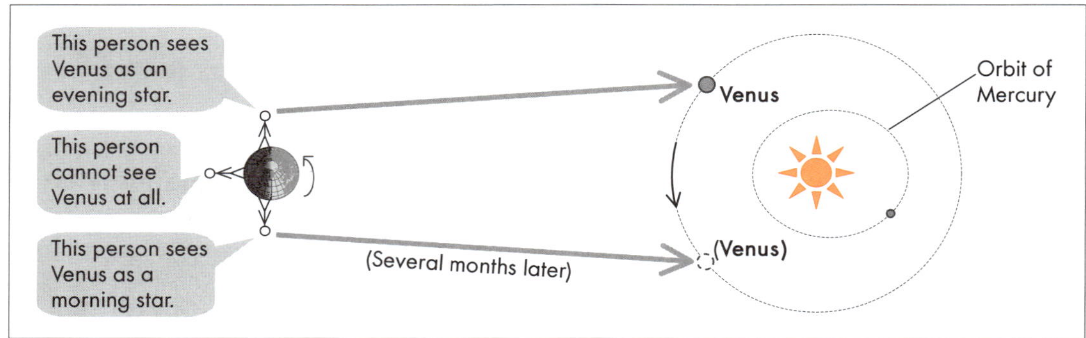


**Appearance of Venus.** Because Venus is an inferior planet, it appears only as an "evening star" or a "morning star." Notice in the diagram above that Venus is beside the sun. As the earth rotates, the sun will drop below the western horizon before Venus does, and Venus will be an evening star. Later, when Venus has moved to the other side of the sun, it will rise above the eastern horizon before the sun does and will be a morning star. When you view the sky in the middle of the night, you see objects that are outside the earth's orbit; therefore, you cannot see Venus at midnight. Of course, in the daytime the brightness of the sun blots out Venus.

Venus varies greatly in brightness. At one place in its orbit, Venus is 160 million miles away (257 million km) on the other side of the sun. Then it looks dim. As it approaches the earth and passes within 26 million miles (42 million km), it looks bigger and therefore brighter. Venus is brightest during its crescent phase. Sometimes it is the brightest object in the sky except the sun and the moon.

You have probably seen Venus many times even if you did not know what it was. In the western sky after the sun set, or in the eastern sky before the sun rose, you saw a bright "star" that was much more brilliant than the other stars. To ancient people, the appearance of Venus in the night sky was a sign that morning would soon come. The Bible refers to Jesus as "the bright and morning star" (Revelation 22:16). Venus certainly does shine out brightly against the darkness of night, just as Jesus shines out brightly in the dark world.

**Venus rotates backward.** Venus takes 225 days to make one trip around the sun. It also rotates on its axis, but not in the same direction as most of the other planets. Venus rotates backward! This means that someone on Venus would see the sun rising in the west and setting in the east.

The backward rotation of Venus is baffling to those who do not believe that God created the world. If the world evolved in the way they think, all the planets should be rotating in the same direction. But opposite rotation is no problem to those who believe the Bible. If God chose to make Venus rotate backward, He could do that since He is all-powerful.

In their own way, the inferior planets bring glory to God their Creator.

## Study the Lesson

7. Give two facts about Venus that make life impossible there.
8. Venus appears as a bright "——— ———" after sunset or a bright "——— ———" before sunrise.
9. You would not see Venus in the sky at midnight, because
   a. the sun would not be shining on Venus then.
   b. Venus is an inferior planet.
   c. Venus would be passing behind the sun.
   d. Venus is orbiting the sun and not the earth.
10. The crescent phase of Venus is brighter than the full phase because
    a. Venus is closer to the earth at crescent phase.
    b. Venus is closer to the sun at crescent phase.
    c. Venus is closer to the horizon at full phase.
    d. Venus is closer to the sun at full phase.
11. What does the Bible call Jesus, which may refer to Venus?
12. What fact about the movement of Venus shows that it was created and did not develop by chance?

## Review Exercises

1. The orbits of the planets, and especially those of the comets, are in the shape of (a circle, an egg, an ellipse). [6]
2. A lunar eclipse occurs when the shadow of the ——— falls on the ———. [4]
3. A solar eclipse is total when the size of the moon appears (equal to, smaller than) the size of the sun. [4]
4. The moon is unsuitable for life because it has no ——— or ——— and because its temperature is both too ——— and too ———. [3]
5. Heat and light travel through empty space by ———. [2]
6. The sun is a steady star and not a ——— star like Mira. [1]

## Apply the Lesson

1. Make a mural of the solar system. Below are the diameters you can use to have the planets in the right proportion to each other (multiply each by 2, 3, or 4 to fit the size of your mural). Since the sun is so big, you may want to simply make an arc of the sun at one end or corner of the mural. Paint the planets according to the way they actually look. For this, you will need to consult an encyclopedia or other source that has colored photographs of the planets.

   Sun (1,392 mm or 1.4 m)
   Mercury (5 mm)
   Venus (12 mm)
   Earth (13 mm)
   Mars (7 mm)
   Jupiter (143 mm)
   Saturn (120 mm; rings 273 mm)
   Uranus (51 mm)
   Neptune (50 mm)
   Pluto (3 mm)

2. Make a notebook of the planets. You could paint the planets or use colored crayons, and include the information about each planet as shown on pages 44 and 45. A short description of each planet will make the notebook even more worthwhile.
3. Be sure to look for Venus in the evening or morning sky. A book about stars may tell you where the planets will be for many years to come. One such book is *Discovering God's Stars,* available from Rod and Staff Publishers. If someone in your community has a telescope, ask if you may use it to see what phase Venus is in. The crescent phase is the most interesting, but it lasts the shortest time.
4. Several spacecraft have been sent to the inferior planets. (As of 2006, only one went to Mercury.) Do some research to find out what has been learned from these space missions.
5. The surface of Mercury becomes very cold during its long night. The night on Venus is much longer—about 121 earth days. (One rotation of Venus is 243 earth days long.) But the surface of Venus does not get cold during its night. Why? Find out what is meant by the greenhouse effect. Your answer to this question will help you understand why it gets colder on a clear night than on a cloudy night.
6. Sometimes Venus is called a twin of the planet Earth. In what ways are the two planets twins? See if you can find out by studying the table of planets on pages 44 and 45. In what ways are they not twins?

## Lesson 8

# Mars and the Asteroids

"For the Lord God will help me; therefore shall I not be confounded: therefore have I set my face like a flint, and I know that I shall not be ashamed" (Isaiah 50:7).

### Vocabulary

**asteroid** (as′·tə·roid′), one of the planet-like rocks between Mars and Jupiter.

**meteor,** a streak of light caused by a speeding rock from space as it enters the earth's atmosphere.

**meteorite,** a rock from space that strikes the earth's surface.

**opposition,** the position of a superior planet when it is in the direction opposite from the sun.

Mars, the Red Planet

South pole with polar ice cap

Some men have thought there was life on Mars. Millions of dollars and thousands of hours have been spent looking for evidence of such life. But God did not make Mars to be inhabited, and men have been confounded in their efforts to find life there. God will never be confounded or ashamed. Mars brings glory to God, not shame.

Mars is the fourth planet from the sun. It is the next one outside the earth's orbit. With telescopes, men have seen white icecaps that come and go with the summers and winters on Mars. Most of Mars looks red, but it also has dark, greenish or bluish gray areas. All of this is very fuzzy even in the best earth telescopes. Men have looked for hours to catch a few short times when the atmosphere of the earth was very clear to give a good view of Mars. They have drawn what they saw or thought they saw.

To many scientists, life on Mars looked like a very real possibility. They saw straight lines on Mars, which some imagined were canals dug by living creatures to bring water from melting polar icecaps to farms and cities. They drew pictures of these canals crisscrossing the planet. They felt that if a closer study were made, it would probably reveal evidence of life on Mars. An observatory was built in Arizona to especially study Mars. Some men fully expected to find life there. This would help to support their idea that the world evolved instead of being created as the Bible teaches. If evolution were true, then life could evolve on planets besides the earth.

In 1976 two unmanned spacecraft landed on Mars. Another one landed in 1997. They all took close-up pictures of the surface of Mars. They analyzed the air and tested the soil. Scientists wanted to find if there was or ever had been life on Mars. But no trace of life was found!

**A hostile environment.** Mars is not at all suited for life. The air on Mars is very thin. Since there is not much air, there is not much air pressure. Air pressure is needed to keep water from boiling at a low temperature. On Mars, water would boil at room temperature. Your body would swell up and your blood would boil with so little air pressure.

The air that is on Mars has almost no oxygen to breathe. There is only a little water on Mars, and the temperature is much too cold for water to stay in liquid form. The water is either a gaseous vapor in the air or a solid in the icecaps. The temperatures on Mars are usually below the freezing point of water. Without liquid water, there can be no rain.

Mars often has huge sandstorms that choke the air with red dust. This fine dust makes the sky look pink instead of blue as on earth. How would you like to live in a world with a pink sky?

**A year on Mars.** It takes 687 days for Mars to make one revolution around the sun. One year on Mars is almost as long as two years on the earth.

Mars is tilted 24° on its axis, which is the imaginary line running through the planet from north pole to south pole. This is just a little more than the tilt of the earth.

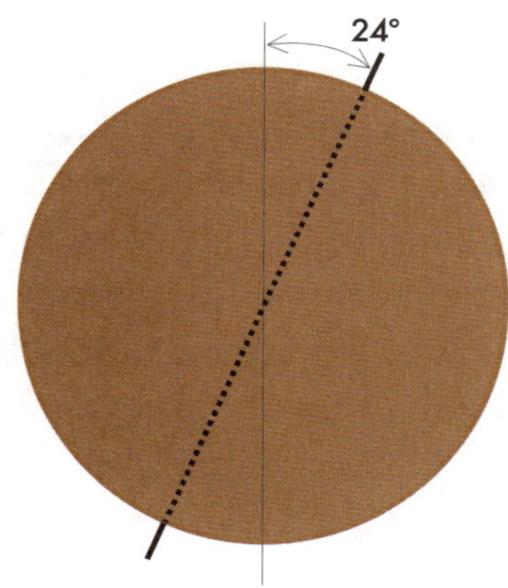


The axis of Mars is tilted 24 degrees.

This tilt of Mars gives it yearly seasons like those on the earth. During half of the year, its northern hemisphere is tilted away from the sun, making winter in the north. The extra cold causes a polar icecap to form. This icecap is made of carbon dioxide, and it can be seen with telescopes on the earth.

As Mars continues through the other half of its orbit, the northern hemisphere tilts toward the sun. Then it is summertime in the north. The Martian north pole warms up so that the ice changes into carbon dioxide as a gas. Summer on Mars is still very cold, with an average temperature of –20°F (–30°C).

A day on Mars is 24½ hours long, just one-half hour more than a day on the earth. But just having seasons like the earth and having a day like the earth does not make Mars fit for living things. Many things need to be right for life to exist. Many things about Mars are not right for life.

## Study the Lesson

1. For years men wrongly thought they had found evidence of ——— on Mars.
2. Which three of these things can be seen on Mars with a telescope?
   a. red areas
   b. canals
   c. polar icecaps
   d. white clouds
   e. mountains and valleys
   f. dark, greenish areas
3. Part of the reason that men expected to find life on Mars was the false idea that living things ——— instead of being ——— as the Bible says.
4. What were some things done by the spacecraft that landed on Mars?

5. Which four of these are reasons why life cannot exist on Mars?
   a. too hot
   b. too cold
   c. no liquid water
   d. no air
   e. not enough gravity
   f. not enough air pressure
   g. almost no oxygen
6. What is the axis of a planet?
7. The tilt of the axis of Mars causes it to have ——— as the earth does.

**Finding Mars in the sky.** Mars is a reddish planet, or "wandering star." Remember that people long ago gave planets that name because the planets move among the stars. They do not stay at a certain place in relation to the stars, as regular stars do.

Where do the planets wander? The sun and the moon travel from east to west along a certain path in the sky. The planets can be found along the same path. So if you see a red "star" along this sky path, and if it moves among the other stars from week to week, then you know you have found Mars.

Sometimes Mars is the brightest "star" in the sky. Sometimes it is very dim. That is because Mars is sometimes much closer to the earth than at other times. Mars is brightest and can best be seen through a telescope when it is on the opposite side of the earth from the sun, in the position of a full moon. Such an opposite position of a superior planet is called an ***opposition.*** An opposition of Mars happens about every two years.

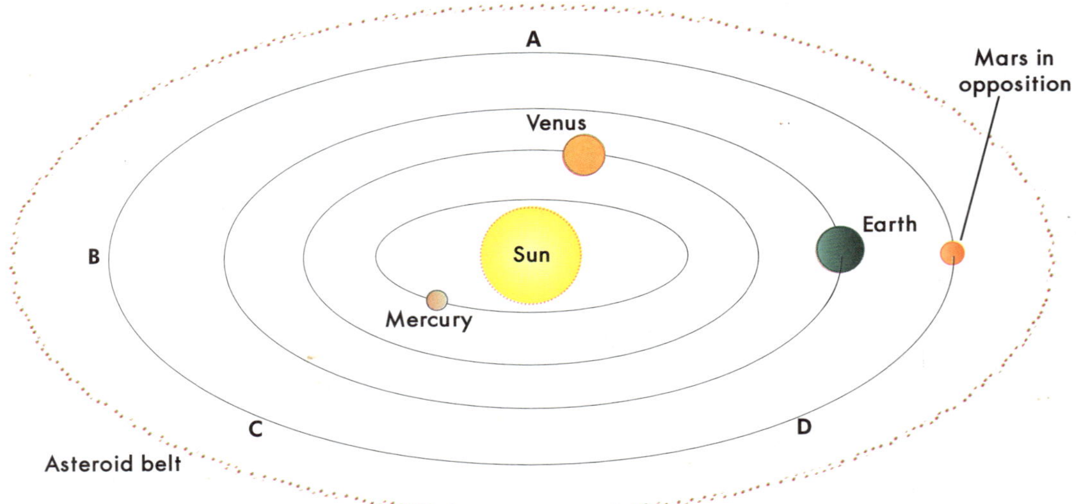


An opposition of Mars occurs only when the sun and Mars are aligned on opposite sides of the earth. If Mars were at positions A, B, C, or D, it would not be in opposition.

The Bible says, "The heavens declare the glory of God" (Psalm 19:1). Mars is part of the created heavens, and it does show us how great and wonderful God is. Do not miss seeing this special part of His handiwork. Do not neglect to give Him glory for His marvelous works.

**Asteroids and meteorites.** There are many small pieces of rock orbiting the sun. Some of these are not much bigger than specks of dust, and a few are hundreds of miles in diameter. Most of the big ones orbit between Mars and Jupiter. They are called ***asteroids,*** which means "starlike objects." But asteroids are not bright like stars or big like planets. They are like small planets orbiting the sun, and for this reason they are sometimes called planetoids. Thousands of large asteroids have been discovered with telescopes, but only God knows how many rock-size asteroids there are.

When watching the stars on a clear night, have you ever seen a bright streak flash suddenly in the sky? Some people call these falling stars, but they are not stars. When a piece of orbiting rock comes close to the earth, the earth's gravity pulls it into the atmosphere. As the rock falls, it moves so fast that friction with the air causes it to burn up. That is what makes the light. The name for these streaks of light is ***meteors.*** Some of the rocks that cause meteors come from the asteroid belt, and some are from comets.

Usually the speeding rocks burn up completely and turn to dust. That is the way God uses the atmosphere to protect us from them. But sometimes a rock reaches the ground, and then it is called a ***meteorite.*** Meteorites are rare and are often displayed in museums. There is no record of a person ever being killed by a meteorite.

Some of the small asteroid rocks in space orbit in bands around the sun. When the earth passes through such a band, a meteor shower occurs. In a few meteor showers, a streak of light can be seen every few seconds.

Meteor Crater is a large crater near Winslow, Arizona. It is 570 feet deep.

In 1947, this meteorite fell in Siberia.

## Study the Lesson

8. Which diagram shows the earth, the sun, and Mars at a time of opposition?

9. Asteroids are studied in a lesson with Mars because
   a. both are small bodies that orbit the sun.
   b. both were once thought to contain life.
   c. both are found in about the same part of the solar system.
   d. both were not discovered before the use of the telescope.
10. Asteroids and meteors are studied together because
    a. both exist between the orbits of Mars and Jupiter.
    b. some meteors are caused by rocks from the asteroid belt.
    c. asteroids were once a kind of meteorite.
    d. both appear as streaks of light in the night sky.
11. Write *asteroid, meteor,* or *meteorite* for each description.
    a. A body that orbits the sun but is much smaller than a planet.
    b. A streak of light caused by a rock entering the atmosphere.
    c. Located between the orbits of Mars and Jupiter.
    d. A special object in a museum.
    e. Sometimes comes with others in a shower.
    f. May be hundreds of miles in diameter.
    g. Sometimes called a falling star.
    h. A rock from outer space that strikes the earth.
    i. Several thousand discovered with telescopes.
    j. May come from a comet.

## Review Exercises

1. The planets located inside the earth's orbit are called ——— planets. [7]
2. The closer a planet is to the sun, the (more slowly, more swiftly) it travels and the (shorter, longer) its year is. [7]
3. A solar eclipse occurs when the shadow of the ——— falls on the ———. [4]
4. The gravity of the moon causes the ——— of the ocean. [3]

5. Dark spots on the sun are called ———, and their number increases and decreases in a cycle of about ——— years. [2]
6. The sun is made mostly of the elements ——— and ———. [2]

## Apply the Lesson

1. Mars has two small satellites. Use an encyclopedia to find out how big they are, how far they orbit from Mars, and how long it takes them to make one orbit.
2. Use *Discovering God's Stars* or a similar book to find where Mars is in the sky right now. When you find it, draw a diagram to show the position of Mars in relation to the nearest stars. Use this drawing to compare its position a week or two later. If a telescope is available, look at Mars through it. You should see a small reddish disk. But except in a very big telescope, you will see almost no details.
3. Meteors may be seen on any clear night. But you are most likely to see some during a meteor shower. Below is information about some of the more interesting showers. Meteors in a shower appear to move outward from a central point in the sky. The name of a shower comes from the name of the constellation (star picture) in which the central point appears to be. Meteor showers can be seen best in the east or southeast after midnight.

| Name of Shower and Constellation | Middle Date of Shower | Duration in Days | Number Per Hour |
|---|---|---|---|
| Orionid (Orion) | October 20 | 8 | 25 |
| Leonid (Leo) | November 16 | 4 | 20 |
| Geminid (Gemini) | December 13 | 6 | 50 |
| Lyraid (Lyra) | April 21 | 4 | 12 |
| Perseid (Perseus) | August 11 | 5 | 50 |

These numbers are approximate. Showers vary from year to year. Some years it is quite rewarding to watch a shower, and other years it is disappointing.

# Lesson 9

## The Outer Planets

"For as the heavens are higher than the earth, so are my ways higher than your ways, and my thoughts than your thoughts" (Isaiah 55:9).

### Vocabulary

**conjunction,** the lining up of planets that makes them appear close together.

**retrograde** (ret′·rə·grād′), in a backward direction.

Distance in space staggers the mind. We must take giant leaps when we study the planets beyond Mars in our journey through the solar system. Even when those planets are closest to us, when we reach Mars, we are only about one-eighth of the way to Jupiter. When we come to Jupiter, we are about halfway to Saturn. When we get to Saturn, we are about halfway to the next planet, Uranus. When we arrive at Uranus, we are about halfway to Pluto. And when we reach Pluto, we would have to go over 1,600 times the same distance to get to the nearest star! God's ways are very high indeed.

All the planets outside the earth's orbit are called superior planets. The first superior planet is Mars, which you studied in Lesson 8. The others are Jupiter, Saturn, Uranus, Neptune, and Pluto. These last five are called outer planets because they are so far away from the sun.

The first three superior planets—Mars, Jupiter, and Saturn—are bright enough to be seen easily without a telescope. They were known to men long before telescopes were invented. In those long-ago days, most people thought all

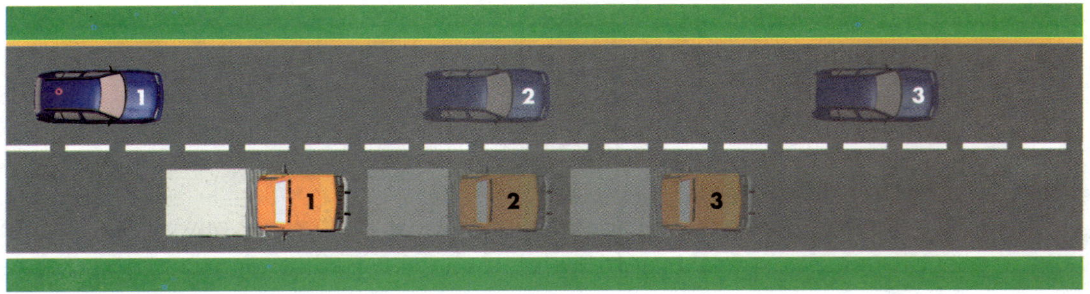


A slow-moving truck seems to be moving backward to the occupants of a passing car. Each set of numbers—for example, the two 3's—represents the same moment of time.

the planets traveled around the earth instead of the sun.

People thought this even though they knew that these three planets appear to move in a strange way. About once a year, the superior planets seem to stop going forward in our night sky and go backward for a time. This is called ***retrograde,*** or backward, motion.

Jupiter, the gas giant. Some of the tiny white dots are moons.

Finally people understood that the sun, not the earth, is the center of the solar system and that the earth itself orbits the sun. About once a year, the earth passes the slower-moving superior planets. Since the earth is moving faster, this makes the slower planets appear to move backward—in the same way that a slow-moving truck appears to move backward when we pass it in a car. That is the reason for retrograde motion.

Now we will take a journey past each of the outer planets and see what wonders they hold for us.

**Jupiter.** This is the biggest of all

The Great Red Spot of Jupiter is a beautiful marvel of the solar system. This storm is about two times as wide as the earth, and it swirls much like a hurricane.

the planets. The diameter of Jupiter is 11 times the diameter of the earth. The planet is so big that even though it is far away, some details can be seen on Jupiter with a medium-sized telescope.

Dark and light bands stretch across the face of this planet. They are caused by streams of gases in the upper part of Jupiter's atmosphere. Many storms rage on Jupiter, some with winds reaching 250 miles per hour. One storm, called the Great Red Spot, is a deep mystery. This spot has been seen for over 300 years. Sometimes it grows dim or even disappears, but then it becomes visible again. Why this spot exists and what keeps it there is one of the many mysteries of the solar system.

Jupiter is slightly flattened at the poles. This huge giant spins on its axis once every 10 hours. Such rapid spinning causes it to bulge out at the equator.

The four brightest satellites of Jupiter have delighted many telescope users. These satellites can be seen easily with just a small telescope. They change position very rapidly. One night two satellites may be on each side of Jupiter, and the next night three may be on one side and one on the other. Sometimes only three satellites are visible. Jupiter is certainly an interesting planet to study.

But Jupiter would not be a pleasant planet to visit. It is much too cold for life, and the air is filled with poisonous gases. Jupiter's gravity would make you so heavy that you could not walk. In fact, Jupiter may not even have solid ground to walk on.

## Study the Lesson

1. Which of these is *not* a superior planet?
   a. Saturn b. Mars c. Venus d. Neptune
2. Understanding that the ——— is the center of the solar system makes it easier to understand ——— motion.
3. What is the reason for retrograde motion of the superior planets?
   a. The sun's gravity pulls the planets backward once a year.
   b. The earth's gravity pulls the planets backward once a year.
   c. The planets turn in circles at the same time they orbit the sun.
   d. The earth orbits faster than the superior planets.
4. What is the Great Red Spot of Jupiter?
5. Suppose you looked at Jupiter through a telescope and saw two satellites on one side and one on the other. How could that be, since Jupiter has four satellites that can be seen in a small telescope?

**Saturn.** Some things are hard to believe even if you see them. Saturn is one of those things. This planet is actually surrounded by a number of thin, flat rings!

Through a telescope, Saturn's rings look like a disk of gold with a hole in the middle and with a golden ball floating in the hole. The rings are made of millions of chunks of icy rocks and other matter. Each chunk travels around Saturn like a tiny satellite. Yet together they form thin and very flat rings. Saturn with its rings is a magnificent sight. It shows the glory of God in an extraordinary way.

Saturn has an atmosphere of poisonous gases, and it bulges outward at the equator. Saturn also has many satellites beyond the rings, but only one of them can be seen with a small telescope. Being so far away from the sun, Saturn is even colder than Jupiter. Saturn is beautiful to look at, but God did not create it to support life.

**Uranus.** The next planet out from Saturn was discovered by accident in 1781. The discoverer thought at first that he had found a new comet. But further study showed that it was a new planet. Uranus (yo͝or′·ə·nəs) is the third largest planet and has twenty-seven satellites.

The axis of Uranus is tilted so much that it is almost level with its orbit. This makes Uranus appear to be rolling along as it travels through space. It also causes very long days and nights on Uranus. During part of its orbit, one hemisphere has day all the time while the other has night all the time.

Uranus rotates backward on its axis, as Venus does. This again speaks of design rather than chance. Since God made the planets, He could make them turn in whichever direction He chose.

**Neptune.** This planet was discovered by the use of mathematics.

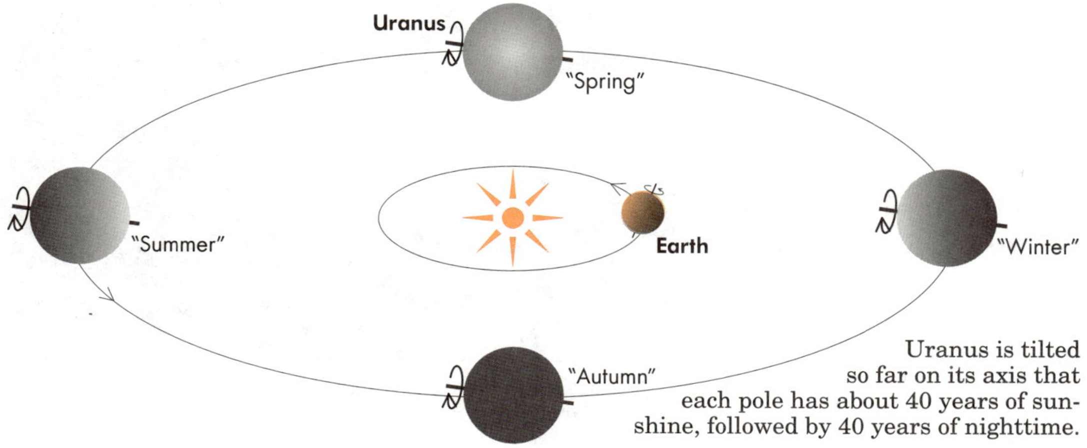


Uranus is tilted so far on its axis that each pole has about 40 years of sunshine, followed by 40 years of nighttime.

The rings of Saturn are the most beautiful feature of the superior planets. A section behind is hidden by Saturn's shadow. The three white dots below Saturn are moons.

Astronomers found that Uranus did not travel in its predicted path. It seemed that the gravity of another planet farther out was pulling Uranus slightly out of course. Between 1843 and 1845, two different astronomers in Europe calculated the position of the unknown planet. An observatory in Germany checked the predicted spot, and there was the new planet!

Uranus is a giant blue ball of gas and liquid. It has 27 moons. Here the five largest moons are enlarged and pasted around the planet.

Neptune is also mostly gas and liquid. The blue clouds are frozen methane crystals.

The discovery of Neptune shows the precision of the laws God established for the universe. They are so exact that people can use mathematics to discover the position of a planet even before pointing a telescope toward the spot.

**Pluto.** This planet is so small and so very far from the sun that it was not discovered until 1930. Pluto is the coldest, smallest, and most distant planet of them all. It is so cold that some of the methane gas in its atmosphere may have frozen into a layer that covers the ground.

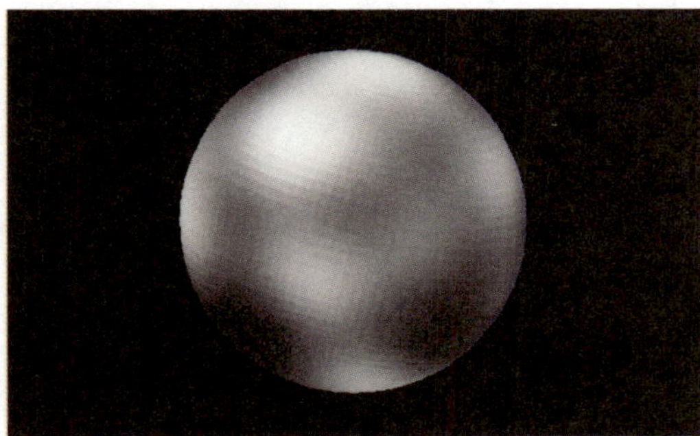

The Hubble Space Telescope gathered light for this picture. Pluto is too far away to show surface detail.

Pluto rotates on an axis that is level with its orbit. The orbit is a very oblong ellipse. About once every 250 years, Pluto passes to the inside of Neptune's orbit. Then for about 20 years, Pluto is actually closer to the sun than Neptune. This unusual part of Pluto's orbit last began in 1979.

Beyond the orbit of Pluto lies the Kuiper (kī′·pər) belt, a region with thousands of small bodies made of rock and frozen gases. The Kuiper belt is so far

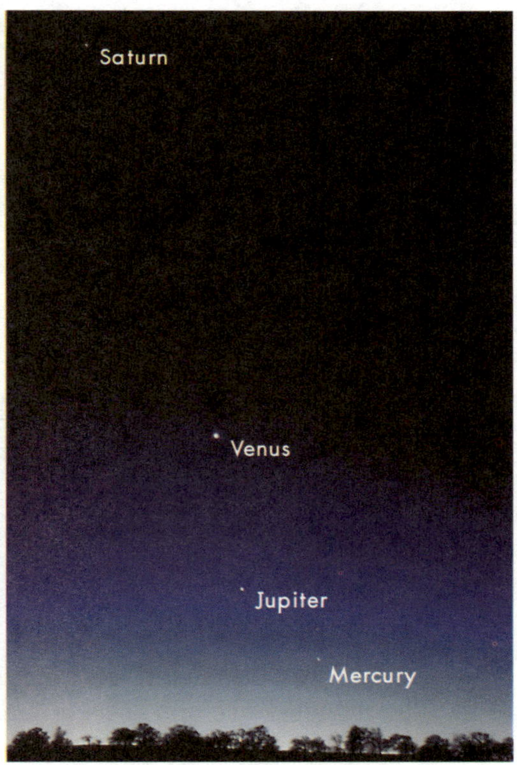


A four-planet conjunction

away that spacecraft from the earth would take about ten years to get there.

**When the planets line up.** Of course you will want to find Mars, Jupiter, and Saturn in the sky. All the planets except Pluto travel nearly the same path through the heavens. Some move faster than others. Sometimes they are in retrograde motion. They are sometimes leaving and sometimes approaching the sun. With all this moving about, two planets sometimes line up in relation to the earth. Then they appear very close together in the sky. Such a lining up of planets is called a ***conjunction.***

Conjunctions are a good time to follow the movement of the planets because changes in their positions can easily be seen from one night to another. On rare occasions, three planets get very close together in the sky to make a triple conjunction. By regularly following the planets, you can witness interesting things happening in the sky.

## Study the Lesson

6. Name the outer planet that fits each description. The number *2* means that two answers should be given.
   a. Has only one satellite that can be seen with a small telescope.
   b. Turns backward.
   c. Position predicted by mathematics.
   d. Bulges at the equator. (2)
   e. Orbit has a very oblong shape.
   f. Has four satellites that can be seen with a small telescope.
   g. Has a system of flat rings.
   h. Discovered by accident.
   i. The largest planet.
   j. The smallest planet.
   k. Axis level or nearly level with orbit. (2)
7. If sometime you see three very bright "stars" close together in the sky, you are probably observing a triple ———.
8. Beyond Pluto lies a region called the ——— ———.

## Review Exercises

1. Mercury is hot on one side and cold on the other because it rotates very (slowly, swiftly). [7]
2. The atmosphere of Venus is mostly ——— ———, and it contains clouds of ——— ———. [7]

3. A solar eclipse is annular when the size of the moon appears (equal to, smaller than) the size of the sun. [4]
4. The moon goes through one cycle of its ———, or different shapes, in ——— days. [3]
5. The best displays of aurora borealis, also called ——— ———, occur during times of (many, few) sunspots. [2]
6. How many earth diameters would it take to equal the diameter of the sun? [1]

## Apply the Lesson

1. Since you have studied all the planets except the earth, now would be a good time to make some comparisons between them. The chart on pages 44 and 45 shows the order of the planets according to their distance from the sun. Use that chart to arrange the planets in the following ways.
   a. from largest to smallest
   b. from shortest year to longest year (Why do they have this order?)
   c. from shortest day to longest day
   d. from coldest to hottest (Use high temperatures only, and remember that negative numbers are backward: –100° is colder than –50°.)
2. A spacecraft can travel 25,000 miles per hour. At that speed, how long would it take to get to Mars, Jupiter, Saturn, and Pluto? (Use their distances from the sun. If you started from the earth, it would make a difference where the earth was in its orbit.) Give your answers in hours and then in years. There are 8,766 hours in a year.
3. One problem in communicating with distant spacecraft is the time it takes for radio waves to travel through space. Radio waves travel at the same speed as light waves—186,000 miles per second. How many seconds would it take for a radio message to get to the earth from the moon? from Mars? from Pluto? (For the planets, use the same distances as in exercise 2 above.)
4. Generally, at least one of the bright planets is in the evening sky at any time. Use a star guide book to find out where the planets are now. Make an observation record of the planets. As you identify one of them, record its location in the sky and the time you observed it. What is the greatest number you will be able to have on your record?

## Lesson 10

# Unit 2 Review

## A. Vocabulary

Write the letter of the correct word for each meaning.

1. Red planet with seasons like the earth.
2. Largest planet; next one after Mars.
3. Smallest planet; last one to be discovered.
4. Next to last planet; discovered by mathematics.
5. Streak made as speeding rock enters the atmosphere.
6. Hot and cold planet closest to the sun.
7. Planet-like rock between Mars and Jupiter.
8. Planet surrounded by large flat rings.
9. Planet with its axis almost level with its orbit.
10. Planet with clouds containing sulfuric acid.
11. Forms a tail as it nears the sun in an oblong orbit.
12. Rock from space that strikes the earth's surface.

a. asteroid
b. comet
c. Jupiter
d. Mars
e. Mercury
f. meteor
g. meteorite
h. Neptune
i. Pluto
j. Saturn
k. Uranus
l. Venus

13. Pull between heavenly bodies.
14. Heavenly body that orbits the sun.
15. Passing of a planet in front of the sun.
16. Orbits the sun inside the earth's orbit.
17. Line around which a planet rotates.
18. In a backward direction.
19. Lining up that makes planets appear close together.
20. Force that keeps an object moving in a straight path.
21. Oval shape of the orbits of planets.
22. Path of a planet or satellite.
23. Orbits the sun outside the earth's orbit.
24. Position of a superior planet when it is in the direction opposite from the sun.

a. axis
b. conjunction
c. ellipse
d. gravity
e. inertia
f. inferior planet
g. opposition
h. orbit
i. planet
j. retrograde
k. superior planet
l. transit

## B. Facts

Write the words that belong in the blanks.

1. If it were not for ———, the planets would crash into the sun.
2. The inferior planets are Venus and ———.
3. The length of Mercury's ——— is much longer than the earth's.
4. When Venus comes close to the earth, it has a ——— phase like the moon.
5. The closer a planet is to the sun, the ——— it will orbit.
6. Almost all the atmosphere of Venus is made of ———.
7. For many years, men thought there might be ——— on Mars.
8. The axis of Mars is ——— about the same amount as the axis of the earth.
9. The superior planets are brightest when they are in a position of ———.
10. A meteor may have come from the ——— belt or from a ———.
11. About once a year, a superior planet like Jupiter goes through ——— motion.
12. Jupiter has ——— satellites that are visible through a small telescope.
13. The ——— of Saturn contain millions of chunks of icy rocks and other matter.
14. The position of Neptune was predicted by the effect of its gravity on ———.
15. Since Venus, Jupiter, and Mars can be very bright, it would be very interesting to see these three planets lined up to form a ———.
16. From memory, write the names of the nine planets in order. You may review them first if necessary.

## C. Concepts

Choose the letter of the best answer in each exercise.

1. Retrograde motion is easy to explain if you understand that
   a. the planets travel in ellipses instead of circles.
   b. the superior planets go backward about once a year.
   c. the planets revolve around the earth, not the sun.
   d. the planets revolve around the sun, not the earth.
2. The fact that Venus and Uranus rotate backward is hard to explain if you believe that
   a. the planets revolve around the sun in ellipses.
   b. the planets evolved over millions of years.
   c. the planets rotate at different speeds.
   d. the planets were created by the word of God.

3. Mercury has extremely high and extremely low temperatures because
   a. it rotates so slowly on its axis.
   b. it is the planet closest to the sun.
   c. it is covered with craters like the moon.
   d. it is one of the smallest planets.
4. The orbit of a comet is most nearly like the orbit of
   a. Earth.
   b. Mars.
   c. Pluto.
   d. Uranus.
5. Which fact is *not* a reason why the planet cannot have life?
   a. The surface of Venus would melt lead.
   b. Mars has very little air pressure.
   c. The atmosphere of Jupiter contains poisonous gases.
   d. Mercury has less than half the gravity of the earth.
6. We do not need to fear being struck by meteorites because
   a. most of them are smaller than a pea.
   b. the rocks usually burn up by friction with the air.
   c. they are moving slowly by the time they hit the ground.
   d. most of them are between the orbits of Mars and Jupiter.
7. Which arrangement of planets is in correct order?
   a. Saturn, Uranus, Neptune
   b. Venus, Mars, Jupiter
   c. Mercury, Earth, Venus
   d. Neptune, Pluto, Uranus
8. Venus is either a morning or an evening star because
   a. the sun shines on only one side of Venus.
   b. it orbits closer to the sun than the earth does.
   c. people are asleep during the rest of the night.
   d. it is a sign that morning will soon come.
9. Mars is similar to the earth in all the following ways *except*
   a. the length of the day.
   b. the occurrence of seasons.
   c. the general temperature.
   d. the presence of polar icecaps.

10. Which pair of planets is *not* related in the way mentioned?
    a. Uranus and Neptune were both discovered with the help of mathematics.
    b. Jupiter and Saturn are both giant planets covered with gases.
    c. Earth and Venus are about the same size.
    d. Mercury and Venus are both inferior planets.
11. Which term names something that could *not* involve Saturn?
    a. conjunction
    b. opposition
    c. retrograde
    d. transit
12. For the next thirty years after Halley's comet is visible from the earth, the comet will be
    a. becoming brighter.
    b. slowing down.
    c. moving around one end of an ellipse.
    d. coming nearer to the sun.
13. The Great Red Spot of Jupiter and the rings of Saturn
    a. are wonders that show the glory of God.
    b. are examples of mysteries that men have explained.
    c. were known by men of Bible times.
    d. help us to understand the laws of God.
14. The distances between the planets in the solar system help us to understand
    a. why men will probably never live on other planets.
    b. how low our thoughts are compared with God's thoughts.
    c. how Jesus is "the bright and morning star."
    d. how the earth was created by God.

# Unit 3

## Earth—the Home for Living Things

You have studied the other planets of the solar system. Now in this unit, you will study a very special planet: the earth. Of course, it is special because you live on it. But it is also special because there is nowhere else to live. Of all the planets, only the earth is fit to be inhabited. That did not come about by chance. The earth was formed by God to be inhabited. That means God knew what would be needed for life, and He made the earth to meet those needs.

"For thus saith the LORD that created the heavens; God himself that formed the earth and made it; he hath established it, he created it not in vain, **he formed it to be inhabited:** I am the LORD; and there is none else" (Isaiah 45:18).

If only one thing were needed for life, we might conclude that the earth just happened to get that way by chance. But many things are necessary for life, and all those things are on the earth but not on other planets. So we must conclude that the earth is the result of wise planning and careful creation by God. That is what God Himself has told us in the Bible. "God himself that **formed** the earth and **made** it; he hath **established** it, he **created** it."

As you study many ways the earth was formed to be inhabited, praise God for His wisdom, thank Him for His care, and love Him for His goodness.

# Lesson 11

## A Climate to Support Life

"I will plant in the wilderness the cedar, the shittah tree, and the myrtle, and the oil tree; I will set in the desert the fir tree, and the pine, and the box tree together: that they may see, and know, and consider, and understand together, that the hand of the LORD hath done this, and the Holy One of Israel hath created it" (Isaiah 41:19, 20).

### Vocabulary

**Antarctic Circle,** the boundary around the southern "land of the midnight sun."

**Arctic Circle,** the boundary around the northern "land of the midnight sun."

**arid** (ar′·id), the kind of climate that is so dry that few plants can grow.

**climate,** the general weather of an area in a year.

**growing season,** the time between the last frost in spring and the first frost in fall.

**polar,** the kind of climate so cold that plants cannot grow.

**semiarid** (sem′·ē·ar′·id), the kind of climate with 10 to 20 inches of rain each year.

**subarctic,** the kind of climate that is dry and cold, but not as cold as the polar climate.

**temperate,** the kind of climate that is neither very hot nor very cold and usually has four seasons.

**tropical,** the kind of climate that is hot and wet.

**tropic of Cancer,** the northernmost latitude of sunlight from straight overhead.

**tropic of Capricorn,** the southernmost latitude of sunlight from straight overhead.

**weather,** the condition of the atmosphere at a certain time.

Why do some parts of the earth grow trees and ferns while other parts contain shrubs and cacti? God made different weather patterns for different kinds of life.

Are you having a warm and sunny day, or is it cool and rainy? Is it windy or calm outside? Sunshine, wind, and precipitation (such as rain or snow) are conditions of the atmosphere that we call ***weather.*** Sometimes there is frost or sleet. Occasionally there will be a thunderstorm or tornado. All of these things are kinds of weather.

The yearly or seasonal patterns of sunshine, wind, and precipitation in a certain area are its ***climate.*** One rain does not make a moist climate, and one dry spell does not make a desert. Different climates have different yearly weather patterns.

You like warm, sunny days. But if every day were sunny, the ground would soon become dry. The grass would turn brown, and finally the trees would die. Then instead of living in a moist climate, you would be living in a desert climate.

**Tropical climate.** The ***tropical*** climate is a hot, wet climate near the equator. The temperature does not drop below 64°F (18°C) even in the coolest month of the year. There are over 40 inches (100 cm) of rain every year. A tropical climate can support an abundance of living things.

**Temperate climate.** Much of the United States and southern Canada, most of Europe, and some of China and South America have an in-between, or ***temperate,*** climate. The yearly rainfall is from 20 to 50 inches (50 to 125 cm). The year-round temperatures are neither very hot nor very cold. Some temperate regions have mild winters with little snow, and some have hard winters with several months of freezing

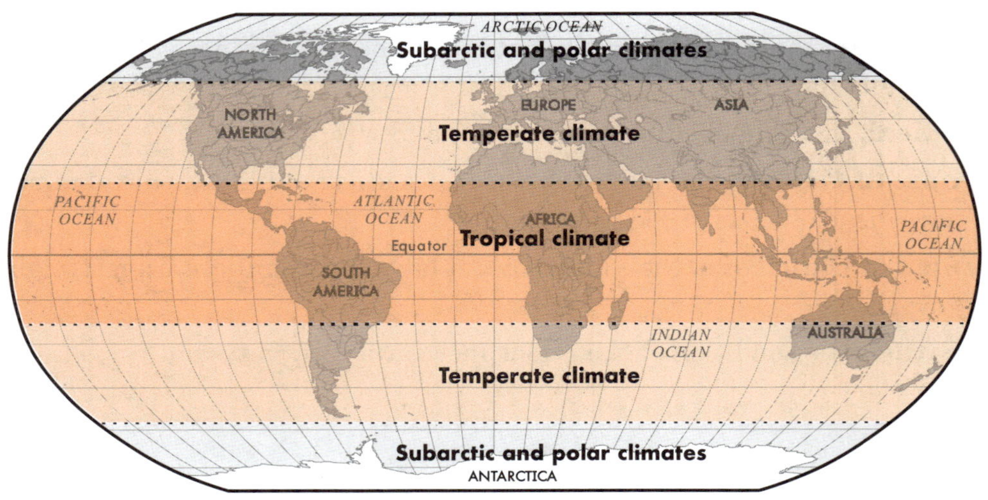

cold and snow. Summers are long enough to be good for farming.

**Subarctic climate.** The ***subarctic*** climate is dry and cold. There is little precipitation, and most of that is snow. Some of the water soaks into the ground, and certain trees can live in this climate.

**Polar climate.** The ***polar*** climate is so cold that not many plants can grow. It has this name because it is in the region of the North Pole or the South Pole. Even the summertime of the polar climate is chilly, and there is snow on the ground most of the year.

**Arid and semiarid climates.** The four climates named above are the main climate zones of the earth. Other climates are named according to the amount of rainfall they have. When an area receives less than 10 inches (25 cm) of rain each year, it is ***arid.*** *Arid* means "very dry." Such desert regions are also hot. Not many plants can live in an arid climate.

If the rainfall of an area is between 10 and 20 inches (25 and 50 cm), the climate is ***semiarid.*** *Semiarid* means "partly dry." Semiarid lands provide hundreds of square miles of tall grass for grazing animals such as beef cattle.

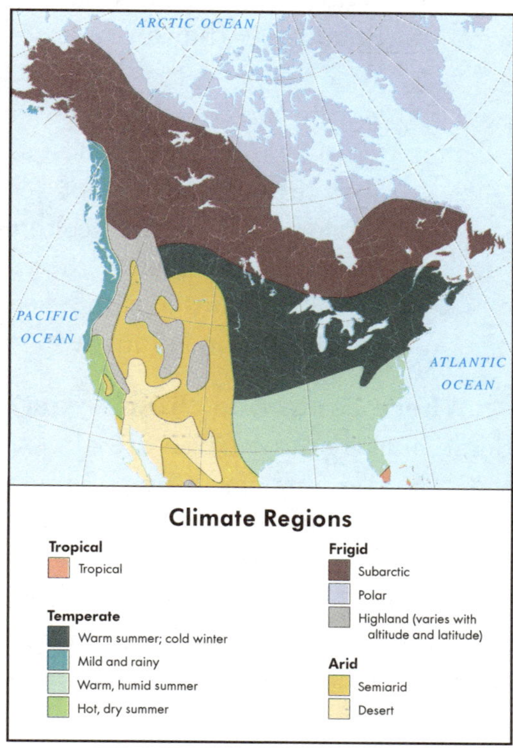


## Study the Lesson

1. Before a planet or a country can be inhabited, it must have a ——— that is suitable for life.
2. Tell whether each of the following describes *weather* or *climate.*
   a. cloudy
   b. 39 inches of rain each year
   c. average annual temperature of 55°F
   d. light snowfall
   e. hurricane
   f. mild winters
   g. 2 inches of rain in 3 hours
   h. hot and wet the year around

3. Write the correct word or word part for each meaning. Use the lesson text or a dictionary if you need help.
   a. Very dry.
   b. Neither very hot nor very cold.
   c. Beneath or almost.
   d. Close to the equator.
   e. Half or partly.
   f. Relating to the North or South Pole.
   g. Very cold.

   arctic
   arid
   polar
   semi-
   sub-
   temperate
   tropical

4. Name the correct climate for each description.
   a. 20 to 50 inches of rainfall a year; good for farming.
   b. Very little plant life; hot; less than 10 inches of rain a year.
   c. Little rain each year; cold; melting snow supports some trees.
   d. Very warm and rainy the year around; much plant life.
   e. 10 to 20 inches of rain a year; cattle graze on grasslands.
   f. So cold that no plants can grow; snow the year around.

**Where can living things exist?** Some places on the earth are almost too hot and dry for living things. Others are almost too cold for living things. Amazingly, there is some life in every land of the earth except near the North and South Poles. Even Antarctica is home for some mosses and penguins.

Deserts also have some plants and animals. The mesquite (me·skēt′) tree has deep roots about 40 feet (12 m) long. Cactus plants gather the little rain they receive and store it in thick stems. Small animals escape the burning daytime heat by burrowing into the ground. The camel has a body designed to conserve water. This allows it to travel several days without needing to drink.

Considering that life exists on no other planet, the earth is indeed a very special creation. God made it with all the necessary conditions and elements to be inhabited by living plants, animals, and people.

In Lesson 1 you saw that the following things help to support life on the earth.

- The sun is the right brightness to produce the right amount of heat.
- The earth is 93 million miles from the sun so that it is not too hot or too cold and so that water is in liquid form.
- The sun is a steady star that gives even heat energy all year long.

Now you will consider more ways in which the earth is suitable to be inhabited.

**The day and the year are the right length.** If the earth turned too slowly on its axis, the ground would become too hot for life in the daytime and too cold for life at night. After 12 o'clock on a summer day, we are glad that the sun moves lower in the sky so the temperature can begin to drop. If our days were several months long, as they are on Mercury, the temperature would keep rising until water would boil and all the plants and animals would die.

The earth turns on its axis once every 24 hours. That makes a good length for our day. The ground has time to get warm enough for plants to grow. At night the ground does not lose too much heat. The length of the day is part of God's wise plan to make the earth inhabitable.

The year is also a good length to support life. In winter the temperatures get colder and colder because of the short days. But then the sun rises higher in the sky each day, and spring comes. "For, lo, the winter is past, . . . the flowers appear on the earth; the time of the singing of birds is come" (Song of Solomon 2:11, 12).

After spring we need the extra heat of summer to grow tomatoes and beans. Many vegetables and farm crops need a growing season several months long. The ***growing season*** is the time from the last killing frost in spring to the first killing frost in fall.

God set the length of the year by the earth's revolution around the sun. It takes the earth 365¼ days to make one journey around the sun. Our year is the right length so that growing seasons are long enough to raise crops in most places on the earth.

**The earth is tilted on its axis.** God made the earth so that most of it could be inhabited. If the earth were not tilted on its axis at all, large areas in the north and south would get so little heat from the sun that crops would not grow there. When the sun shines at a slant, the same amount of

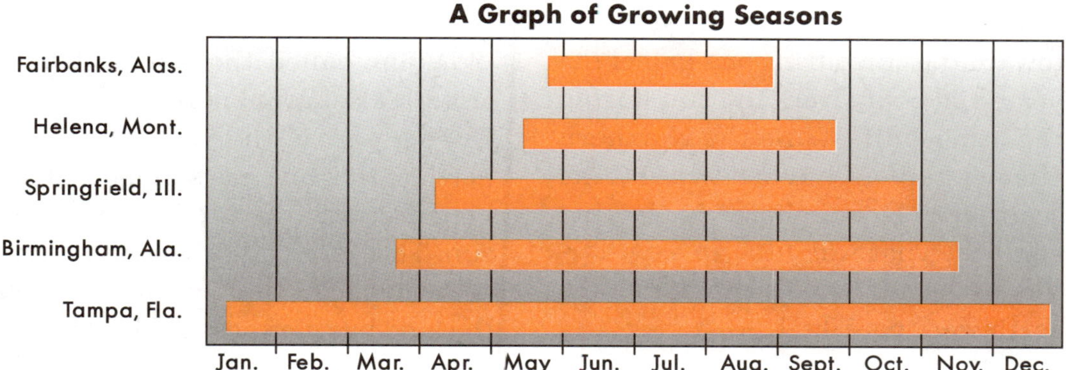

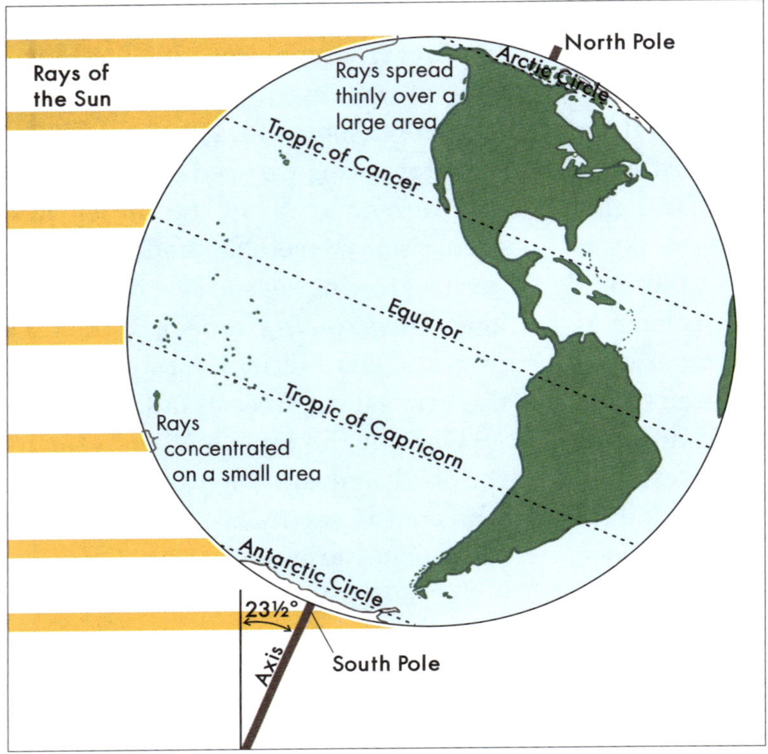


sunlight spreads out over a greater area than if it were coming straight down. Then the ground does not get as warm.

As the earth travels around the sun, its tilt causes different seasons. The Northern Hemisphere tilts toward the sun during one-half of the year, and away from the sun during the other half. While the Northern Hemisphere is having winter, the Southern Hemisphere is having summer. That way life can exist farther to the north and south than if the earth were not tilted.

A globe is a model of the earth. A globe is mounted so that its axis has the same slant as the earth's tilt. That slant is 23½ degrees. Most globes are circled by five special lines. One of them is the equator, which goes around the exact middle of the globe. Between Florida and Cuba is a line called the ***tropic of Cancer.*** This line marks the northernmost latitude on which the sun shines from straight overhead.

The ***tropic of Capricorn,*** which goes through the middle of Australia, is the southernmost latitude on which the sun shines from straight overhead. The area between the tropic of Cancer and the tropic of Capricorn has mostly tropical climate.

A line called the ***Arctic Circle*** crosses Alaska and northern Canada. During part of the year, the region north of this line has sunlight all day long because it is tilting toward the sun. That is why it is called the "land of the midnight sun." Six months later, the land has darkness all day because then the region tilts away from the sun. Around the continent of Antarctica is the ***Antarctic Circle.*** The region south of this line also has days of all sunshine and all darkness.

North of the equator, the temperate climate lies between the Arctic Circle and the tropic of Cancer. South of the equator, the temperate climate lies between the Antarctic Circle and the tropic of Capricorn. Most of the land regions of the earth lie in these tropical and temperate climates. This pattern of climates is part of God's wise plan for living things.

**Extremes of the Earth's Climate**

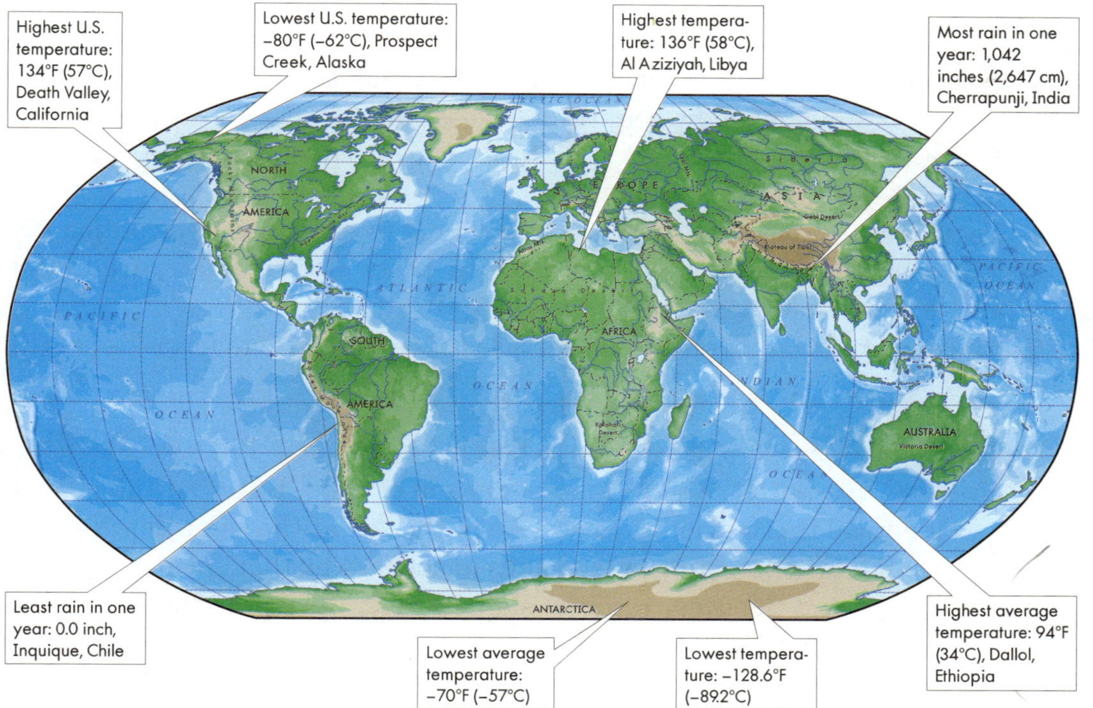


## Study the Lesson

5. The earth turns completely around on its axis once every ——— hours to make one ———.
6. a. Why would the earth be less suited for life if the day were longer?
   b. Why would it be less suited if the year were shorter?
7. The earth revolves around the sun every ——— days to make one ———.
8. The earth's axis is tilted ——— degrees, and this causes the ——— of the earth.

9. Why is the ground cooler when the rays of sunlight are slanted?
10. To be at a place that has sunshine at midnight, you would need to go either north of the ——— or south of the ———.
11. When the North Pole is at its greatest tilt toward the sun, the sun is directly above the ———.
12. This lesson tells about five special lines that circle the globe.
    a. Between which two lines does most of the tropical climate occur?
    b. Most of North America is in the north temperate region. Between which two lines is this region?

## Review Exercises

1. Four of Jupiter's ——— can be seen with a small telescope. [9]
2. Saturn is surrounded by beautiful ——— that look like a disk of gold. [9]
3. Between the orbits of Mars and Jupiter are thousands of small bodies called ———. [8]
4. Venus rotates ——— on its axis, which cannot be explained by evolution. [7]
5. The orbits of the planets, and especially those of the comets, are in the shape of (a circle, an egg, an ellipse). [6]
6. The sun produces its energy as particles of ——— unite to form ———. [2]

## Apply the Lesson

1. Test the relationship of latitude to heating by the sun. Fill two cake pans the same size with the same kind of dry soil or sand. Bury the bulb end of two identical thermometers slantwise in the soil at the same depth. On a clear day, let the sun shine on the pans in such a way that one pan receives direct rays and the other receives slanted rays. Check the thermometers after half an hour. Between what two lines on the earth is the land like that in the pan receiving direct sunlight? Between what two lines is the land like that in the pan receiving slanted sunlight?
2. Use a dictionary or an encyclopedia to learn why Cancer and Capricorn are used to name the tropic lines.
3. At the South Pole, the sun is in the sky all day long for several months of the year. Why does the air not become so warm that it melts the huge icecap on Antarctica?

## Lesson 12

# Water to Support Life

"For I will pour water upon him that is thirsty, and floods upon the dry ground: I will pour my spirit upon thy seed, and my blessing upon thine offspring: and they shall spring up as among the grass, as willows by the water courses" (Isaiah 44:3, 4).

### Vocabulary

**aquifer** (ak′·wə·fər), a layer of broken rock or soil containing water.

**atom,** the smallest possible particle of an element.

**capillary action** (kap′·ə·lar′·ē), the upward movement of water by making surfaces wet.

**compound,** a material made of more than one element.

**fresh water,** water that is not salty like the ocean.

**molecule,** the smallest possible particle still having the properties of a substance.

**oasis** (ō·ā′·sis), a place in a desert with enough water for plants.

**solvent,** a liquid that dissolves other materials.

**wetland,** a place where the underground water level is near the surface.

All living things must have water. This is true for all plants and animals, from the one-celled bacterium to the 5-ton elephant. Without water there can be no life. Water makes the difference between a field of tall, growing corn and a barren desert.

God made the cactus to need very little water. Its roots lie close to the surface of the ground to quickly absorb water from light showers. The inside of its fleshy trunk soaks up water like a sponge. A waxy skin on the cactus helps to keep the water from evaporating.

God made the camel to live several days without water. As it uses fat in its hump, water is released. A hump of fat can provide over ten gallons of water. The cactus and the camel can live in lands with very little water; but they must have some water, or they too will die.

God made your mouth so that you feel thirsty when your body needs more water. Only water can quench that thirst. God created living things to need water, and He provided abundant water on the earth to meet that need.

Saguaro cacti

**What is water?** If you could divide a water droplet again and again until you had the smallest possible particle of water, you would have one ***molecule*** of water. A molecule of water can be divided into three parts: one ***atom*** of oxygen and two atoms of hydrogen. But if the molecule were divided, it would no longer be water. That is why we say a molecule is the smallest possible particle of water.

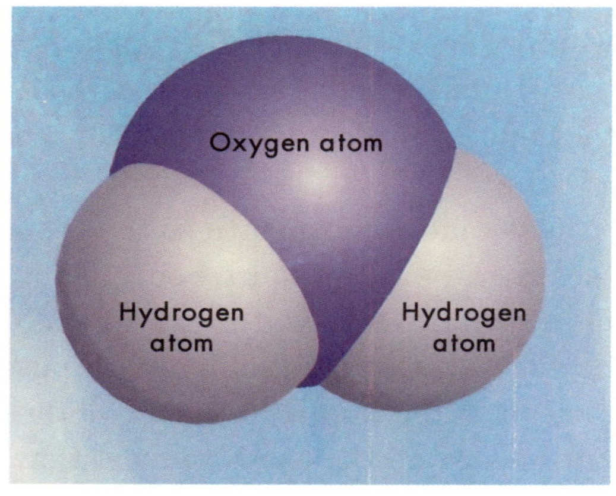

A water molecule

Any material, such as water, that is made of two or more different ingredients is a ***compound.*** The compound water consists of two parts of hydrogen and one part of oxygen, or in abbreviated form, we sometimes say $H_2O$.

Many materials such as sugar and salt dissolve easily in water. For this reason, water is called a ***solvent.*** Water works as a solvent in blood. During digestion, the starches, proteins, and fats in food are changed into materials that will dissolve. Only dissolved materials can be absorbed into the blood. The water in your blood carries this dissolved matter to the cells and takes dissolved wastes away. The kidneys use water to remove the wastes from the blood.

Being a solvent also makes water important to plants. Only dissolved minerals can go into a plant through

Copper sulfate is a blue salt that dissolves in water. As these grains of "rock" dissolve, the water turns into a transparent blue.

the roots. Minerals in soil and fertilizer dissolve in water to feed the plants. All life depends on water being a good solvent.

Living things cannot use water unless it is liquid. Only between the freezing and boiling points of water can it be liquid. God has placed the earth at just the right distance from the sun for water to be a life-sustaining liquid.

God made your body to sweat when it gets hot. The evaporation of sweat is a cooling process that keeps your body from overheating when you work or play.

The wetting action of water causes water to climb a small distance up the sides of a glass. If the sides are very close together in a glass tube, the water will actually climb up the tube. This is called ***capillary action.*** Capillary action helps carry water up the capillaries (tiny tubes) in the stems of plants. Capillary action also brings water up through the particles of soil from underground water. Without this, plants would die for

Water in the dish rises up the soil by capillary action and waters the plant roots.

lack of water a few days after a rain.

The slippery property of water is important to man and animals as a lubricant. Water lubricates the food as it slips down your throat. Water lubricates your joints and allows the muscles to move smoothly. If the eye does not have enough water, it will not move easily in the eye socket. This condition, called "dry eye," can be painful.

Water is a good cleaning agent. Clean clothes, food, and bodies help to reduce sickness. The water of your eye cleans the eye and also lubricates it. If you get dirt in your eye, it will begin to water to help clean the dirt out.

Water makes up 65 percent of a person's body weight. About 6 percent of the body water is in the blood, and 63 percent is in the cells. Much water fills in the spaces of the body. If a person loses 20 percent of his body water, he is likely to die. A man can live over two months without food, but he cannot live more than a week without water.

You must have water to live. All plants and animals must have water to live.

## Study the Lesson

1. Write whether each statement is *true* or *false*.
   a. Most living things need water to stay alive, but there are a few exceptions.
   b. The cactus stores water to use over long periods of dry weather.
   c. Cactus plants have deep roots that bring up water from underground.
   d. The hump of a camel contains a pouch full of water that helps it to survive in the desert.
   e. Thirst helps you know when your body needs more water.
2. Explain what is meant when water is called $H_2O$.
3. Before a material can be absorbed into the blood, it must be ———.
4. Your body needs water to carry materials in the ——— and to help the ——— remove wastes.
5. Animal hair is very high in nitrogen, which plants need. Since hair does not dissolve in water, it makes a (good, poor) fertilizer.
6. God planned for the ——— of sweat to cool our bodies.
7. In what two ways is capillary action helpful to plants?
8. Your body needs water to ——— the joints and eyes, and to ——— the eyes.

**The earth has plenty of water.** The earth has 326 million cubic miles (1,358 million $km^3$) of water. A cubic mile is a cube one mile wide, one mile long, and a mile high. If the surface of the whole earth were flat with all the water on top, the whole earth would be covered to a depth of more than 1½ miles (2.4 km). That is a lot of water! Think of it—of all the planets in the solar system, only the earth has enough water to support life. And what a great quantity of water there is! God created the earth to be inhabited. He placed water here because life needs water.

**The distribution of water.** Some places have more water than others. In a ***wetland,*** the level of underground water is near the surface of the land. These marshes are the home of many plants and animals. Alligators live in swamps or marshes in Florida. Cattails grow in wetlands. Low areas along oceans and streams make wetlands teeming with life.

Because of low rainfall and hot temperatures, a desert has very little water for living things. If a river runs through a desert, as in Egypt, people can raise crops by irrigation. At some places in a desert, there are spots with enough water for trees and other vegetation. Such an area of vegetation in a desert is called an ***oasis.*** Understanding how an oasis gets water will help you understand an important way God provided for the storage and distribution of water.

When rain falls, much of the water soaks into the ground. It seeps downward until it reaches a layer of solid rock. Since it can sink no farther, the ground above the rock fills with water. Some ground water flows out of the ground in the form of springs. Some water may flow horizontally through a layer of broken rock or soil called an ***aquifer.*** An aquifer can carry water for many miles under the ground. If an aquifer comes to the surface in a desert, it forms an oasis.

Even in lands with plenty of rainfall, aquifers are a valuable source of water. Wells are drilled into the aquifer, and water is pumped out for drinking, washing, and irrigation. Maybe the water at your school or home comes from an aquifer.

The illustration on page 92 shows that the oceans contain most of the water on the earth. But ocean water is not fit for drinking and irrigation because it contains salt and other materials that are harmful to plants, animals, and man. God provided a very wonderful way for ocean water to be purified. When sunlight warms the ocean, only water evaporates into the atmosphere. The salt and harmful materials are left behind. The evaporated water then falls in showers to water crops and to feed underground aquifers. Water in aquifers, rivers, and

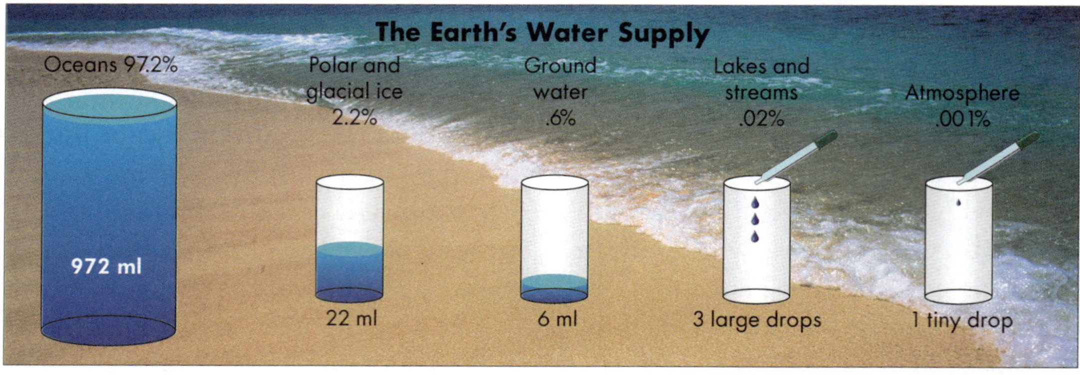


If all the earth's water were represented as one liter, the water would divide into these portions.

lakes is called ***fresh water*** because it has been purified by evaporation from the oceans.

**Water makes the earth beautiful.** Water is a very useful material. Life needs water. We use water for washing and putting out fires. Falling water generates much electricity. The oceans and rivers are used for transportation. We are also thankful for the beauty that water gives the earth. People travel many miles to see a waterfall. Streams and rivers, lakes and oceans also attract tourists. Pictures on calendars often show a beautiful scene that includes water. None of these things can be found on any other planet. Only God could provide so much from a single material. Water is a very special part of the way God made the earth for our health and enjoyment.

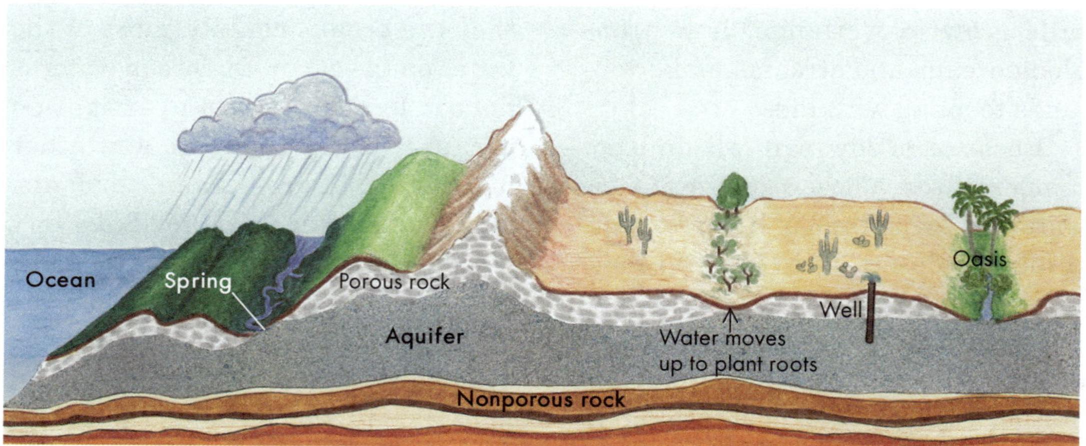


The water in an aquifer feeds springs, wells, and plants and flows on out to the ocean.

Sand dunes are slowly filling this low oasis in Algeria, leaving only treetops visible.

Water makes beautiful rice paddies in Indonesia. A mountain aquifer provides water to flood the terraces.

## Study the Lesson

9. Write the correct vocabulary word for each sentence.
   a. Water is a good ——— because many materials dissolve in it.
   b. Water is called a ——— because it is made of more than one element.
   c. A thirsty traveler in a desert is glad to find an ———.
   d. For a compound such as water, the smallest possible particle is a ———.
   e. For an element such as oxygen, the smallest possible particle is an ———.
   f. Plants need ——— ——— rather than salty water like that in the ocean.
   g. An ——— is an underground layer that may carry water for many miles.
   h. Underground water moves upward by ——— ———.
   i. Another name for a swamp or marsh is a ———.
10. What harm would be done by draining a wetland?
11. How did God provide for rainwater to be pure?
12. Besides being useful, water also helps to make the earth ——— for our enjoyment.

## Review Exercises

1. The earth's axis is tilted ——— degrees, and this causes the ——— of the earth. [11]
2. The axis of Uranus is almost (level, vertical) in relation to its orbit. [9]
3. The location of Neptune was predicted by the use of ———. [9]
4. The closer a planet is to the sun, the (more slowly, more swiftly) it travels and the (shorter, longer) its year is. [7]
5. The moon is unsuitable for life because it has no ——— or ——— and because its temperature is both too ——— and too ———. [3]
6. A solar eclipse is total when the size of the moon appears (equal to, smaller than) the size of the sun. [4]

## Apply the Lesson

1. Experiment with the dissolving ability of water. Weigh one-half glass of water. (Subtract the weight of the glass.) Dissolve salt until no more will dissolve. Weigh the glass of water again. How much salt dissolved in comparison with the weight of the water?
2. Here are some experiments you can do with capillary action.
   a. Put two tablespoons of water in a glass, and add a few drops of red food coloring. Cut off the bottom end of a celery stalk that has leaves on it, and set the stalk in the glass for several hours. You will see the colored water traveling up the small tubes in the celery.
   b. Roll up some brown paper (such as from a grocery bag), and place one end in a glass with a little water at the bottom. Notice how fast the water rises. This is the way water rises in the soil by capillary action.
   c. Observe the turned-up edge of water in a clear glass. Get two flat pieces of glass about 6 inches square, and use tape to hinge them together along one vertical side. Open the other side very slightly, and lower the pieces of glass into a tray of colored water. This will show that the closer together the pieces are (along the hinged edge), the higher the capillary action will raise the water.
3. Do some research in an encyclopedia on methods of desalting ocean water. Are any of the methods similar to God's method of purifying ocean water? Why do countries not desalt enough water for large-scale irrigation? How does this show the wonder and wisdom of God's method?

# Lesson 13

## The Protecting Atmosphere

"They shall not hunger nor thirst; neither shall the heat nor sun smite them: for he that hath mercy on them shall lead them, even by the springs of water shall he guide them" (Isaiah 49:10).

### Vocabulary

**infrared** (in′·frə·red′), the kind of rays that produce heat.

**magnetosphere** (mag·nē′·tō·sfir′), the magnetic region above the atmosphere that protects the earth from the solar wind.

**mesosphere** (mez′·ə·sfir′), the layer of the atmosphere where rocks from space become meteors and burn up.

**ozone** (ō′·zōn′), a gas in the atmosphere that filters out ultraviolet light.

**stratosphere** (strat′·ə·sfir′), the layer of the atmosphere that filters out ultraviolet rays.

**troposphere** (trō′·pə·sfir′), the lowest layer of the atmosphere, where weather occurs.

**ultraviolet,** the kind of invisible, cancer-causing rays from the sun.

Have you ever felt as if the sun were smiting you on a hot summer day? You know that the rays of the sun are very strong. We need the heat from those rays to warm the earth, but the sun also gives off particles and rays that are dangerous to life. The verse above is a promise of protection from the smiting power of the sun.

Did you know that God provided the earth with special filters to protect living creatures from the sun's harmful rays?

**The atmosphere is a blanket of air surrounding the earth.** Like a thick comforter, the atmosphere protects the earth and helps to keep it warm. But the atmosphere is different from other blankets in that it has no upper surface. With higher altitudes, the air gets thinner and thinner until at more than 600 miles (1,000 km) there is no air at all. In this lesson you will study things about the atmosphere that God designed to help make the earth inhabitable.

**The atmosphere gives us oxygen to breathe.** The air is mostly a mixture of two elements: about four-fifths nitrogen and one-fifth oxygen. We can be thankful that both nitrogen and oxygen are colorless and odorless so that the sky is clear and the air is refreshing to breathe. You could live only a few minutes without breathing. Your body needs the oxygen from the air. God put plenty of oxygen in the atmosphere, and breathing is all you need to do to get it.

The oxygen in the atmosphere is also needed to light fires. Wood, gasoline, and coal need oxygen to burn. But if the atmosphere were 100 percent oxygen, fires could not be controlled. Even steel will burn in pure oxygen. When God made the oxygen we need for breathing and burning, He wisely mixed it with nitrogen that will not burn.

**The atmosphere gives us air pressure.** Air has weight and pushes down on the earth. With miles of air above you, the atmosphere makes helpful pressure. The air pressure pushes the air into your lungs when you take a breath. The pressure pushes the milk up a straw when you suck on it. Air pressure keeps water from boiling at a low temperature. We must have air pressure surrounding us to live.

## Study the Lesson

1. One-fifth of the air is ———, which we ——— to stay alive.
2. Four-fifths of the air is ———, which makes it possible to control ———.
3. Because air is ———, we can see clearly through it. Because air is ———, it is refreshing to breathe.
4. If the atmosphere were only a few miles thick, there would be so little air ——— that we could not breathe, drink with a straw, or even live.

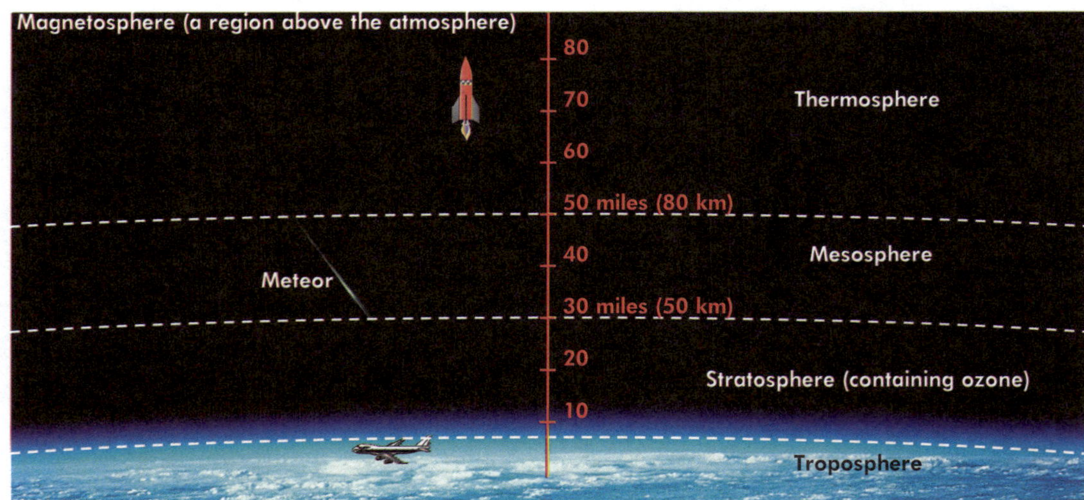


The layers of the atmosphere

**The atmosphere protects us.** The atmosphere has a number of layers. You can see these layers in the diagram above. Different things happen in each layer. We want to especially see how the atmosphere protects life from various kinds of harmful radiation.

The ***magnetosphere*** has no air and therefore is not actually part of the atmosphere. But this region above the atmosphere is an important part of what is overhead to protect living things from harm. The magnetosphere, which is part of the earth's magnetic field, protects us from the solar wind. Charged particles like colorless smoke stream away from the surface of the sun, traveling 1 million miles per hour (1.6 million km/h). This wind would be harmful to life if it reached the earth's surface. But the magnetic field pushes aside the charged particles like a car driving through a smoke cloud, and they continue harmlessly into outer space. See the diagram on page 20.

The ***mesosphere*** protects us from pieces of rock that are called meteorites if they reach the ground. More than a million of these rocks plunge into the atmosphere every day. Even small ones would be as dangerous as bullets fired from a gun. But few of them get closer than 30 miles from the earth. They become so hot from friction with air in the mesosphere that they burn up and turn into a fine dust that floats harmlessly to the ground.

The ***stratosphere*** filters out the sun's harmful ***ultraviolet*** rays. Although we cannot see ultraviolet rays, they can do us much harm. On warm summer days, these rays tan your skin. Too many ultraviolet rays can damage living cells and cause cancer and blindness. If the atmosphere did not screen out most of the ultraviolet rays, the earth would not be a safe place to live.

The material in the stratosphere that filters out ultraviolet rays is ***ozone***. This gas is a special form of oxygen, different from the oxygen we breathe. Ozone is poisonous, but in the stratosphere it helps us stay alive by protecting us from ultraviolet rays.

The bottom layer of the atmosphere where we live is called the ***troposphere.*** More than three-fourths of the air in the atmosphere is squeezed into the 6–10 miles (10–16 km) of the troposphere. Only in this layer is there enough air pressure to breathe. Even in the upper troposphere, the passenger compartment of an airplane must be pressurized so that people can breathe well.

Weather occurs in the troposphere. All the clouds you see are less than 10 miles high. Highest of all are the thin, wispy cirrus clouds. The fluffy cumulus clouds are much lower. Even

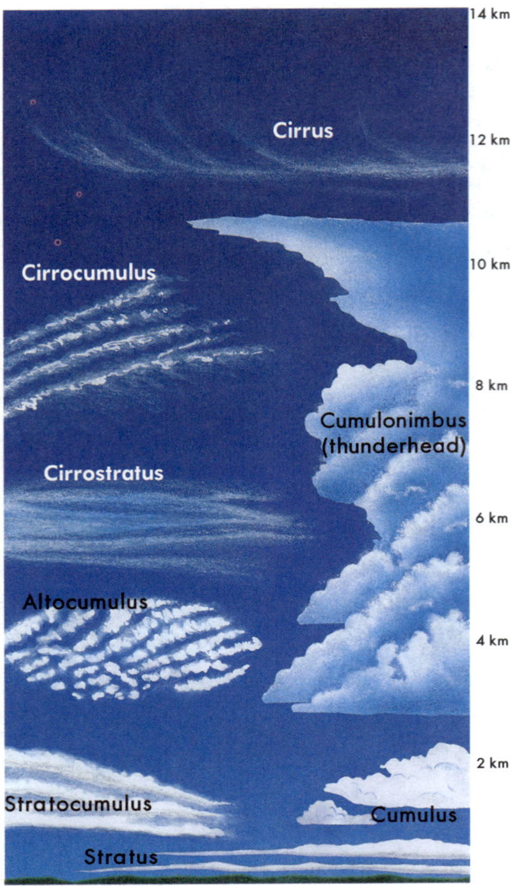

Different clouds are seen at various altitudes.

lower are the stratus clouds, which form layers not far above the ground. Rain and snow come from the clouds. They are an important part of God's plan for distributing water with the water cycle.

The clouds also help to keep the earth warm. Maybe you thought their shade helped to keep it cool. We do appreciate the shade of clouds on a summer day. But at night, the clouds help to keep heat from escaping. Knowing about ***infrared*** rays will help you understand how this works.

A warm object gives off infrared rays, or heat rays. Hold your hand close to a hot kettle, walk past a fire, or stand in front of a heater. Infrared rays make you feel warm, even though you do not touch the kettle or the heater. Infrared lamps are sometimes used for keeping animals or pipes warm in winter.

During the day, the earth soaks up heat from the sun. At night, the earth gives off heat in the form of infrared rays. The clouds act as a blanket to reflect the infrared rays back, and this helps to keep the earth warm. On a cloudless night, more infrared rays escape into space and temperatures drop much lower. In the spring and fall, we sometimes have frost on clear nights because there are no clouds to reflect the heat back to the ground.

Twilight at Memphis, Tennessee. How will these clouds warm the city during the night?

God's wisdom in creating the atmosphere is evident in many ways. The atmosphere is the right thickness to give us good air pressure. It is made of the right materials. An outer shell causes harmful particles to flow around the earth. The mesosphere burns up the rocks flying in from space. The ozone layer protects us from harmful rays. The winds and clouds of the troposphere bring us pure, life-sustaining water. Truly, God made the atmosphere wisely for the good of all living creatures.

## Study the Lesson

5. For each layer of the atmosphere, write what item it protects us from. You will not use all the choices.

| | | |
|---|---|---|
| a. stratosphere | infrared rays | solar wind |
| b. mesosphere | meteorites | ultraviolet rays |
| c. magnetosphere | pressure | |

6. Write the correct word or phrase from your lesson for each description.
   a. Cancer-causing rays that tan our skin.
   b. Stream of high-speed particles from the sun.
   c. Poisonous form of oxygen that takes out ultraviolet light.
   d. Heat-producing rays that warm the earth.
7. The passenger compartment of a high-flying airplane must be pressurized because
   a. this protects the passengers from poisonous ozone.
   b. the outside air is too thin to breathe.
   c. the plane would be crushed without the extra pressure inside.
   d. the extra pressure is needed to operate the controls.
8. Clouds help to keep the ground warm because
   a. they store heat from the sun.
   b. they protect the ground from the cold of outer space.
   c. they send warm rain to the ground.
   d. they reflect heat rays that come from the earth.
9. In spring and fall, you can expect to see frost in the morning
   a. when the sky was clear during the night.
   b. when the sky was clear the day before.
   c. when the sky was cloudy during the night.
   d. when the sky was cloudy the day before.

## Review Exercises

1. Water is called $H_2O$ because each molecule has two atoms of ——— and one atom of ———. [12]
2. To be at a place that has sunshine at midnight, you would need to go north of the ——— ——— or south of the ——— ———. [11]
3. Sometimes the superior planets appear to move backward in relation to the stars. This is called ——— motion. [9]
4. The axis of Mars is ———, which causes it to have ——— as the earth does. [8]
5. Mercury is hot on one side and cold on the other because it rotates very (slowly, swiftly). [7]
6. A lunar eclipse occurs when the shadow of the ——— falls on the ———. [4]

## Apply the Lesson

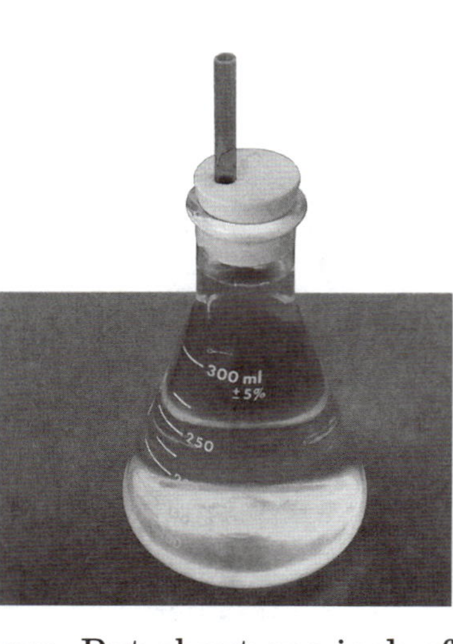


1. Show that without air pressure you cannot use a straw to drink water. Get a bottle with a small opening, and fill it completely with water. Put a glass tube through a one-hole stopper that fits the opening of the bottle. (A three-hole stopper with two holes sealed shut will work too.) Put the stopper in the opening. Try to draw water out of the bottle by sucking on the glass tube.
2. Only about one-fifth of the air is oxygen. You can do a demonstration to show that most of the air is not oxygen. Use melted candle wax to fasten a four-inch candle in the center of a pan. Put about one inch of water in the pan. Light the candle, and quickly cover it with a quart jar so that the mouth of the jar is in the water. How long does the candle continue to burn? Why does it go out?
3. Ozone is an interesting and useful gas. Do some research in an encyclopedia or a chemistry book on what is special about this form of oxygen. What are some practical uses for it? How is it made? Perhaps you have even smelled this gas. Where?

# Lesson 14

## The Moderating Oceans

"Sing unto the LORD a new song, and his praise from the end of the earth, ye that go down to the sea, and all that is therein; the isles, and the inhabitants thereof" (Isaiah 42:10).

### Vocabulary

**current,** a large stream of slowly moving ocean water.

All the natural works of God praise Him. The oceans praise God by their greatness and by the wonderful way they help to make the world inhabitable. Without the oceans, there would be no inhabitants. The oceans not only provide a home for "all that is therein," but they also supply water for all the islands and continents "and the inhabitants thereof." That includes you. We should praise God for the oceans.

**Oceans contain life-supporting water.** As you have learned, living things must have water to stay alive. The oceans have plenty of water!

**Facts About the Ocean**

Size: 140,000,000 square miles (361,000,000 km²)

Amount of water: 322,000,000 cubic miles (1,347,000,000 km³)

Deepest spot: 36,198 feet (11,033 m) at Challenger Deep, in the Mariana Trench, in the western Pacific

Temperature at surface: about 28°F to 86°F (–2°C to 30°C)

Taste: very salty (3½%), mostly "table salt"

Even if you live hundreds of miles from the nearest ocean, you need its water to stay alive. The water you drank this morning was in the ocean not long ago.

The water running down the streams and rivers goes into the ocean. The water of the ocean then evaporates and rises high into the air to form clouds. Rain from the clouds brings life-supporting water to lands far from the ocean.

If you fill a cake pan with water and let it sit uncovered long enough, all the water will leave by evaporation. You would not want to wait for a drink until enough water evaporated from one cake pan to fill a glass. That would probably take a week or more! If you filled an entire meadow with pans of water, each pan would give only a little by evaporation, but the total from the entire field would be a large amount of water.

The oceans are big evaporating pans that supply plenty of fresh water for the rest of the earth. About 72 percent (almost three-fourths) of the earth's surface is covered with oceans. If you should spend two hours along the Gulf of Mexico on a warm summer day, more than 10 billion gallons of water would evaporate while you were there. Without this water from the oceans, the lands would become dry and barren. God made the lands for man to live on, and He made the oceans to supply those lands with water.

**Oceans contain many forms of life.** The ocean is teeming with plants and animals. Fishing is an important industry that supplies a healthy source of food. Cod, halibut, mackerel, salmon, and tuna are only a few of the many valuable fish in the ocean.

The ocean is the home of whales, the largest animals. There are many kinds of whales, but the largest is the blue whale. It may reach a length of 100 feet (30 m) and a weight of 150 tons (135 MT). Whales are different from fish in two important ways. Fish use gills to take oxygen from the water. But whales breathe air, so they must come to the surface every five to ten minutes. Fish are cold-blooded, but whales are warm-blooded. A whale's body is insulated with a thick layer of fat called blubber.

Many strange creatures inhabit the ocean. The squid and the octopus have long arms covered with round sucking disks. Jellyfish with stinging tentacles, coral with rocklike homes, sponges with rubbery bodies, sea anemones with flowerlike heads, eels that look like snakes—these all make the ocean a zoo of animal wonders.

Many strange plants live in the ocean. The tiny diatoms in geometric

Anemone fish in a sea anemone

The leopard shark is a predator fish.

A blue ribbon eel

A lionfish and a starfish among cup coral

Yellow sea lilies are plantlike animals.

shapes are a kind of one-celled algae. Coarse brown kelp is a seaweed that can grow up to 100 feet (30 m) in length. Sargassum is a leafy seaweed with air bulbs that keep it afloat in the middle of the ocean. The large Sargasso Sea in the middle of the North Atlantic Ocean gets its name from this plant, since this part of the ocean has large beds of sargassum. Red algae is long seaweed that grows along seacoasts. If you visit an ocean shore, watch for seaweed, especially around rocks when the tide is out.

## Study the Lesson

1. Almost ——— (what fraction?) of the earth is covered with water.
2. The water for rain comes from ocean water that ———.
3. We would have less rain if the oceans were
   a. bigger.
   b. smaller.
   c. deeper.
   d. not as deep.
4. Name each ocean-dwelling plant or animal described below.
   a. Breathes with gills and is a good source of food.
   b. Is a large warm-blooded animal that breathes air.
   c. Has eight long arms with sucking disks.
   d. Has a flowerlike head.
   e. Has a rubbery body that can be used for washing.
   f. Has a rocklike home that builds up large reefs.
   g. Is a kind of alga with a tiny, geometric-shaped body.
   h. May be coarse and brown, and may grow 100 feet long.
   i. Has air bulbs that keep it floating.

**Oceans moderate the temperature of the earth.** You have probably heard of solar energy collectors that are on the roofs of some houses. Often water is used in solar collectors to hold the heat absorbed from the sun. Water is one of the best materials to store heat. Water can take in or give off a large amount of heat without a large change in temperature. A pound of water can hold about nine times as much heat energy as a pound of iron.

The oceans are giant solar collectors. The direct sunlight of summer falls on ocean water, which stores huge amounts of heat. Then during winter, the oceans give up some of their heat to the air above them. The warmed air blows over the surrounding lands and helps to keep their winters from becoming so cold. This is why farmers in Delaware and New Jersey can begin growing crops earlier in the spring than farmers in Pennsylvania can.

But on warm summer afternoons, the ocean does not warm up as fast as the land. Then the ocean is like an air conditioner as cool ocean breezes blow inland. These breezes keep summer temperatures from rising as high as they do farther inland. The oceans help to moderate both summer and winter in lands along the sea. In this way they make those places more pleasant to be inhabited.

**Ocean currents move heat.** As winds blow over the ocean, they tend to make the ocean water rotate in huge circles. For example, winds over the northern part of the North Atlantic Ocean usually blow from west to east. Farther south, the winds usually blow from east to west. This causes the whole North Atlantic Ocean to rotate slowly in a clockwise direction. A large stream of moving ocean water is called an ocean ***current.***

The water in the Gulf of Mexico receives much warmth from the sun. This warm water is carried by an ocean current north and then east to surround England with warm water. As a result, England has a milder climate than would be expected of a country so far north. England is as far north as areas of Canada that have severe winters. Yet England has moderate winters with temperatures rarely as low as 10°F (–12°C).

The current that warms England is called the Gulf Stream. It is one example of how an ocean current carries heat from one part of the earth to another.

Some ocean currents are cool. An example is the Peru Current along the coast of Peru and Chile, which brings cold water northward from near the South Pole. The cool air above this current holds little moisture, with the result that very dry land lies along the coast where the Peru Current flows.

This desert region is so dry that some parts may have no rain for ten years or more.

God wisely provided the oceans to make the earth inhabitable. They give us water. They contain many kinds of living things. They store heat to help warm us in winter. They help to cool our summers. They move heat from one place to another. We thank and praise God for the helpful oceans.

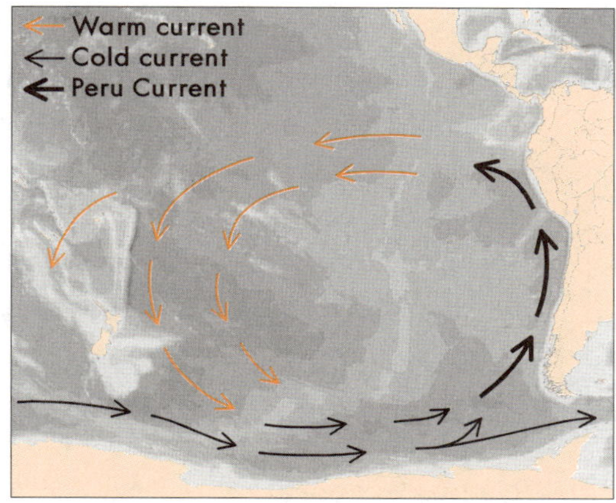

South Pacific Ocean currents

## Study the Lesson

5. If you wanted to keep your feet warm in bed, would you get more heat from 5 pounds of water at 150°F or from 5 pounds of iron at 150°F?
6. The largest solar collector in the world is the ———.
7. The oceans help to make the surrounding land (warmer, colder) in winter and (warmer, cooler) in summer.
8. A ——— is a movement of ocean water from one place to another.
9. What word describes the direction that the North Atlantic Ocean rotates?
10. The Gulf Stream is a (warm, cool) ocean current.
11. Why would you expect England to have a cold climate? Why does it have a moderate climate?
12. The Peru Current is a (warm, cool) ocean current that causes (much, little) rain to fall on nearby land.

## Review Exercises

1. Four-fifths of the air is ———, and one-fifth is ———. [13]
2. Water moves upward through soil by a process called ——— ———. [12]
3. The planets located inside the earth's orbit are called ——— planets. [7]
4. A solar eclipse is annular when the size of the moon appears (equal to, smaller than) the size of the sun. [4]
5. The moon goes through one cycle of its ———, or different shapes, in ——— days. [3]
6. Water must be in the ——— state for life to exist. [1]

## Apply the Lesson

1. Experiment with things that affect the rate of evaporation. Get four cake pans of the same size, one larger pan, and one smaller pan. Put one cup of water in each pan.

   Place the smaller pan, the larger pan, and one of the other pans on a table in the room. Of the remaining pans, place one in a cooler place, such as in the basement, and one in a warmer place, such as on a radiator. Use a fan to blow air lightly over the last pan.

   Which pan will become dry first? Which one will be last? What do the results tell you about God's wisdom in designing the oceans? When do the oceans evaporate most rapidly? Why will the ocean never evaporate dry?
2. Find a piece of iron that weighs about 1 pound. Weigh out an equal weight of water. Put a gallon of cold water in each of two plastic buckets. Now put both the piece of iron and the equal weight of water in a pan, and slowly heat them together until the water is just about too hot to put your hand into. Pick out the hot iron, and put it into one of the buckets. Pour the hot water into the other bucket. Let them sit for about a minute.

   Check the temperature of the water in each bucket after the heat is absorbed. Which is warmer? You could perform a similar experiment with lead, aluminum, brass, and alcohol (put the alcohol in a small jar when warming it in the water). Find out the meaning of *specific heat.* Try to find a table of specific heats. What does this demonstration have to do with the ocean?

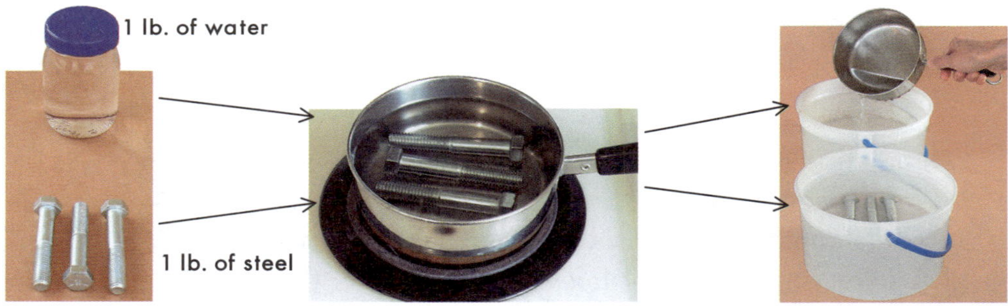


3. Use a reference book to find how currents move in the oceans of the world. Then write *clockwise* or *counterclockwise* to complete the following statements about the general direction of ocean currents.
   a. North of the equator, the ocean rotates ———.
   b. South of the equator, the ocean rotates ———.

# Lesson 15

## The Renewing Cycles

"The rain cometh down, and the snow from heaven, and returneth not thither, but watereth the earth, and maketh it bring forth and bud, that it may give seed to the sower, and bread to the eater" (Isaiah 55:10).

### Vocabulary

**legume** (leg′·yo͞om′), a plant that puts nitrogen compounds into the soil.

**nitrate** (nī′·trāt′), a compound with nitrogen in a form that plants can use.

**nitrogen fixation,** the process of putting nitrogen from the air into compounds that plants can use.

**protein,** a compound containing nitrogen and other important elements that are used by the body for growth and repair.

**renewable,** able to be used over and over.

**water table,** the underground level to which the soil is soaked with water.

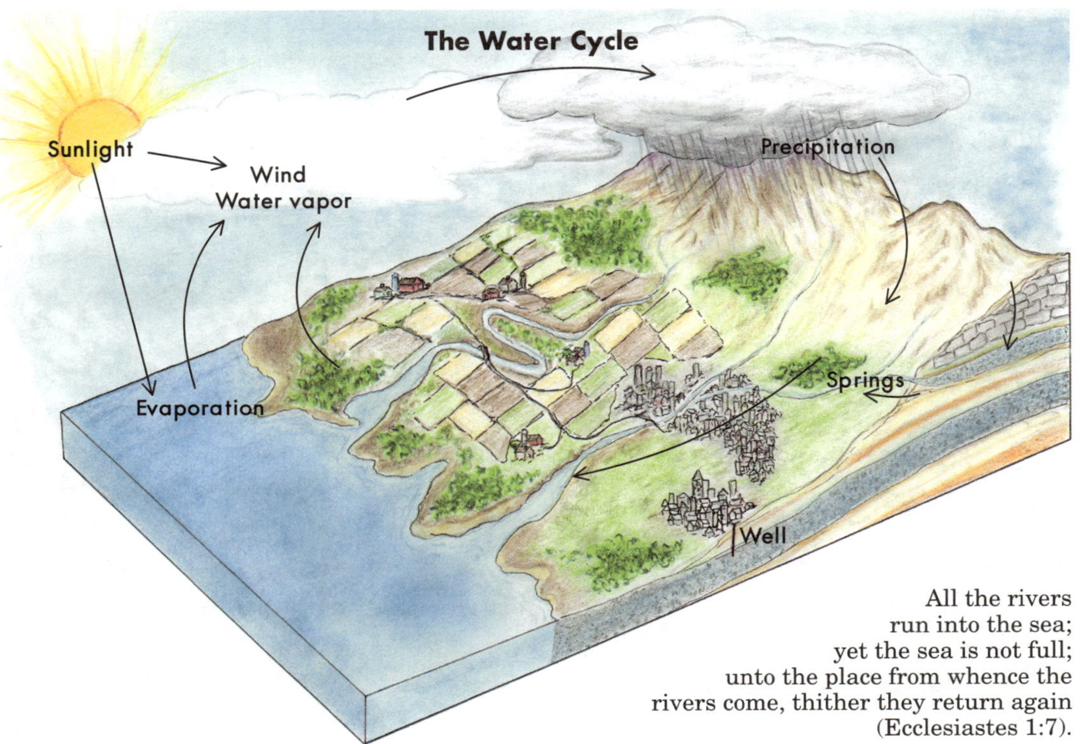


All the rivers
run into the sea;
yet the sea is not full;
unto the place from whence the
rivers come, thither they return again
(Ecclesiastes 1:7).

God placed many natural resources on the earth for man to use. Rocks and timber are useful building materials. Coal, oil, iron, copper, and zinc are useful fuels and metals found in the earth. Soil, wind, and water are all around us. These are but a few of the resources God supplied for us.

Many resources cannot be replaced or recycled once they have been used. For example, coal is dug from the ground and used to heat people's homes in winter. The smoke goes into the air, and the ashes are dumped outside. That coal can never again be used to produce heat. But even if all the coal were used up, there would still be living things on the earth.

Some resources are necessary to sustain life on the earth, and God made these to be ***renewable.*** This means they go through a series of events in which they are used again and again. Water, oxygen, and nitrogen are three renewable resources that are used over and over in cycles. In contrast, materials such as rocks and metals are not needed for life and are not recycled.

Why is coal a nonrenewable resource?

**The water cycle.** When rain falls, some of it soaks into the ground and supplies water that plants need to live. What will happen to the plants after all the water has come out of the clouds? Will all the land become a desert? Of course not. God has wisely planned that the water goes through a cycle to be used over and over again.

In the last lesson, you saw that large amounts of water evaporate from the oceans. This can be considered the beginning of the water cycle. Oceans are large storage areas for water. Of course, some water evaporates from lakes and rivers too.

As water vapor rises from the oceans, winds carry it over land areas, where it cools to form clouds. Job said, "He bindeth up the waters in his thick clouds" (Job 26:8).

Then "if the clouds be full of rain, they empty themselves upon the earth" (Ecclesiastes 11:3). In other words, rain falls when the air in the clouds becomes so full of water vapor that it cannot hold any more moisture. If the temperature is cold enough, the moisture may fall as snow, sleet, or hail.

After the water soaks into the

ground, some of it goes into the roots of plants. Some of the water trickles into underground streams to be carried to nearby springs. And some just stays in the ground to maintain the ***water table.*** During dry spells, water flows upward from the water table (through capillary action) to keep plants growing.

Visiting a wet cave is a good way to see an underground stream.

Underground streams carry the water to springs, wells, streams, lakes, and rivers. This network provides for the needs of people and animals, and eventually it carries the water back to the ocean, where it can start the cycle over again.

**The oxygen cycle.** The air in the atmosphere consists mostly of nitrogen and oxygen. Every time you draw a breath, you take both of these into your lungs. But your body can use only the oxygen. When you breathe out, you put carbon dioxide into the air. Carbon dioxide is a compound of carbon and oxygen, which your body releases as a waste product.

There is such a tremendous amount of oxygen in the atmosphere that you would have to breathe a long time before you used it all. But remember that you are not the only breather. Millions of people and millions of animals are also using oxygen. And every fire uses oxygen. Slowly but surely, all the free oxygen would be changed to carbon dioxide if God had not made a way for it to be renewed.

That is exactly what God did. He created multitudes of green plants, which use carbon dioxide to make food and release oxygen as a waste product. So even though multitudes of people and animals use oxygen every day, the supply is continually being renewed by the even greater number of green plants.

Oxygen is given off not by just one kind of green plant but by thousands of different plants in the world. Forests of giant trees, huge fields of crops, broad grasslands, and weeds all help to renew the oxygen supply in the air.

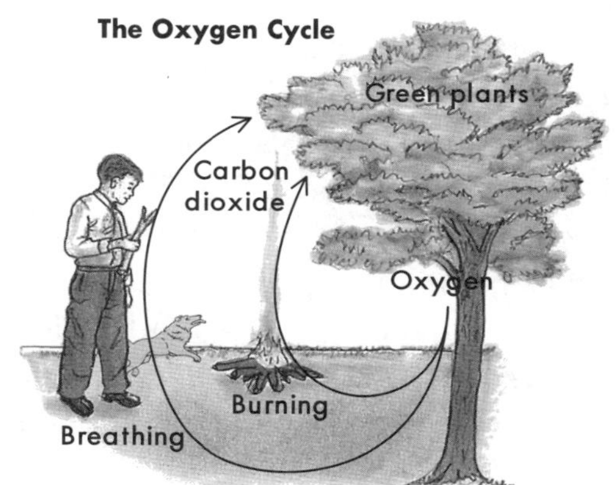

## Study the Lesson

1. Write the words that belong in the blanks.
   a. If a resource can be used over and over, it is said to be ———.
   b. A system in which things return to where they began is a ———.
   c. A waste product of breathing is ——— ———.
   d. Plants release ——— as a waste product.
2. There are no renewing cycles for materials such as coal and iron. Why not?
3. Write the missing words in each cycle. Use the diagrams in the lesson for help.
   a. ocean, ———, wind, clouds, rain, ———, streams, ocean
   b. plants, ———, animals, ——— ———, plants
4. For each cycle in number 3 above, name the important material for life that is being used over and over.
5. What would happen to a material such as oxygen if God had not made a cycle for it to be renewed?

**The nitrogen cycle.** You read in Lesson 13 that about four-fifths of the air is nitrogen. Plants, animals, and people all need nitrogen to grow, but none of them can use nitrogen directly from the air. Our lungs cannot absorb nitrogen as they absorb oxygen. The nitrogen must first go through a process called ***nitrogen fixation,*** in which it is changed into a ***nitrate.***

Nitrogen fixation happens in two main ways. One way is with the help of lightning. When the electricity of lightning goes through the air, it causes some of the nitrogen to combine with oxygen. Raindrops then carry this natural fertilizer to the ground, where plants can use it.

Nitrogen fixation also happens through the work of special bacteria in the soil. The bacteria form small knoblike growths on the roots of ***legumes,*** which are plants such as peas, beans, peanuts, clover, and alfalfa. Legumes take nitrogen from the air and carry it to their roots. There the bacteria change the nitrogen into nitrates and put them in the soil.

Plants take nitrates from the soil and turn them into ***proteins.*** The

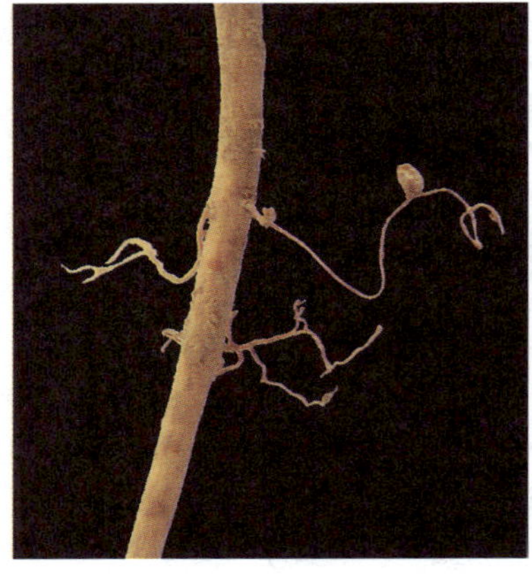

A nodule of bacteria on an alfalfa root.

bodies of animals and people use proteins to grow and repair themselves. When animals and people eat vegetables, they take in these proteins. The digestive system breaks them down, and the body uses the nitrogen in the proteins to produce new cells. We also get proteins from animal products such as meat, eggs, and milk because they come from animals that eat plants and store the proteins in their bodies.

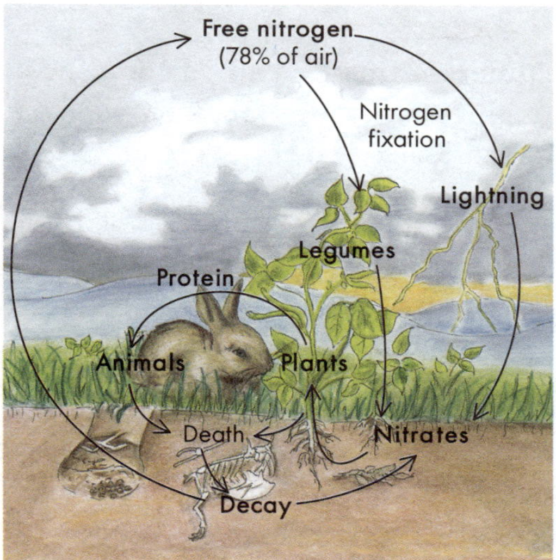

The nitrogen cycle

The last part of the nitrogen cycle is death. If plants and animals are not eaten, they die and decay. The bodies of people also die and decay. The decaying process releases nitrogen from the proteins stored in the body. Some of the nitrogen changes to nitrates for plants to use again, and the rest is released into the air to start the cycle over again.

The most important resources for life are renewable. Water, oxygen, and nitrogen are a few of them. If any one of these could be used up, all living things would die and the earth would no longer be inhabited. It would be a great mistake if one of these requirements for life could be used up. But God makes no mistakes! He made every one of these important life materials to be renewed in a cycle. The materials go round and round the cycles, being used over and over again.

## Study the Lesson

6. Write the correct word from the lesson for each description.
   a. A compound with nitrogen in a form that plants can use.
   b. A compound containing nitrogen and used to build cells.
   c. A source of electricity to combine oxygen and nitrogen.
   d. A kind of plant that puts nitrogen compounds into the soil.
   e. The making of compounds from nitrogen in the air.
7. Give two natural methods of nitrogen fixation.
8. A ——— like alfalfa has nitrogen-fixing bacteria on its ———.
9. How did the renewing cycles come about?

## Review Exercises

1. Almost what fraction of the earth is covered with water? [14]
2. The atmosphere protects the earth from most ———, which are speeding rocks from outer space. [13]
3. The earth's axis is tilted ——— degrees, and this causes the ——— of the earth. [11]
4. Four of Jupiter's ——— can be seen with a small telescope. [9]
5. Between the orbits of Mars and Jupiter are thousands of small bodies called ———. [8]
6. Heat and light travel through empty space by ———. [2]

## Apply the Lesson

1. Show that the air you breathe out is different from the air you breathe in. Put several tablespoons of lime into a pint jar of water. Shake it well, and then let it stand overnight. The lime will settle to the bottom, leaving clear limewater.

   Carefully pour some limewater into a clean glass. Bubble air from your breath through a straw into the limewater. What happens to the limewater after you do this for half a minute? This is a test for carbon dioxide.

   With the blowing end of a vacuum cleaner, carefully blow air through a straw into another glass of limewater. Do this for at least a minute. Explain the difference.

2. Show in yet another way the difference between the air you breathe in and what you breathe out. Collect a quart of "breath" by displacing water. Fill the jar with water, cover it with a lid, and turn it upside down in a pan of water. Use tubing to carry your breath into the jar. Cover the jar of breath with a lid, and turn it right-side up. Set another jar of ordinary air beside it.

   Light a wooden match, and lower it into the "breath" jar first. Then lower a burning match into the ordinary air. What difference do you observe? Explain the reason for the difference.

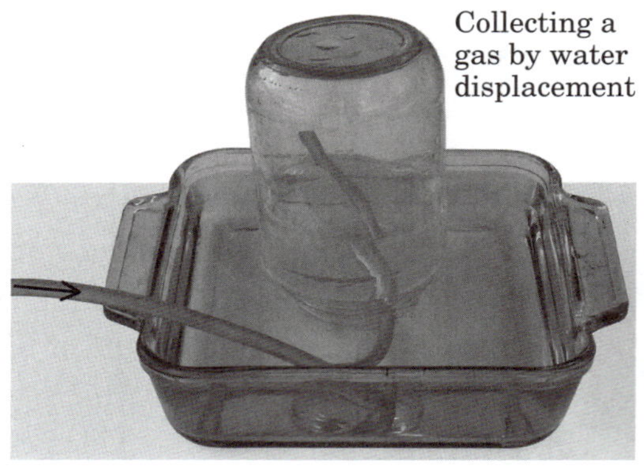
Collecting a gas by water displacement

# Lesson 16

## Unit 3 Review

### A. Vocabulary

Write the letter of the correct word for each meaning.

|  |  |
|---|---|
| 1. Kind of invisible, cancer-causing rays from the sun. | a. aquifer |
| 2. General weather of an area in a year. | b. climate |
| 3. Kind of climate so cold that plants cannot grow. | c. current |
| 4. Southernmost latitude of sunlight from straight overhead. | d. fresh water |
| 5. Liquid that dissolves other materials. | e. growing season |
| 6. Layer of broken rock or soil containing water. | f. polar |
| 7. Layer of the atmosphere where weather occurs. | g. protein |
| 8. Large stream of slowly moving ocean water. | h. renewable |
| 9. Able to be used over and over. | i. solvent |
| 10. Body-building compound that contains nitrogen. | j. tropic of Capricorn |
| 11. Time between the last frost in spring and the first frost in fall. | k. troposphere |
| 12. Life-supporting liquid that is not salty like the ocean. | l. ultraviolet |

|  |  |
|---|---|
| 13. Kind of climate with 10 to 20 inches of rain each year. | a. Arctic Circle |
| 14. Boundary around the northern "land of the midnight sun." | b. capillary action |
| 15. Gas that filters out ultraviolet light. | c. compound |
| 16. Upward movement of water through the soil. | d. infrared |
| 17. Place where the underground water level is near the surface. | e. legume |
| 18. Compound with nitrogen in a form that plants can use. | f. magnetosphere |
| 19. Material made of more than one element. | g. nitrate |
| 20. Kind of rays that produce heat. | h. nitrogen fixation |
| 21. Overhead region protecting the earth from the solar wind. | i. oasis |
| 22. Plant that puts nitrogen compounds into the soil. | j. ozone |
| 23. Place in a desert with enough water for plants. | k. semiarid |
| 24. Process of putting an element in the air into compounds that plants can use. | l. wetland |

## B. Facts

Write the words or numbers that belong in the blanks.

1. God created not the earth in vain, but "he formed it to be ———."
2. About one-fifth of the air is ———.
3. The United States has a ——— climate.
4. The earth rotates on its axis once every ——— hours to make one ———.
5. God uses the ——— of sweat to cool our bodies.
6. About ——— (what fraction?) of the earth's surface is covered with water.
7. The largest solar collector in the world is the ———.
8. Warm, rainy lands near the equator have a ——— climate.
9. The tilt of the earth's axis is ——— degrees.
10. God made cycles to renew water, ———, and nitrogen, which are three materials necessary for life.
11. A pound of water can hold more ——— than a pound of iron.
12. A ——— of water contains two atoms of hydrogen and one atom of oxygen.
13. Before the ——— in the air can be used by plants, it must be put into a compound.
14. A ——— is a speeding rock from outer space that burns up in the mesosphere.

## C. Concepts

Choose the letter of the best answer in each exercise.

1. The earth has seasons because
   a. it has different climates.
   b. it is tilted on its axis.
   c. it is sometimes closer to the sun and sometimes farther away.
   d. the year has 365¼ days.
2. If the year were shorter, the earth would be less suitable for life because
   a. the summers would be too warm.
   b. the days would be too short.
   c. the growing season would be too short.
   d. the winters would be too cold.
3. The temperate climate is found in most lands between
   a. the tropic of Cancer and the Arctic Circle.
   b. the equator and the tropic of Capricorn.
   c. the tropic of Cancer and the tropic of Capricorn.
   d. the equator and the Antarctic Circle.

4. The climate of England is different from what you would expect because
   a. high mountains protect it from frost.
   b. the North Atlantic Ocean rotates clockwise and brings warm water there.
   c. warm winds from the east blow across it.
   d. the atmosphere causes greater pressure in England.
5. If the oceans were smaller, all the following things would be true *except*
   a. the earth would have less rain.
   b. the summers would be warmer.
   c. the winters would be colder.
   d. the oxygen in the air would be less.
6. At night, the clouds help to keep the ground warm because
   a. they reflect infrared rays back to the earth.
   b. the water of the clouds contains stored heat.
   c. they send warm moisture to the ground.
   d. they keep the cold of space from reaching the earth.
7. The ocean is a benefit for all the following things *except*
   a. evaporation. b. heat storage. c. food. d. fixation.
8. Which list describes the nitrogen cycle?
   a. rain, ground, rivers, ocean, air, clouds, rain
   b. air, lightning, plants, food, animals, decay, air
   c. breathing, air, green plants, air, breathing
9. Which phrase describes something about climate?
   a. rain from cumulus clouds
   b. one inch of rain in one hour
   c. 29 inches of rain in one year
   d. sleet mixed with rain
10. The ground gets warmest when the sun is directly overhead because
    a. the sun's rays are warmer.
    b. there are fewer shadows.
    c. the rays are spread over less space.
    d. less ultraviolet light is filtered out.
11. Which statement is true?
    a. Tuna and sea anemones are a good source of food from the ocean.
    b. Corn and soybeans are good crops to improve the nitrogen level of the soil.
    c. Cactuses and camels can live in deserts because they are designed to conserve water.
    d. Fish and whales get their oxygen from the water they live in.
12. Which statement about the value of water is *not* true?
    a. Because water is slippery, we do not have the pain of "dry eye."
    b. The wetting action of water helps plants to live between rains.
    c. Water as a solvent makes it useful to carry materials in the blood.
    d. Evaporation of water keeps enough oxygen in the air for breathing.

# Unit 4

# Food for Living Things

"To every thing that creepeth upon the earth, wherein there is life, I have given every green herb for meat: and it was so" (Genesis 1:30).

The earth could be suitable for life in every other way, but if there were no food, all living things would die.

God makes no mistakes. From the beginning, He planned for green herbs to be the source of food for people and animals. He did not make just one kind of green plant. God made such variety that plants can grow in many different climates and suit the appetites of many different creatures.

The great variety gives us what we need for a balanced diet. The variety of flavors and textures makes eating enjoyable.

Prayer before our meals is certainly fitting. You should thank and praise God for His wonderful way of providing food. "He causeth the grass to grow for the cattle, and herb for the service of man: that he may bring forth food out of the earth" (Psalm 104:14). To God be the glory!

## Lesson 17

# Photosynthesis, the Food-making Process

"For the waters of Nimrim shall be desolate: for the hay is withered away, the grass faileth, there is no green thing" (Isaiah 15:6).

### Vocabulary

**carbohydrate** (kär′·bō·hī′·drāt′), a sugar or starch, with two hydrogen atoms for each oxygen atom.

**chlorophyll** (klôr′·ə·fil), the green material in plants that makes food when light shines on it.

**chloroplast** (klôr′·ə·plast′), a small plate containing chlorophyll in a plant cell.

**photosynthesis** (fō′·tō·sin′·thi·sis), the process of making food by putting water and carbon dioxide together with the power of light.

Life depends on green things. Green hay, green grass, green trees, and green vegetables have one thing in common. They all make their own food. No animal or person can make his own food. All the food you eat comes from green plants. Even a beefsteak comes from green plants. The beef came from a steer. The steer ate green grass. The green grass made its own food. This marvelous food-making process of green plants is the creation of God to sustain life on the earth.

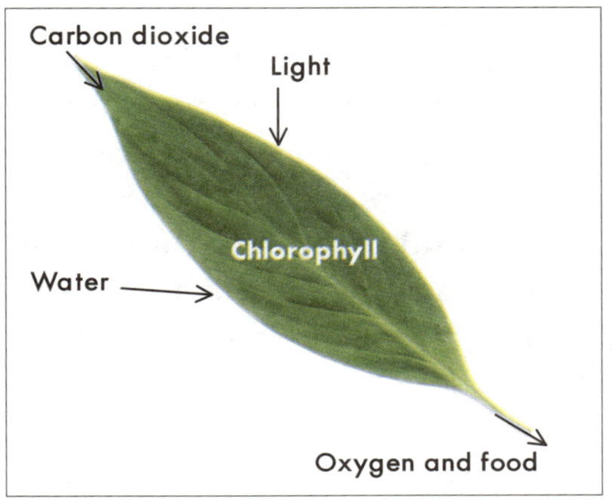

God can make a simple leaf factory much better than men can make a complex steel factory.

**Sunlight produces food from water and carbon dioxide.** The food-making process in green plants is called ***photosynthesis.*** *Photo* means "light." *Synthesis* means "putting together." Photosynthesis is the process of putting water and carbon dioxide together with the power of light to make food. Photosynthesis is a chemical reaction that changes water and carbon dioxide into sugar and oxygen.

You can think of green leaves as food factories. The raw materials they take in are water and carbon dioxide, and the product they manufacture is food. Men have built complex factories to make many wonderful things, but none of them are as wonderful and important as the green leaves created by God.

Photosynthesis is an ideal manufacturing process that includes three things: free, abundant raw materials; a free, unlimited source of energy; and products that are all useful, with no pollution. Men have never invented such an ideal process. Here again we see the wisdom of God in providing for life. We could not live without photosynthesis, and there is no substitute for it. Let us examine this wonderful process called photosynthesis.

**Free and abundant raw materials.** You have already seen that about 70 percent of the earth is covered with water. You know the wonderful way God made the water cycle to carry fresh water over the land and drop it as rain on the soil. The plants absorb the water through their roots and carry it through veins in the stems to their leaves. As long as there is enough water in the soil, plants have all the water they need as one of the two raw materials for photosynthesis.

The other raw material for photosynthesis is carbon dioxide. You are supplying this chemical every time you breathe out. To people and animals, carbon dioxide is a waste product, and the body wants to get rid of it. But what you give off as waste is just what green plants need to make sugar. Carbon dioxide is also given off by fires that burn wood, coal, gasoline, and other things.

Only about 0.035 percent ($\frac{7}{20,000}$) of the atmosphere is carbon dioxide. But that is plenty of raw material for photosynthesis. And since breathing and burning give off carbon dioxide, the supply is continually renewed.

Carbon dioxide enters a leaf through tiny pores on its underside.

**Free and unlimited source of energy.** The sun is a giant and steady producer of light. Just as gasoline provides energy for a car engine to run, so the sun provides energy to combine water and carbon dioxide to make sugar in green plants.

## Study the Lesson

1. What would be different about the earth if there were no green plants?
2. Write the missing words for each sentence.
   a. The raw materials for photosynthesis are ——— and ——— ———.
   b. The products of photosynthesis are ——— and ———.
   c. The energy for photosynthesis comes from the ———.
   d. People and animals put carbon dioxide into the air by ———.
3. What three things make photosynthesis an ideal manufacturing process?

**Manufacturing sugars.** Scientists have only a partial understanding of how photosynthesis works. They have found that leaf cells contain many tiny plates called ***chloroplasts.*** Each chloroplast has a special green coloring material called ***chlorophyll.*** When sunlight strikes the chlorophyll, it generates a little electricity. As this electricity flows from one place to another in the chloroplast, it causes a series of chemical reactions that produce sugar for the plant.

Remember that water molecules and carbon dioxide molecules come together in the leaf cells. This happens in the chloroplasts. Each molecule of water is made of two atoms of hydrogen and one atom of oxygen ($H_2O$). Each molecule of carbon dioxide has one atom of carbon and two atoms of oxygen ($CO_2$). (*Di* means "two.")

The electricity generated by sunlight breaks up water molecules and carbon dioxide molecules into groups of six. The hydrogen (H) atoms and the carbon (C) atoms join together with a few oxygen (O) atoms to form one molecule of sugar. The leftover oxygen atoms join in pairs and are released into the air for us to breathe.

**All useful products.** The oxygen released by photosynthesis goes out of the leaf through the same pores that bring in carbon dioxide. Also, some of the water brought up from the roots evaporates in the warm sunshine. It has been estimated that during a typical growing season, a sizable oak tree gives off 28,000 gallons of water.

The sugar produced by photosynthesis fills several purposes. First it provides food for the plant to grow. Some of the excess sugar is stored in the plant and gives strawberries, peaches, and even carrots their sweet flavor. Bees collect sweet nectar from flowers, change the sugar to a different form, and store it as honey. Granulated sugar sold in stores comes from the stem of a tall grass called sugar cane or from the roots of sugar beets.

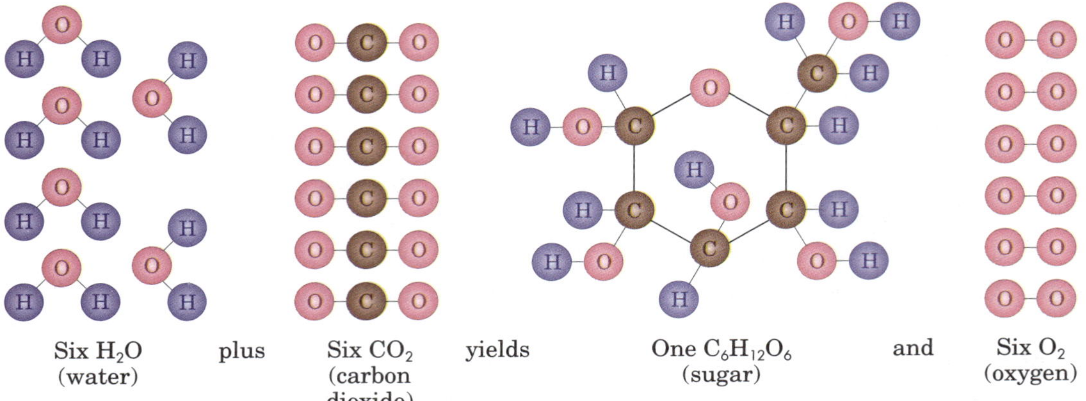


Did you notice from the illustration above that sugar and water have something in common? Each sugar molecule ($C_6H_{12}O_6$) is similar to each water molecule ($H_2O$) in that it has twice as many hydrogen atoms ($H_{12}$) as oxygen atoms ($O_6$). This is why sugars are called ***carbohydrates.*** *Hydrate* refers to water, and *carbo* refers to carbon. Carbohydrates are a combination of carbon and water.

Plants change some of the sugar into starch, which is also a carbohydrate. The plant then stores the starch

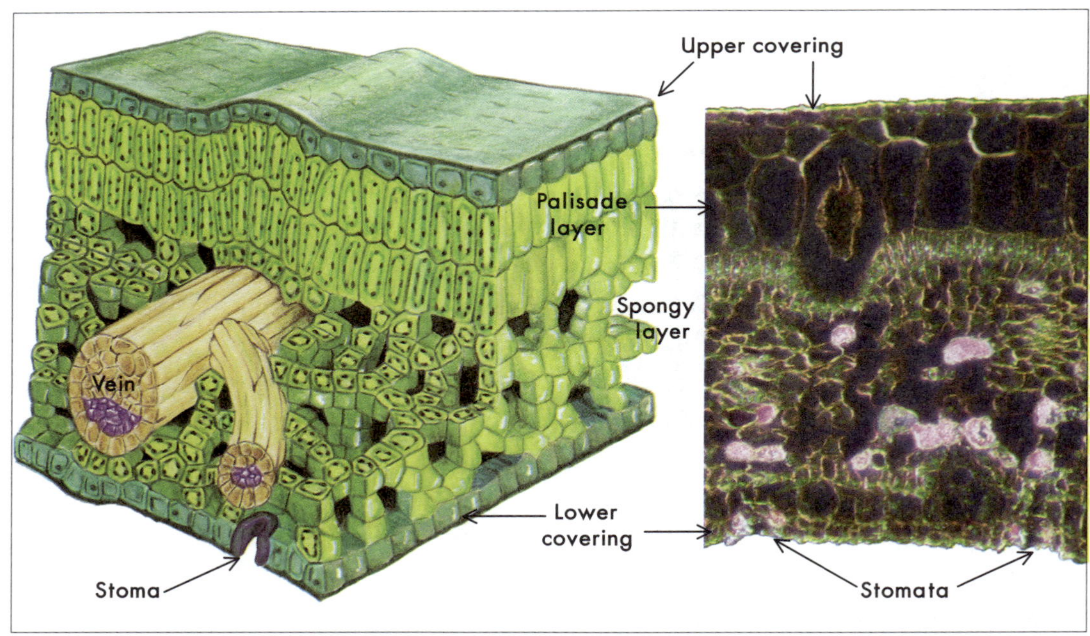


A cross section of a leaf. On the left is a drawing; on the right is a photo taken through a microscope.

in its fruit: seeds (as in corn), underground stems (as in white potatoes), or roots (as in sweet potatoes). That is why these plant parts make good food. In digestion, your body turns the starch back to sugar that your body can use.

God made living things to need food. He provided photosynthesis to make a good supply of food. The next time you eat a starchy banana or slice of bread, remember that starch came from water and carbon dioxide put together in green chloroplasts with energy from the sun. How wise God is!

Can you identify each kind of atom in this sugar molecule?

## Study the Lesson

4. For each compound, choose the correct chemical formula.

| | | |
|---|---|---|
| a. water | $O_2$ | $CO_2$ |
| b. oxygen | $H_2O$ | $C_6H_{12}O_6$ |
| c. sugar | $H_2$ | |
| d. carbon dioxide | | |

5. For each word part, choose the correct meaning on the right.

| | | |
|---|---|---|
| a. *photo* | two | hydrogen |
| b. *synthesis* | water | put together |
| c. *di* | light | |
| d. *hydrate* | | |

6. Plants that carry on photosynthesis have green ——— in small plates called ———.
7. The sweetness of fruits and vegetables comes from stored ———.
8. The sugar that stores sell in bags comes from ——— or ———.
9. Most of the food we get from photosynthesis comes from sugar that has been changed to ——— and stored in some part of the plant.
10. Give at least one way that photosynthesis shows the wisdom of God.

## Review Exercises

1. In the water cycle, water falls from clouds as ——, streams and rivers carry it to the ——, and then it —— to form clouds again. [15]
2. The oceans help to make the surrounding land (warmer, colder) in winter and (warmer, cooler) in summer. [14]
3. Water is called $H_2O$ because each molecule has two atoms of —— and one atom of ——. [12]
4. Saturn is surrounded by beautiful —— that look like a disk of gold. [9]
5. The axis of Mars is ——, which causes it to have —— as the earth does. [8]
6. The atmosphere of Venus is mostly —— ——, and it contains clouds of —— ——. [7]

## Apply the Lesson

1. Observe how darkness affects green plants. Select two growing potted plants of the same kind and about the same size. Place one where it can get a good amount of sunlight every day. Put the other in darkness at the same temperature (perhaps covered with a cardboard box). Keep each plant watered the same amount. Compare the plants each day in dim lighting. When do you begin to see a difference in the plants? What differences do you see? Continue this observation for several weeks.
2. Plants can be grown under light from bulbs. How much would it cost a farmer to raise one acre of crops under fluorescent lights? Use the following steps to calculate the answer.
   a. Four 40-watt fluorescent bulbs are enough for plants covering a space 8 feet by 3 feet. How many square feet is that?
   b. Divide 43,560 (the square feet in an acre) by the answer found in step *a*. This tells you how many sets of bulbs it would take to light an acre.
   c. Each set of bulbs would use about 230 kilowatt-hours of electricity during a typical growing season. Multiply 230 by the answer in step *b* to find how much electricity an acre of bulbs would use.
   d. Multiply the answer in step *c* by $0.08 (per kilowatt-hour) to find the cost of the electricity.
   e. The answer in step *d* does not include the cost of bulbs, wire, light fixtures, and installation of such a lighting system. By comparison, how much does the farmer pay for the sunlight to raise one acre of crops?

## Lesson 18

# Soil, a Support for Green Plants

"Doth the plowman plow all day to sow? doth he open and break the clods of his ground? When he hath made plain the face thereof, doth he not . . . cast in the principal wheat and the appointed barley and the rie in their place?" (Isaiah 28:24, 25).

### Vocabulary

**cultivation,** the action of breaking up the soil.

**fertile** (fûr′·təl), rich in the nutrients needed by plants.

**humus** (hyōō′·məs), decayed plant and animal material in the soil.

**hydroponics** (hī′·drə·pon′·iks), a method of growing plants without soil.

**nutrient,** one of the soil chemicals that plants need to grow.

**percolation** (pûr′·kə·lā′·shən), the downward movement of water through the soil.

**pH,** a measure of how acid or base a soil is.

**soil,** a mixture of finely ground rocks and humus, in which the roots of plants can grow.

When God made the world, He covered most of the land areas with a mixture of fine materials called ***soil.*** The soil and the roots of plants were made to work together. In a number of important ways, we can see the wisdom of God in making soil. You read in past units that different things must be present to make the earth a suitable place for life. The soil is another part of the earth that is needed to make it inhabitable.

It is possible to raise plants without soil. Some tomatoes and other vegetables are grown by ***hydroponics,*** a method of raising plants without soil. The plants need to be tied up or held by wire screens. The roots grow in a bed of water or coarse material surrounded by water. The farmer must be sure the water has all the minerals that the plants need, and he must be very careful to give the plants enough but not too much of these minerals. God's plan for growing crops in soil is much more practical.

**The soil can be cultivated.** The verse at the beginning of this lesson asks, "Doth the plowman plow all day to sow? doth he open and break the clods of his ground?" This is talking

*Left:* Tomatoes in a hydroponic greenhouse. *Right:* Basil growing in hydroponic trays. A little bit of soil in the roots and the shape of the trays help to hold the plants in place.

about the ***cultivation*** of soil to prepare it for planting a crop. Plowing, disking, and harrowing are various ways in which the farmer breaks up the soil to make a loose bed for plants.

Cultivation makes the soil loose so that seeds can sprout easily and spread roots underground. It also allows rainwater to soak into the soil instead of running off. Cultivation loosens the soil so that air can get to small living things in the soil. These living organisms, including the earthworm, help to break down dead plants and make the soil better for growing plants.

Plowing turns the old plant stalks under the ground so that they can rot more quickly and help to improve the soil with their ***humus.*** Cultivation also destroys the competition of weeds and weed seeds by turning them under the ground.

If the soil is not plowed for several years, it may become hard and make a poor seedbed. The people of Old Testament times understood the importance of cultivation. "Break up your

Plowing the old stalks under the ground.

fallow ground, and sow not among thorns" (Jeremiah 4:3).

Modern farmers sometimes grow crops with a no-till method instead of cultivating the soil. They use special planters with heavy cutters that break open the soil to receive the seed. This method depends on using strong chemicals to kill the weeds. While the no-till method works, it is not wise to use this method on the same fields for many years in a row. God made the soil to be cultivated. Cultivation requires more work than no-till farming, but it is better for the soil, it helps to control weeds, and it does not depend as much on the use of harmful chemicals.

No-till corn planting. No-till farming works best in well-drained fields.

## Study the Lesson

1. Besides water, what two things must be provided when raising vegetables by hydroponics?
2. What wise provision did God make that is better than hydroponics?
3. Complete these sentences to tell the value of cultivating the soil.
   a. During cultivation, the ——— and their ——— are buried, which makes fewer of them.
   b. Cultivation makes a loose bed of soil that makes it easier for the ——— to sprout and the ——— to spread out.
   c. During cultivation, dead and living plant material is buried so that it can ——— and add ——— to the soil.
4. Which one of these is *not* a disadvantage of no-till farming?
   a. More acres can be farmed with the same amount of effort.
   b. Control of weeds can be a greater problem.
   c. There is danger from the use of strong chemicals.

**Soil holds water needed by the plants.** If the soil did not hold and supply water for plants, they would die between one rain and the next. The soil acts as a giant storage basin for water. Good, loose soil will allow water to sink deep. The passing of water downward through the tiny spaces of the soil is called ***percolation.*** Soil that has much hard clay in it does not allow water to percolate well. Sometimes a farmer uses a chisel plow or subsoiler to dig deep into the soil and break up the tight ground. This improves percolation.

God also provided a way for the water to come back up through the soil. Water makes things wet because it sticks to the surface of other materials. As water wets one particle of soil, it comes in contact with another particle and makes that particle wet too. In this way the water moves upward by capillary action from one particle to another. Capillary action is a slow process, but it is fast enough to bring up much-needed water to the roots of the plants. Water moves downward by percolation, and it comes back up by capillary action to supply water for plants during dry spells between rains.

Soil near the surface can hold much water if it has a large amount of humus in it. Humus acts like a sponge and soaks up water. Gardeners and farmers like to have much humus in their soil. This helps the soil to stay loose and hold moisture.

Several things will add humus to the soil. Plowing down dead plants from the previous year adds humus. A farmer may plant a crop of rye or clover and then plow it down to add humus. Farmers spread manure on the fields to add humus. Sometimes a gardener will mulch his garden with straw, peat, or grass clippings. This not only holds the moisture in and keeps down weeds, but it also adds more humus when it is plowed down the next year. Compost piles, made from rotting leaves, plants, and kitchen scraps, are a good source of humus for gardeners.

Sandy soil percolates better than what farmers usually like. The rainwater sinks too quickly and leaves the surface dry too soon. But if sandy soil has much humus, the soil will hold moisture better.

A fertilizer spreader is used to sprinkle fertilizer uniformly on fields.

**Soil holds nutrients for the plants.** Plants need water and carbon dioxide to produce food by photosynthesis. But plants also need some other materials to grow. The main fertilizers a plant needs are compounds of nitrogen, phosphorus, and potash (potassium). Plants also need magnesium, manganese, and iron compounds. These soil chemicals that help plants to grow are called ***nutrients.*** When plants decay and become humus, they return these nutrients to the soil.

Sometimes the soil is lacking the three main fertilizers. Then the farmer or gardener can add a mixture that contains nitrogen, phosphorus, and potash. When a soil has all the right chemicals for plants to grow well, it is said to be ***fertile.*** Soil can be made more fertile by adding humus and fertilizer.

Sometimes farmers also spread lime on their fields to "sweeten" the soil. Normal farming practices and plenty of rainfall raise the level of acids in the soil. A few crops such as blueberries and strawberries grow well in soil that is acid, or sour. But most grain crops grow best in soil that is sweeter, or more base.

The level of acids in the soil is called the ***pH*** of the soil. A soil test can tell the farmer what the pH of his soil is. The test results are compared to a scale of numbers on which *7* is neutral, halfway between acid and base. A pH lower than *7* is acid (sour). A pH higher

**The pH Scale**

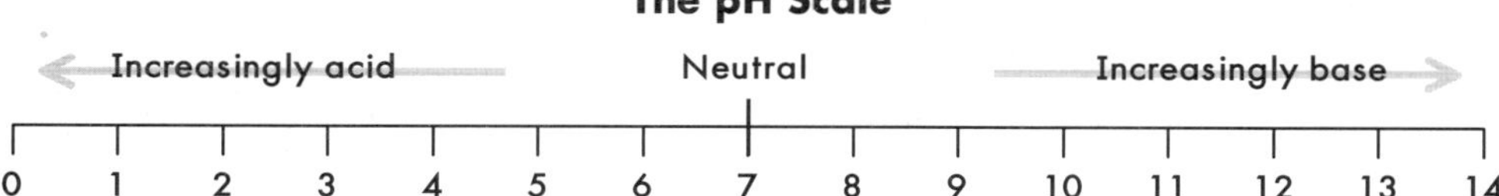

than 7 is base (sweet). Many crops grow best in soil with a pH between 6 and 7, or slightly acid.

**Soils anchor the plants.** A tall tree can sway back and forth in the wind without falling over. Its roots go deep into the soil and are held tight. Even small plants need roots to hold themselves upright. God made most soil to be loose enough for percolation and capillary action, yet tight enough to be a good anchor for roots. Of course, sandy soil will not anchor plants as well because it is so loose.

As you have seen in this lesson, soil is a very valuable natural resource. The dark top layer containing humus is especially valuable for growing plants. We must have green plants to get food. So we depend on the soil for food. This was God's wise plan for us to live. Even the work that is required to cultivate the soil is part of God's plan for our welfare. God told Adam that "in the sweat of thy face shalt thou eat bread" (Genesis 3:19).

Prop roots on a cornstalk help to keep it from blowing over.

## Study the Lesson

5. Deep cultivation helps to improve the ——— of water down into the soil, and the ——— ——— that brings it back up to the top.
6. What material in the soil holds water, even in sandy soil?
7. Give three ways that humus can be added to the soil.
8. If crops do not grow well, a farmer may use ——— to increase the nutrients in the soil, or he may spread ——— to improve the pH.
9. If soil has a pH of 4, the soil is too ———.
10. In addition to letting water percolate too easily, what is another disadvantage about the looseness of sandy soil?
11. Choose the correct word for each description.

| | |
|---|---|
| a. Breaking up of soil. | cultivating |
| b. Decayed plant material in the soil. | fertile |
| c. Chemicals in the soil that plants need. | humus |
| d. Downward movement of water through soil. | hydroponics |
| e. Measure of how acid or base a soil is. | nutrients |
| f. Raising of plants with water and no soil. | percolation |
| g. Kind of soil in which plants grow well. | pH |

## Review Exercises

1. In the process called ———, plants use ——— and ——— ——— in the presence of sunlight to make sugar. [17]
2. In the oxygen cycle, people and animals breathe out ——— ———, which plants use, and plants give off———, which people and animals breathe. [15]
3. A ——— is a movement of ocean water from one place to another. [14]
4. Water moves upward through soil by a process called ——— ———. [12]
5. The axis of Uranus is almost (level, vertical) in relation to its orbit. [9]
6. The location of Neptune was predicted by the use of ———. [9]

## Apply the Lesson

1. Many states require that a percolation test be done before a septic system is installed. A drain field for the system cannot be installed if water percolates too rapidly (letting the sewage water flow directly into underground streams) or if it percolates too slowly (allowing the sewage water to come to the surface). You can do such a "perk test" on the school grounds. (Be sure to get the school board's permission first.)

   Dig a hole 22 inches deep and 6 to 8 inches in diameter. Push a nail partway into the side of the hole one foot above the bottom. Fill the hole with water to that level, and let it soak away overnight. The next morning, again fill the hole to the nail and record the time. After 30 minutes, measure the distance in inches from the nail to the top of the water. Divide 30 minutes by that distance to obtain the percolation rate in minutes per inch.

   Percolation of 6 to 90 minutes per inch is suitable for a drain field in the subsoil—the lower the rate, the better. (Rates above or below that range either require finding a more suitable site or else using a special septic system.)
2. A flowerpot often has a hole in the bottom. Put a few stones in the bottom of such a pot to keep the soil from falling out. Fill the pot with fine, dry soil. Press the soil firmly together. Place the pot in a pan containing about two inches of water. How long does it take for the water to reach the top of the soil? How does the water get to the top? You may need to add water to the pan from time to time. You can plant some seeds in the soil and grow some plants with water that rises through the soil.
3. If you have access to a soil test kit, you can test some soil for its pH. Add a little lime, and test it again. Does the pH go up or down?

## Lesson 19

# The Food Chain

"Thou shalt sow the ground withal;... and it shall be fat and plenteous: in that day shall thy cattle feed in large pastures" (Isaiah 30:23).

### Vocabulary

**carnivorous** (kär·niv′·ər·əs), a kind of animal that kills other animals for food.

**food chain,** the passing of food from one living thing to another.

**herbivorous** (hûr·biv′·ər·əs), a kind of animal that eats plants for food.

**omnivorous** (om·niv′·ər·əs), a kind of creature that eats plants and animals.

**predator,** an animal that kills other animals for its food.

**prey,** an animal that a predator seeks for its food.

**scavenger** (skav′·ən·jər), an animal that seeks dead animals for food.

Why do people go to such great effort to feed and house chickens, cattle, and hogs? Are they trying to be kind to the animals? A good farmer does try to treat his animals well, but his main reason for raising livestock is to provide food for himself and others. The farmer wants the eggs, milk, and meat that these animals provide for food.

This is part of God's plan to feed man. God told Noah, "Every moving thing that liveth shall be meat for you; even as the green herb have I given you all things" (Genesis 9:3). So man has two main sources of food: plants and animals.

**Only green plants can produce food.** As you saw in Lesson 17, green plants make food from water and carbon dioxide by using light energy from the sun. The nutrients in the soil that help plants to grow are not really food for man. You could not live on fertilizer. But you can live on the sugars, starches, and proteins produced by plants.

The same is true for animals. Cattle cannot live by eating fertilizer. They must be allowed to eat grass in a pasture, or dried grass called hay. They may also eat corn silage, haylage, or dry grains, such as soybeans, corn, oats, or barley. Cows, like people, are consumers of food—not producers. Only green plants can produce food. For this reason, plants can be thought of as the first link in every food chain.

A lynx. What two things help carnivorous animals eat flesh?

**People and animals consume food.** Some animals, like rabbits, squirrels, deer, and cows, eat only plants or the fruit of plants. They are ***herbivorous,*** since they eat only herbs (green plants). They do not kill other animals for food. They get all their food from plants.

Foxes, owls, and lions are ***carnivorous.*** Almost all of their food comes from animals that they kill. *Carnal* means "of flesh." A carnivorous animal eats the flesh of other creatures. (The *vor* part of *herbivorous* and *carnivorous* means "eat." Compare the word *devour*.)

God has designed the bodies of herbivorous and carnivorous animals especially for the kind of food they eat. A cow does not have front teeth in its upper jaw. It does not bite off food as you do. It tears the grass loose, chews it only a little, and then swallows it. By contrast, carnivorous animals, such as tigers, have long, pointed front teeth useful in tearing the meat of their prey. Their powerful jaw muscles can crunch even the bones as they eat.

The digestive systems of these animals are very different too. The cow brings partially digested food back up to its mouth and chews the softened grass. This is called chewing its cud. Then the cud is swallowed again, and it goes through other parts of the stomach. The stomachs of carnivorous animals can break down meat into food that their bodies can use without needing to chew a cud.

Also consider the feet of these animals. Herbivorous animals, such as deer and cattle, have hooves for walking on the ground. Rabbits and woodchucks have feet designed for digging in the ground. But animals in the cat and dog families have paws and claws to attack and tear their prey.

God created some animals to be ***omnivorous.*** The *omni* part of this word means "all." Omnivorous animals eat both plants and animals. They include bears, hogs, opossums, and raccoons.

People are also omnivorous. We have canine teeth, but they are not as long as in carnivorous animals. God gave us the intelligence to cook our meat before we eat it. That makes the meat easier to chew. But we do not depend on meat alone for our food. Much of our diet comes directly from plants in the form of fruits, vegetables, and grains.

Herbivorous animals

## Study the Lesson

1. True or false? The sun helps to provide our food. Explain your answer.
2. All animals are (consumers, producers) of food.
3. Tell whether each of these is herbivorous (*H*), carnivorous (*C*), or omnivorous (*O*). Use an encyclopedia for additional help.
   a. dog  d. rabbit  g. lion
   b. cow  e. man  h. sheep
   c. cat  f. elephant  i. bear
4. You would expect to see long canine teeth in an animal that is ——.

**Most animals are either predators, prey, or scavengers.** An animal that seeks other animals for food is called a ***predator.*** The animals that it catches are its ***prey.*** The cat is a predator, and the mouse is its prey. Predators are carnivorous animals, while most prey are herbivorous animals.

When an animal is killed on the road or dies in a field, it is usually not long until vultures (often called buzzards) come to eat the dead animal. The vulture is called a ***scavenger***

Vultures help clean up dead bodies.

because it eats animals that it finds dead. Scavengers are helpful in consuming dead animals. Think of how unpleasant it would be if all the animals killed along the road would need to rot away.

Each living thing has its place in God's great plan. There is a plentiful source of food from green plants. Some animals eat the green plants directly as food. Carnivorous animals get their food by eating herbivorous animals. Scavengers get their food by eating animals that have died.

**Food follows a chain.** The food chain starts with green plants. A rabbit eats green clover. A fox catches the rabbit and eats it. The fox dies, and a vulture eats it. Such passing of food from one living thing to another is called a ***food chain.*** Food chains may be long or short.

Here is an example of a long chain. A caterpillar eats the leaves of a green plant. The caterpillar develops into a butterfly that is eaten by a dragonfly. A frog flicks out its tongue and catches the dragonfly for food. A snake swallows the frog whole. A hawk swoops down and catches the snake to eat.

Here is a very short food chain. The green algae in the ocean make food that is eaten by very small animals such as protozoans and water fleas. These small animals and the algae together form a floating mixture called plankton. The plankton becomes the food of baleen whales, whose mouths have baleen hanging from the upper jaw. (Baleen is hundreds of thin plates made of a material like that in fingernails.) A baleen whale eats by taking a mouthful of seawater and using its tongue to force the water through the baleen. The baleen strains out the plankton, which the whale swallows.

**Food is the source of energy for living things.** The energy of the sun is changed into food energy by green

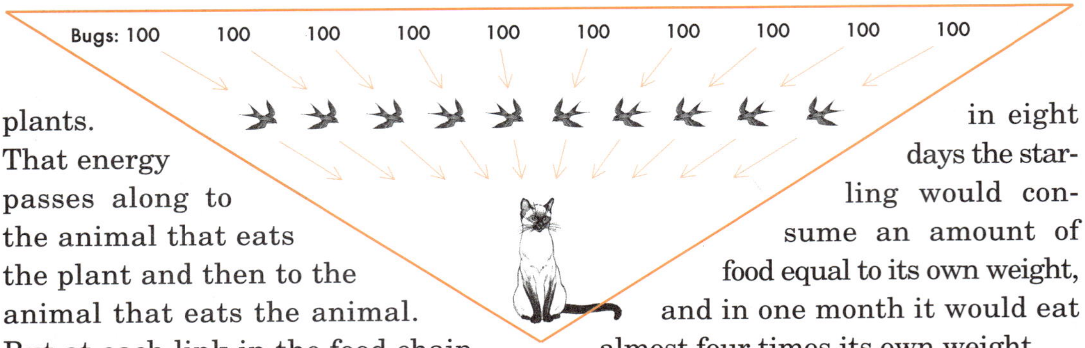

Bugs: 100 100 100 100 100 100 100 100 100 100

plants. That energy passes along to the animal that eats the plant and then to the animal that eats the animal. But at each link in the food chain, some of the energy is lost. Not all the energy in food is stored up in the body of the animal that eats it. The animal uses some of the energy to live and move.

Not only does the amount of energy drop at each link in the food chain; the number of animals also drops. Hundreds of insects and worms become food for one bird. Dozens of birds would be needed to feed one cat for even a few months. The upside-down triangle above illustrates this pattern in the food chain.

In pounds of food, the food chain is also an inverted triangle. Every day a starling eats food equal to about one-eighth of its body weight. That means in eight days the starling would consume an amount of food equal to its own weight, and in one month it would eat almost four times its own weight.

To make one pound of meat in a beef cow, it takes about seven pounds of grain in addition to the grass and hay that it eats. That is what makes meat an expensive source of food. That is why the same land can feed more people if they use it to raise corn for themselves, than if they raise corn to feed cattle and then eat the meat. We get valuable protein and minerals from meat, but most of our food comes directly from plants.

When we pray for our daily bread, we are recognizing our dependence on God for the food we eat. Let us give Him praise and thanksgiving for His wise plan to provide food for us and for all other living things.

## Study the Lesson

5. Choose the correct word for each description.
   a. Feeding only on plants.
   b. Animal that seeks dead animals to eat.
   c. Animal that kills and eats other animals.
   d. Feeding on both plants and animals.
   e. Animal that is sought for food.
   f. Feeding mostly on animals.

carnivorous
herbivorous
omnivorous
predator
prey
scavenger

6. To the snake, a frog is its (predator, prey).
7. To the fly, a frog is its (predator, prey).
8. We are glad that God made some animals to be scavengers because
   a. they help to keep fields and roadsides clean.
   b. they help to control the rat population.
   c. they eat many harmful insects.
   d. they help to destroy many weeds.
9. Put this list in the right order for a food chain.

   frog, hawk, snake, dragonfly, green plant, butterfly
10. A mixture of small living things called ——— provides food for baleen whales.
11. What two things become less at each link in a food chain?
12. If a country found it hard to feed its people, would it be better for the people to eat mainly meat or food from plants?

## Review Exercises

1. Dead plant materials improve the soil by decaying to form ———. [18]
2. In many plants, sugar is changed to ——— and stored in some part of the plant. [17]
3. Plants called ——— build up nitrogen compounds in the soil through a process called ——— ———. [15]
4. Four-fifths of the air is ———, and one-fifth is ———. [13]
5. To be at a place that has sunshine at midnight, you would need to go north of the ——— ——— or south of the ——— ———. [11]
6. Venus rotates ——— on its axis, which cannot be explained by evolution. [7]

## Apply the Lesson

1. Use reference books to make a list of animals in each of the following groups: *Herbivorous, Carnivorous, Omnivorous,* and *Scavenger.* This could be done as a class project, with students adding to the lists on the chalkboard.
2. Look up the vocabulary words of this lesson in a dictionary that gives etymologies (word histories). Try to find the relationship of the vocabulary words to the following words: *devour, carnality, omnipotent, herbalist.*
3. Make a few more food chains that you know. Remember, man can be the final link in a food chain. Why do you think we never eat meat that comes from a scavenger? Why would meat from a woodchuck probably be safer than meat from a dog?

## Lesson 20

# The Balance of Life

"Their roaring shall be like a lion, they shall roar like young lions: yea, they shall roar, and lay hold of the prey, and shall carry it away safe, and none shall deliver it" (Isaiah 5:29).

### Vocabulary

**ecology** (i·kol′·ə·jē), the study of living things in relation to their surroundings.

**environment,** all the things and conditions around a living thing.

**host,** the source of a parasite's food.

**lichen** (lī′·kən), a scaly growth on rocks, consisting of a fungus and algae.

**parasite,** a living thing that lives in or on another living thing.

**population,** the number of living things of one kind.

**symbiosis** (sim′·bē·ō′·sis), the living together of two different things for certain benefits.

God created the earth to be inhabited. He not only created different living things, but He also planned that they would stay in balance. That is, He planned that the ***population*** of each kind of living thing would not become so great that it would destroy other kinds of living things.

God wisely made some animals to be herbivorous and some to be carnivorous. Suppose all animals would eat only green plants. Then none of the animals would be prey to other animals. They would keep multiplying and eating green plants until most of the plants were gone, especially in dry places. Then there would be a lack of food since plants are food producers.

You may have seen the problem of overpopulation if potato beetles are allowed to multiply without control. The potato beetles will eat all the leaves of the potato plants. Then the plants cannot grow and produce good potatoes.

**God provided a balance of life.** Several things help to control the population of each kind of living thing. Every living thing has certain natural enemies that keep the population of that living thing from getting too high.

These lions are eating a cape buffalo. Lions help control the buffalo populations in Africa. Too many buffaloes can destroy the grass by grazing it to the bare ground.

For example, several *predators,* such as cats and hawks, keep the mouse population under control. Otherwise, mice would eat many of the crops in the field and much grain in storage bins. But as the mouse population increases, the hawks have more food. Then the hawks can multiply, and more mice will be killed. So predators are one thing that keeps populations in control and produces a balance of life.

The *food supply* is another limiting factor. If the population of hawks keeps increasing, eventually there will not be enough mice to feed them all. This slows the increase of the hawk population and produces a balance between the number of mice and the number of hawks.

Plants are limited by the *competition* of other plants. If weeds are allowed to grow freely in a cornfield, the weeds compete with the corn for sunlight, moisture, and soil nutrients. Then less corn will be produced, and there will be fewer seeds to grow the next year.

*Parasites* help to balance the population. A ***parasite*** is a living thing that gets its food by living in or on another living thing. Several kinds of

A sea lamprey lives on fish by attaching itself to the side of a fish.

worms are internal parasites that live in the intestines of animals and cause diseases. The living thing that provides the food for the parasite is called its ***host.***

The eellike sea lamprey is an external parasite to fish. It has a round mouth with many sharp teeth, as well as a tongue with teeth on it. The lamprey attaches itself to the side of a host fish and sucks blood and other fluids from the fish.

*Disease* also helps to control the population of living things. Japanese beetles were first seen in the United States in 1916. Only a few could be found. But by 1950, Japanese beetles were a major problem in the eastern United States. In the grub stage, they ate roots; and in the adult stage, they ate leaves and fruit. Then came disease germs that killed many grubs and greatly reduced the Japanese beetle population.

Sometimes *extreme weather* reduces a population. When a winter is very cold or a summer is very dry, some living things will not survive.

## Study the Lesson

1. The fact that some animals are carnivorous and some are herbivorous helps to control the ——— of each kind of living thing and to produce a ——— of ———.
2. For each example, choose the term that tells how the growth of population is being limited.

| | |
|---|---|
| a. Mice killed by hawks. | competition |
| b. Sea lamprey on a fish. | disease |
| c. Germs affecting Japanese beetles. | parasites |
| d. Weeds in a cornfield. | extreme weather |
| e. Hawks depending on mice. | limited food supply |
| f. Intestinal worms in animals. | predators |
| g. Many birds dying in a cold winter. | |

3. A parasite gets its food by living in or on another living thing called its ———.
4. Mice and hawks control each other's population. Which *two* give reasons for this?
   a. As the hawks increase, the mice increase.
   b. As the hawks decrease, the mice increase.
   c. As the mice increase, the hawks decrease.
   d. As the mice decrease, the hawks decrease.

Penguins are well insulated with water-tight feathers to swim in the icy cold waters.

When chased by an enemy, the chuckwalla slips into a crevice in a rock and wedges itself tightly by filling its lungs with air.

**Living things and their surroundings.** Every living thing is in a part of the world with other living things. All the things and conditions around a living thing are its ***environment.*** Weather is just one part of that environment. Environment includes the soil, the water, the plants, the animals, and the seasons. The earth contains countless different environments.

Different living things are suited for different environments. Penguins survive very well in the cold environment of Antarctica. The chuckwalla feels quite at home in hot, rocky deserts of the southwestern United States. Alligators live best in the swampy areas of Florida. Bighorn sheep are sure-footed enough to climb the jagged ridges of the Rocky Mountains. Dolphins need the saltwater environment of the ocean. Perch live in the freshwater environment of streams and rivers.

Even around your house, there are many different environments. A carefully mowed lawn provides the right environment for many creatures. Maybe you have seen low ridges where moles burrowed through the sod, searching for earthworms and insects. Lift a rock, and you will see the creatures inhabiting that environment. A vegetable garden is a different environment. A rotting log makes a good environment for a host of living things. Maybe you will find mushrooms springing up at the base of a dead tree.

The study of living things in relation to their environment is called ***ecology.*** Ecologists try to understand how a living thing is suited to its environment and what changes in the environment may upset the balance of life.

**Man can spoil the balance of life.** Sometimes people think they can improve an environment by introducing

Dall sheep can relax on top of a steep mountain peak. Stagnant swamp water is quite inviting to a Florida alligator.

a new kind of living thing. This sometimes causes a serious imbalance in nature.

In 1890 some well-meaning people released sixty starlings from Europe in a park in New York City. Forty more were released the next year. Those who did this were pleased to find that the new birds began multiplying in their new home. Today, farmers and city officials battle multitudes of these hungry and dirty birds. People wish that all starlings had been kept in Europe.

Rabbits were not native to Australia. Men took wild rabbits to that continent, thinking that they would be a good source of food. The rabbits multiplied so rapidly that they soon caused serious damage to the grasslands used for grazing sheep and cattle. After 1945, men brought in a disease that helped to bring the wild rabbits under control.

The importation of starlings and water hyacinths spoiled the balance of life. The water hyacinth has pretty flowers, but it is such a nuisance that it has been called the purple curse.

Plant populations can also get out of control when they are introduced into a new environment. In 1884 a water hyacinth was brought to New Orleans for a special exposition. Visitors liked this beautiful flower and took cuttings to plant in streams and ponds near their homes. But water hyacinths spread fast, and they often cover a river with such a thick mat that boats cannot get through.

It was thought that a certain kind of cactus would make a good cattle fence in Australia. It grew wild and took over about 60 million acres. An insect was then found that would bring it under control.

Why do living things in a new environment sometimes have a runaway population growth? It is because they do not have enough natural enemies.

We marvel at how well-balanced God made the natural world. If an area has not been touched by man for hundreds of years, it can abound in a great variety of plants and animals living together in balance. One kind of plant or animal does not become so numerous that it destroys other kinds of living things. Rather, the food chain operates for the good of all. For each kind of living thing, the number of enemies, the food supply, and the competition are just right to maintain a good population.

**Living together.** All living things depend on other living things. Often two kinds of living things will live close together. This is called ***symbiosis,*** from *sym* (together) and *bio* (life). The parasite–host relationship is one kind of symbiosis. The parasite lives in or on another living thing at its expense.

In another kind of symbiosis, plants or animals live together for the benefit of both. Oxpeckers are birds that live around big animals, such as cape buffalos in Africa. The buffalo

Nuisance flies, ticks, and maggots on this cape buffalo are food for the two oxpeckers.

These lichens are green algae and gray fungi that support each other.

allows the oxpecker to perch on his hide, and the oxpecker rids the buffalo of parasites and warns him of danger.

Another example of symbiosis can be found on rocks. You have probably seen rocks with scaly growths called ***lichens.*** A lichen is actually two kinds of plants living together. One kind is green algae that can make food in sunlight, and the other is a fungus that lives on this food. The algae receive water and protection from the fungus. The two kinds of plants need each other to live on the surface of rocks.

God made many different living things. Each fills a place in God's great plan for the earth to be inhabited. Who but God could have provided such a balance of life!

## Study the Lesson

5. Garden soil makes a good ——— for earthworms.
6. The study of how living things in a certain place live together is called ———.
7. In each group, choose the one that you would not expect to find in the same environment with the rest.
   a. whale, perch, plankton, dolphin
   b. rabbit, alligator, cactus, kangaroo
   c. penguin, mole, grass, earthworm
   d. cape buffalo, bighorn sheep, oxpecker, giraffe
8. Give two examples that show how man has spoiled the balance of life in certain places.
9. The lichen is a good example of ———, in which the living things help each other.
10. How do a cape buffalo and an oxpecker help each other?

## Review Exercises

1. In the ——— ———, a small animal is eaten by a larger animal, and the larger animal is eaten by a still larger animal. [19]
2. A farmer may spread ——— to increase the nutrients in the soil, or he may spread ——— to improve the pH. [18]
3. Almost what fraction of the earth is covered with water? [14]
4. The atmosphere protects the earth from most ———, which are speeding rocks from outer space. [13]
5. A solar eclipse occurs when the shadow of the ——— falls on the ———. [4]
6. The sun is about ——— miles away from the earth. [1]

## Apply the Lesson

1. Choose one of the following places, and do research to learn what kind of environment it has. Find out what flora (plants) and fauna (animals) live in that environment. Write a report, or give an oral report, as your teacher directs.

| | | | |
|---|---|---|---|
| Alaska | Australia | Egypt | Philippines |
| Antarctica | Brazil | Hawaii | |

2. Be an ecologist for a while. Make a study of an environment available to you. What living things are there? What do the living things eat? Can you discover any food chains? What keeps their populations in balance? Does the environment have any problems of control? This can be done as a class project, in small groups, or individually.

## Lesson 21

# Unit 4 Review

## A. Vocabulary

Write the letter of the correct word for each meaning.

1. Green material that uses light to make food.
2. Scaly fungus and algae on rocks.
3. Sugar or starch, with two hydrogen atoms for each oxygen atom.
4. Number of living things of one kind.
5. Animal that kills other animals for its food.
6. Action of breaking up the soil.
7. Process of making food by using light and carbon dioxide.
8. Downward movement of water through the soil.
9. Dead plant material in the soil.
10. Small plate containing chlorophyll in a plant cell.
11. Living together of two different things for certain benefits.
12. Method of growing plants without soil.

a. carbohydrate
b. chlorophyll
c. chloroplast
d. cultivation
e. humus
f. hydroponics
g. lichen
h. percolation
i. photosynthesis
j. population
k. predator
l. symbiosis

13. Natural mixture in which roots can grow.
14. Source of a parasite's food.
15. Living thing that lives in or on another living thing.
16. Kind of animal that eats plants for food.
17. Passing of food from one living thing to another.
18. One of the soil chemicals that plants need to grow.
19. What a predator seeks for its food.
20. Measure of how acid or base a soil is.
21. Kind of animal that kills other animals for food.
22. Kind of soil in which plants grow well.
23. Animal that seeks dead animals for food.
24. All the things and conditions around a living thing.
25. Study of living things in relation to their surroundings.

a. carnivorous
b. ecology
c. environment
d. fertile
e. food chain
f. herbivorous
g. host
h. nutrient
i. parasite
j. pH
k. prey
l. scavenger
m. soil

## B. Facts

Write the words that belong in the blanks.

1. Green plants make sugar from the common materials ——— and ———.
2. The sugar sold in stores comes from plants called sugar ——— and sugar ———.
3. When we eat corn, bananas, or potatoes, we are eating the carbohydrate ——— that was made from sugar and was stored by the plant.
4. Soil can hold much water if it has plenty of ———.
5. Besides making the soil loose, cultivation helps to control ———.
6. If soil has a pH of 5, it would be good to add some ——— to raise the pH.
7. For plant roots to get water between rains, God provided ——— action.
8. Plowing down plants, spreading manure, and adding compost are all ways of adding ——— to the soil.
9. Green plants are the first link in the ——— ———.
10. There is a ——— of ——— between the predator and the prey.
11. A limited ——— ——— will keep a population from becoming too large.
12. Weeds in a cornfield make it hard for the corn to grow because of ———.
13. The Japanese beetle was brought under control by use of a disease ———.
14. Man sometimes upsets the ——— of ——— by introducing a new kind of living thing to an area.
15. A fish is the ——— to a sea lamprey attached to its side.

## C. Concepts

Choose the letter of the best answer in each exercise.

1. Photosynthesis is an ideal process for all of the following reasons *except*
   a. all the products are useful.
   b. the steps are few and simple.
   c. the energy is free and unlimited.
   d. the raw materials are free and abundant.
2. Which material named is followed by its correct chemical formula?
   a. water: $HO_2$
   b. sugar: $C_{12}H_6O_{12}$
   c. carbon dioxide: $CO_2$
   d. oxygen: $O_2H$

3. Which word part is *not* followed by its correct meaning?
   a. *photo:* picture
   b. *hydro:* water
   c. *carn:* flesh
   d. *sym:* together
4. Green plants provide us with both food and
   a. oxygen.
   b. nitrogen.
   c. carbon dioxide.
   d. hydrogen.
5. Hydroponics shows us that
   a. plants can be grown more easily without soil.
   b. plants need more water and nutrients than soil can provide.
   c. soil contains chemicals that are harmful to plants.
   d. soil provides support, water, and nutrients.
6. A farmer may add fertilizer to the soil to increase the
   a. pH.
   b. humus.
   c. nutrients.
   d. percolation.
7. A main disadvantage of no-till farming is
   a. more work is required.
   b. the plants do not grow as well.
   c. strong chemicals must be used.
   d. the weeds cannot be controlled.
8. Sandy soil has better ——— than people usually want.
   a. nutrients
   b. percolation
   c. acids
   d. capillary action
9. Which one of these statements is *not* correct?
   a. Man is omnivorous.
   b. Cats are herbivorous.
   c. Dogs are carnivorous.
   d. Vultures are scavengers.
10. More people can be fed with corn than with beef because
    a. more people would rather eat corn products than beef.
    b. it is easier to prepare food from corn than from beef.
    c. various kinds of plants can be fed to beef cattle.
    d. with beef, there is a greater loss in the food chain.

11. We can be thankful for scavengers because
    a. they help to keep the land clean.
    b. they are an important link in the food chain.
    c. they do not compete with herbivorous animals for food.
    d. they help to control the rat population.
12. Plankton and lichens are similar in that
    a. both are found in ocean water.
    b. both are parasites to animals.
    c. both are made of more than one kind of living thing.
    d. both are an important source of food for birds.
13. Which statement is *not* true about animals and the food they eat?
    a. Some whales strain their food with baleen.
    b. Rabbits have long canine teeth for tearing flesh.
    c. Cows have several parts to their stomachs.
    d. Oxpeckers do a good service to cape buffalos.
14. A good example of symbiosis is
    a. the relationship between hawks and mice.
    b. fungus supplying water, and algae supplying food.
    c. the introduction of starlings to America.
    d. the cow chewing her cud.

# Unit 5

## Energy—Harnessing Its Sources

"And the posts of the door moved at the voice of him that cried, and the house was filled with smoke" (Isaiah 6:4).

Without energy, nothing moves. If something moves, there is energy to make it move. When you move a box, your muscles are the source of the energy. When you mow the lawn, the gasoline in the engine is the source of energy that turns the blade to cut the grass.

Sometimes it is difficult to know what produces the motion. The wind makes the leaves on a tree move, but what makes the wind blow? The water racing through a turbine is used to generate electricity, but what gives the water its energy?

When Isaiah saw a vision of the Lord, the posts of the temple door moved. What was the source of energy to make those posts move? It was the voice of God. He can make things move by speaking. When God created the world, He said "Let there be" and it was. This is the way He created the sun, the main source of energy for us. This is the way He set the planets spinning and moving around the sun. The voice of God has great energy. There is no limit to the energy of God. He is almighty. He is omnipotent, which means that He is all-powerful.

God is the source of all energy. Even the energy that you use to push a box is from God. To get energy for your body, you eat food. The food is made by green plants. The green plants get their energy from the sun. God put the energy in the sun at Creation. So the source of all the energy in the universe is God.

## Lesson 22

# The Energy Chain

"Behold, I have created the smith that bloweth the coals in the fire, and that bringeth forth an instrument for his work" (Isaiah 54:16).

### Vocabulary

**energy,** the ability to make something move or change.

**kinetic energy,** energy in motion.

**law of conservation of energy,** the fact that energy cannot be created or destroyed.

**law of thermodynamics,** the fact that energy moves from a higher level to a lower level.

**potential energy,** stored energy.

At the Creation, God placed energy in the sun, and He put energy in the materials of the earth. ***Energy*** is what causes changes and makes things move. Without energy, nothing would happen. The earth would be barren and uninhabitable, for no one would be able to move or even to live.

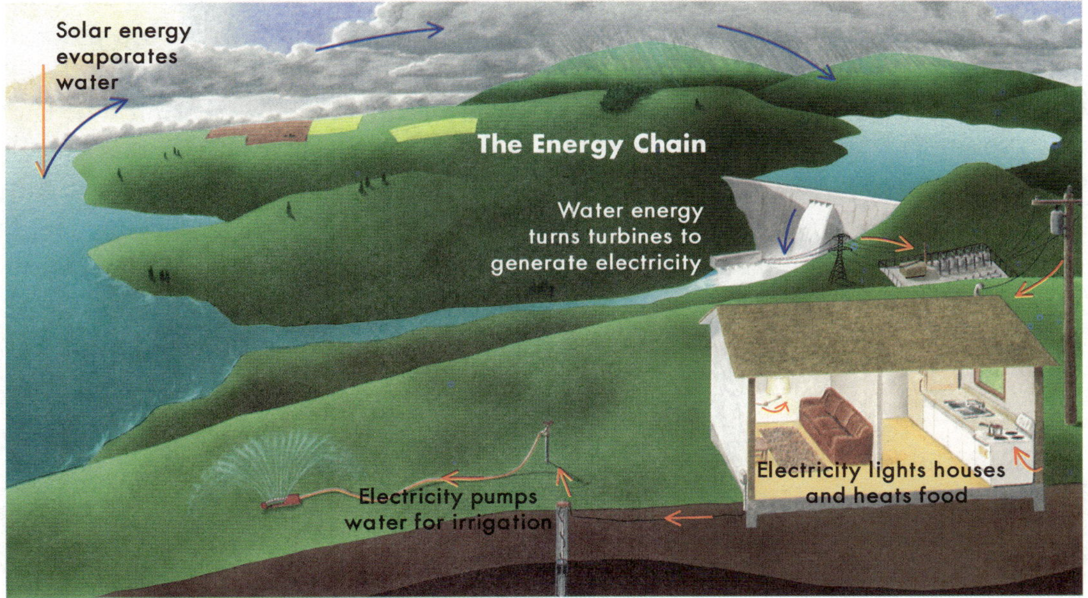

The blacksmith uses heat energy from a fire to soften iron so that he can shape it. A moving car, burning wood, and boiling water all show energy in operation. Life itself must have energy.

**Forms of energy.** There will never be a factory that can make energy. No machine can convert a small amount of energy into a large amount of energy. For example, an electric motor cannot run a generator that produces more electricity than the motor uses.

Scientists call this principle the ***law of conservation of energy.*** This law says that energy cannot be created or destroyed. It applies only to man, not to God. God created energy when He said, "Let there be light."

Though man cannot create energy, he can change it from one form to another. Light energy from the sun changes to heat energy that warms the water in the ocean and causes it to rise into the air. The water falls as rain and then flows down a river. The mechanical energy of the flowing water turns generators at power plants, which produce electrical energy. We use electrical energy to light our homes, cook our food, pump our water, and do many other things.

The number of times that energy can change from one form to another is endless, but only God can create or destroy energy.

**The energy chain, a one-way street.** In Lesson 15 you saw that some things are used over and over in cycles. Three of these are the water cycle, the oxygen cycle, and the nitrogen cycle. But energy was not made to be recycled. Energy passes through a chain similar to the food chain in Lesson 19. The food chain is actually an energy chain.

God created the sun to be the source of energy. A green plant uses energy from the sun to live and grow through photosynthesis. An animal eats the plant to get energy to live, and a predator may eat that animal. So the energy from the sun passes through the food chain as it goes from a plant to an animal to another animal. But the energy stays on the earth; it never goes back to the sun.

Energy always goes "downhill" in its chain. For example, if you place a piece of hot metal against a piece of cold metal, which direction will the heat energy go? Will the hot metal draw energy out of the cold metal and become hotter? Of course not. Heat energy always goes from the hot object to the cold object.

This is a law of thermodynamics. *Thermo* means "heat." *Dynamics* means "motion." Heat is just one form of energy, but the law applies to all energy. The ***law of thermodynamics*** states that energy always moves from a higher level to a lower level: from hot to cold, from the fire to boiling water, from the sun to the earth, from digesting food to muscles. This law is often called the second law of thermodynamics; the law of conservation of energy is the first law of thermodynamics.

These are two very important laws of science. They apply to all parts of the universe and to all the different subjects of science. Because there are no exceptions to these laws, they are some of the best scientific evidences that the world was created by God. It could not have come into being through evolution.

## Study the Lesson

1. Before something can move or happen, there must be ———.
2. In each pair, write the number of the statement that is true.
   a. (1) Energy passes around a continuous cycle.
      (2) Energy begins at a source and passes along a chain.
   b. (1) No new energy is being produced.
      (2) New energy is regularly added.
   c. (1) Energy moves from a hot area to a cold area.
      (2) Energy moves from a cold area to a hot area.
   d. (1) Energy comes from the sun to the earth and does not return.
      (2) Energy goes back and forth between the earth and sun.
3. Put each list in the right order for an energy chain.
   a. green plants, man, beef cattle, sun, light
   b. fire, train wheels, steam engine, coal, steam
   c. electricity, waterfall, stove, generator, hot food
4. Where did the sun get its energy?
5. What is the law of conservation of energy?
6. What is the (second) law of thermodynamics?
7. Since we have energy and man cannot create energy, we know ——— has created it.
8. Energy always goes from a higher level to a lower level. This is strong, scientific evidence that
   a. energy is affected by gravity.
   b. the world was created by God.
   c. things in the universe happen by chance.

**Two kinds of energy.** When you move a box, your muscular energy is in motion. This is called ***kinetic energy.*** Any energy in motion is kinetic energy. The wind, a car moving down the highway, a fire heating a kettle of water, and light coming from a light bulb are examples of kinetic energy.

God planned for ways to store up energy. Photosynthesis stores light energy in the fruits of plants. Your body stores energy from digesting food in your muscles. Stored energy is ***potential energy.*** Potential energy is not in use but is ready for use, such as the food in your lunch box, gasoline in a tank, electrical energy in a battery, or the compressed spring of a mousetrap.

Before potential energy can be useful to us, it must be changed to kinetic energy. Gasoline is potential energy. It is changed to kinetic energy when we burn it. This kinetic energy must be harnessed before it will do us any good. For example, the energy of burning gasoline needs to power the engine of a tractor before it can be used to plow a field. In this unit you will study some ways energy is changed from potential to kinetic and then harnessed. The word *harnessed* comes from the practice of putting harnesses on horses so their energy can be used to pull things.

Examples of kinetic energy

Examples of potential energy

The energy in fuel is much more concentrated than the energy in wind.

**Good sources of energy.** Some sources of energy are better than others. An ideal source of energy should have the following four qualities.

*Convenient.* The source of energy is easy to obtain, handle, and transport. Coal is a good source of energy, and for years it was the main fuel for train locomotives. But diesel fuel is much more convenient. Diesel fuel can be stored in tanks or pumped long distances through hoses and pipes. Diesel fuel is a more convenient source of energy than coal.

*Concentrated.* Wind is a free source of energy, but it is not very concentrated. Long ago, sailing ships needed huge sails so they would move through the water. One gallon of fuel is a much more concentrated source of energy. One gallon of fuel will move a car about 30 miles. It would take a strong wind and big sails to move a car that far.

*Convertible.* Before a source of energy can be useful, it must be changed or converted into the form we need. If you need electricity, it is much easier to harness waterpower to turn a generator than to convert energy from plants to electrical energy.

*Clean.* Wind turning a windmill is a clean source of energy; it produces no ashes, no exhaust, and no pollution. Gasoline is a convenient, concentrated, and convertible source of energy. But when gasoline burns in an engine, it produces poisonous gases. These gases will pollute the air unless they are changed by a catalytic converter.

No source of energy is always best in all four ways. We can be thankful to God for giving us such a variety of energy. People use energy to work, travel, and run their factories. We need to use energy sources wisely and avoid wasting them.

Two sources of energy are harnessed to make electricity—wind and coal. Which one is cleaner? Which one is more concentrated, or takes up less space?

## Study the Lesson

9. Tell whether each one is an example of *potential* or *kinetic* energy.
   a. a falling rock
   b. a gallon of diesel fuel
   c. a flashlight battery
   d. water behind a dam
   e. water from a fire hose
   f. the spring of a mousetrap
   g. a car going down a highway
10. Each sentence below is followed by two of the four qualities of a good energy source. Choose the quality that is illustrated in that sentence.
    a. One pound of uranium fuel has as much energy as 1,500 tons of coal. (concentrated, convenient)
    b. Wind energy can be harnessed with blades fastened to a rotor. (concentrated, convertible)
    c. Natural gas can be used to cook food, heat water, and heat the house. (clean, convenient)
    d. Harnessing solar energy does not pollute the air, water, or land. (clean, convertible)

11. For each of these sentences, choose the *missing* quality of a good energy source.
    a. Burning high-sulfur coal produces a poisonous gas. (clean, concentrated)
    b. It would take 500 windmills over 60 feet in diameter to supply electricity for a town. (concentrated, convertible)
    c. Angel Falls in Venezuela is the highest waterfall in the world, but it is very difficult to get there by land. (clean, convenient)

## Review Exercises

1. The study of living things in relation to their surroundings is called ———. [20]
2. An animal that feeds mostly on plants is (carnivorous, herbivorous, omnivorous). [19]
3. In the water cycle, water falls from clouds as ———, streams and rivers carry it to the ———, and then it ——— to form clouds again. [15]
4. Water moves upward through soil by a process called ——— ———. [12]
5. Sometimes the superior planets appear to move backward in relation to the stars. This is called ——— motion. [9]
6. The orbits of the planets, and especially those of the comets, are in the shape of (a circle, an egg, an ellipse). [6]

## Apply the Lesson

1. Energy has become a major part of modern life. We use energy for transportation, communication, manufacturing, farming, cooking, and heating. Where does all the energy come from? Do research to find out how much energy is used and what percent comes from the various sources. How much has the use of energy increased in the last one hundred years? An encyclopedia, the *World Almanac,* and *Information Please* give interesting information on energy use.
2. The second law of thermodynamics makes perpetual motion machines impossible. What is a perpetual motion machine? Why will such a machine never be invented?

## Lesson 23

# Harnessing Wind, Water, and Sunlight

"The trees of the wood are moved with the wind" (Isaiah 7:2).

### Vocabulary

**dam,** a barrier in a river that concentrates the energy in water by collecting it and raising its height.

**hydroelectric,** the kind of power produced when water turns a generator.

**solar cell,** a device that uses sunlight to produce electricity.

**solar energy,** the energy from the sun.

**water turbine,** a device for harnessing energy in moving water to drive a generator.

**wind turbine,** a device for harnessing energy in moving air to drive a generator.

Energy is required to make things move. If the leaves of a tree move, the energy of the wind is pushing them. Sometimes the wind energy is so strong that the entire tree sways back and forth. A stormy wind can even uproot a tree. Wind has little or much energy, depending on how fast the air is moving.

**Wind energy can be harnessed to do work.** The same wind that pushes the leaves on a tree can push aside a blade fastened to a shaft. In a windmill, many blades are fastened to

A windmill pumps water.

Turbines on this wind farm generate electricity.

one shaft. Each blade is slanted the same way so that each one helps to turn the shaft in the same direction. The turning windmill can then be made to do useful things, such as pumping water from wells or turning stones to grind corn and wheat to make flour.

Today most windmills turn electric generators and are called ***wind turbines.*** Wind turbines often have only two or three long blades. They are mounted on tall towers, which hold the wind turbines high where the wind is blowing faster. In California and some other areas, hundreds of wind turbines are set up together at places called wind farms.

As you know, the energy to run a wind turbine is free. As the turbine turns, it does not pollute the air at all. Why then are not more wind turbines used to harness this clean, cheap source of energy?

The wind is not always blowing, and in most places it does not blow fast enough to make a wind turbine practical. The wind must blow at an average of 12 miles per hour (19 km/h) or more to be useful for generating electricity. Wind is not a very concentrated form of energy, so the blades of a wind turbine may have a length of 20 feet (6 m) or more.

Such long blades are heavy and spin very fast. This makes strong forces that can bend or break the rotor and wear out the bearings. Sometimes the wind blows too fast. A storm can wreck a wind turbine unless it is made very well. So while it is easy to make a simple wind turbine, it is difficult to make one that will harness the energy of the wind for years in all kinds of weather.

**Moving water is an excellent source of energy.** Water is heavy and pushes with great force as it falls. Many years ago, large water wheels harnessed water energy by catching the water in buckets. The buckets of a

An old water wheel

Modern hydroelectric turbines

water wheel were full of water on one side and empty on the other side. The weight of the water on one side caused the wheel to turn. The shaft of the wheel could then be used to pump water, saw wood, or grind flour.

Today the energy of moving water is usually harnessed with ***water turbines.*** A water turbine has a shaft with curved blades extending from it. As moving water pushes the blades, it makes the shaft spin at high speed. This speed is what is needed to generate electricity. Places that generate electricity with waterpower are called ***hydroelectric*** plants.

Hydroelectric plants can be built only at certain places. Two things are needed. There must be a large amount of flowing water, and the water must fall a great distance. Only at a waterfall in a river are both of these needed things found naturally. A famous place for hydroelectric plants is Niagara Falls. Both the Americans and the Canadians take water from above the falls and use it to generate electricity as it descends to the river below the falls.

Most hydroelectric plants are built at ***dams.*** A dam backs up the water and makes it rise many feet so that it will have much energy as it flows through the water turbines. The highest dams in the world cause the water to rise over 800 feet (250 m).

Moving water is a much more concentrated source of energy than the wind. The water energy is free and easily convertible into useful electrical energy, and it causes no pollution. Why then do we not get all of our electric energy from hydroelectric plants?

Most of the good places to harness moving water are already being used. Some rivers and waterfalls would be useful if they were closer to the places where the electricity is needed. There are many hydroelectric plants in the United States, but they supply only about 8 percent of the energy that is needed.

The Itaipú Dam in Brazil is one of the world's largest hydroelectric projects.

## Study the Lesson

1. If you see something move, you know that ——— made it move.
2. What things were windmills of long ago used for?
3. What are most modern wind turbines used for? How many blades do they have, and how long are they?
4. Why might your area be a poor place to build a wind turbine?
5. A 10-foot waterfall turns a water wheel better than a 5-foot waterfall because
   a. more water strikes the wheel.
   b. the water falls a greater distance.
   c. the water moves faster.
6. If a hydroelectric plant is built in your area, what two things must be present?
7. The main purpose of a dam at a hydroelectric plant is
   a. to back up the water for many miles.
   b. to store a large amount of water for use during dry seasons.
   c. to protect the hydroelectric plant from floods.
   d. to make the water rise higher.

**Solar energy is another free source.** All the energy of wind and moving water comes from the sun. Wind is produced as the sun heats the earth and causes air to circulate. Water power is produced as heat from the sun, first of all, evaporates ocean water. Then winds carry the moist air over the land, where it falls as rain and flows back toward the oceans. The flowing water gives us hydroelectric energy.

Energy from the sun also goes into green plants that make food and wood. The energy of a burning piece of wood comes from the sun. The sun is our most important source of energy. The energy of the sun costs us nothing. God causes the sun to shine as a free gift.

The energy from the sun is called ***solar energy.*** Can solar energy be harnessed directly to run our machines? Yes, but not very well. We get much sunlight in a day, but it is not very concentrated. It is spread over many square miles. A big problem in harnessing solar energy is to collect a large amount of it. Perhaps you have seen large solar energy collectors on roofs of houses. These collectors heat water or air, but they do not run machines.

There are two main ways to convert solar energy into electrical energy. One way is to use the sun to heat water and make steam. The steam

A greenhouse captures the sun's energy. As radiant sunlight heats the contents inside, the shell keeps the heat from escaping.

drives a steam turbine to generate electricity. But it takes many large mirrors to collect enough sunlight and focus it on boilers so that they will run a steam turbine.

A more practical way to harness solar energy is to use ***solar cells.*** Solar cells are made of special material that produces electricity when sunlight falls on it. Many solar cells can be connected together to produce a useful amount of electricity from a large area of sunlight.

The electricity needed in satellites is produced by solar cells. Solar cells are also useful to run a calculator, an electric fencer, or a telephone far from a regular source of electricity. But solar cells are very expensive, so they are used mainly where just a small amount of electricity is needed.

Of course, solar cells cannot produce electricity at night, and they do not work well on cloudy days. That is why solar cells are usually connected to storage batteries. The solar cells charge the batteries, and the batteries provide electricity both day and night.

Sunlight falls on the earth whether or not people use it as a power source. This is a clean, free source of energy,

*Left:* A solar-powered sensor notifies motorists when deer are near the highway. The batteries are above the solar panel. *Right:* A solar-powered road construction sign. The solar panel is tilted back on top of the sign. The batteries are in the orange compartment below the sign.

and harnessing it does not use up irreplaceable resources like coal and petroleum. Yet solar energy is the least harnessed source used today. However, men are seeking better ways to harness this valuable source of energy.

**God gives us the energy we need.** In this lesson you have thought about wind, moving water, and solar energy. In the next lesson you will consider fuel as a source of energy. Man cannot create any of this energy. God created all of it. You cannot turn to the next page without the solar energy that makes food.

When we ask God to "give us this day our daily bread," we are looking to God to supply the energy we need to live and work. We should remember that the many sources of energy are gifts from God. As with all other gifts, we must receive them with gratitude and use them properly.

## Study the Lesson

8. The heat from sunlight can produce electricity if it is first used to make ______.
9. Give three common uses for the electricity produced by solar cells.
10. Why are solar cells often connected to storage batteries?
11. Write the matching term for each word or definition.

| | |
|---|---|
| a. sun | turbine |
| b. water | energy |
| c. control to do work | solar |
| d. ability to make things move | harness |
| e. device with blades fastened to a shaft | hydro |

12. Write *wind, moving water,* or *solar energy* for each description. More than one answer may be correct.
    a. No pollution from harnessing it.
    b. The most concentrated.
    c. The least harnessed today.
    d. A free gift from God.
    e. Electricity produced with it.
13. What should be our response to God for the sources of energy?

## Review Exercises

1. The law of conservation of energy states that energy cannot be ——— or ———. [22]
2. An animal that kills and eats other animals is (carnivorous, herbivorous, omnivorous). [19]
3. Dead plant materials improve the soil by decaying to form ———. [18]
4. In the oxygen cycle, people and animals breathe out ——— ———, which plants use, and plants give off ———, which people and animals breathe. [15]
5. The oceans help to make the surrounding land (warmer, colder) in winter and (warmer, cooler) in summer. [14]
6. The planets located inside the earth's orbit are called ——— planets. [7]

## Apply the Lesson

1. Design a simple windmill, using cardboard, wood, or metal. What problems must you solve so that the wind will actually turn the windmill? If you were making a big windmill, what additional problems would you need to solve? Think of several ways to get the energy of the turning windmill at the top of the tower down to do work at the bottom of the tower.
2. Design a simple water wheel. Small plastic or metal containers could be wired to a wooden disk. Can you think of other ways to accomplish the same purpose? What is the main purpose? What conditions do you need for your water wheel to function in a natural setting?
3. a. Experiment with a solar-powered calculator. One that shows individual solar cells will be best. How close must you be to a 100-watt bulb for the calculator display to work?
   b. In a brightly lit room, lay a small paper on a part of each cell. If you cover a fourth of each cell, can you still see the display? If you cover a half of each? Three-fourths?
   c. Now try this: Cover one whole cell. Did the display disappear? Cover two cells, then three cells. Compare the resulting fractions from *b* and *c*. Can you explain the results?
   d. Cover just enough of the solar cells to make the display disappear. Now do a complete calculation. Remove the cover. Does the answer appear? What does this tell you about the energy needed to display compared with the energy needed to calculate?

# Lesson 24

## Harnessing Fuel Energy

"When the melting fire burneth, the fire causeth the waters to boil" (Isaiah 64:2).

### Vocabulary

**choke,** the device on an engine that blocks the airflow to increase fuel added to air.

**combustion,** the burning of a material.

**crankshaft,** a shaft that changes the up-and-down motion of pistons to rotary motion.

**cylinder,** in a gasoline engine, a round space with a piston moving up and down inside.

**exhaust valve,** a valve that lets burned gases out of a cylinder of a gasoline engine.

**fuel injector,** a device that mixes fuel with air for a gasoline engine.

**intake valve,** a valve that lets the fuel–air mixture into a cylinder of a gasoline engine.

**piston,** a round part that slides up and down inside a cylinder of a gasoline engine.

**spark plug,** a device that makes a spark to cause combustion in a gasoline engine.

**throttle,** a device that controls the speed of a gasoline engine.

**Steam Engine**

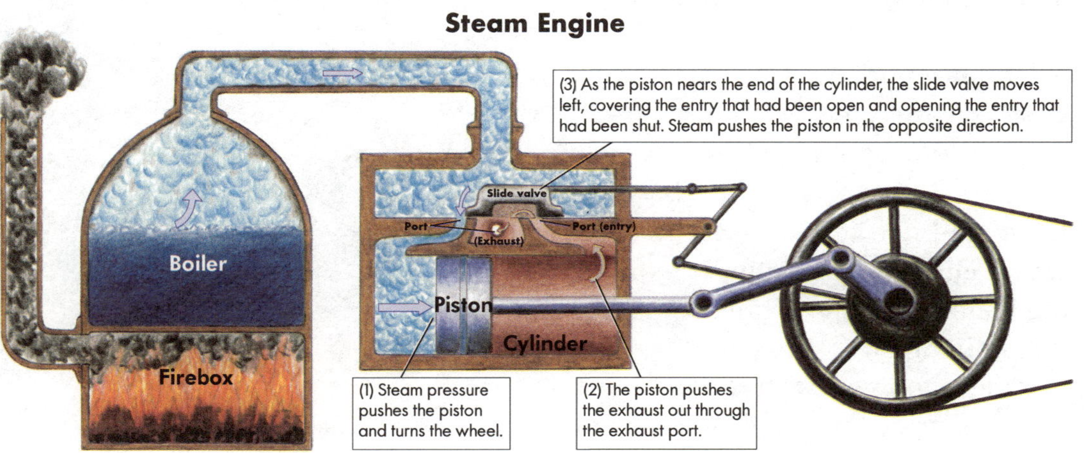

Anything that will burn is fuel. Wood, leaves, and straw are fuel that comes from plants. Tons and tons of coal are mined every year to burn as fuel. Thousands of gallons of petroleum are pumped every year from deep oil wells. The energy in all fuel comes from God.

A ton of coal and a thousand gallons of oil do you little good until they are burned. Fuel is a form of potential energy. The fuel is changed into useful kinetic energy when it is burned to produce heat.

Sometimes we make direct use of the heat from burning fuel. Fire is useful to heat our houses and cook our food. Fire can be used to melt iron and glass to make useful products. But the greatest use for fuel is to run our machines.

**How can fuel be harnessed to run a machine?** The basic way to harness fuel energy is to burn it in such a way that a gas (air) expands and pushes against a movable engine part.

At one time this was done mostly with steam engines. In a steam engine, fuel is burned in a firebox beneath a water supply. The heat from this fire makes steam. When water changes to steam, it expands (becomes bigger). This expanding steam is piped to the engine, where it gives the push to run machinery. In a steam turbine engine, it pushes against the blades of the turbine. In a steam piston engine, it pushes against the piston.

You likely did not get to school with energy from a steam engine. With the invention of the modern gasoline engines, steam piston engines have become nearly obsolete. They are too heavy, clumsy, and inefficient. They need a constant supply of not only fuel but also water.

In modern piston engines, the fuel burns inside rather than outside, as with a steam engine. The burning fuel causes gases to expand. These gases give the push that runs our machinery.

There are many different kinds of engines that burn fuel. Jet engines power airplanes. Diesel engines are in tractors and big trucks. Little two-cycle engines are used on chain saws. The rest of this lesson discusses how a four-cycle gasoline engine works.

This gasoline engine for a propeller airplane has nine cylinders arranged in a circle.

This is a very common engine used in cars, small trucks, lawn mowers, and small tractors. Your parents probably have one or more four-cycle gasoline engines. You may have started and used one yourself. Now you will learn how they harness the energy of gasoline.

**An engine needs fuel, air, and spark.** For the energy of gasoline to be useful in an engine, it must burn. Another name for burning is ***combustion.*** Combustion will happen only when fuel becomes hot enough to unite with oxygen in the air. Cold gasoline in a can does not burn. But when it evaporates and mixes with air, the mixture is highly explosive. Yet even then it does not burn unless some part of it is made very hot. Then there is a *boom,* and fire flashes in every direction. That is why it is very dangerous to light a match near gasoline. In a gasoline engine, the spark from a ***spark plug*** causes the combustion.

So a gasoline engine needs three things in order to run: fuel, air, and spark. If the gasoline tank is empty, if the air intake is clogged, or if there is no spark, the engine will not run.

**The fuel injector puts fuel into the air.** As air rushes into a gasoline engine, a ***fuel injector*** sprays tiny droplets of gasoline into the air. This makes an explosive mixture that burns readily inside the engine.

In a lawn mower engine, the fuel and air are mixed in a device called a carburetor.

The right amount of gasoline must be mixed with the air. When a cold engine is started, the injector is electronically adjusted to make the mixture especially rich in gasoline so that it burns easily.

A lawn mower engine uses a ***choke*** to partly close off the airflow so that more gasoline is added to the air. After the engine is warmed up, the choke must be fully opened so that the

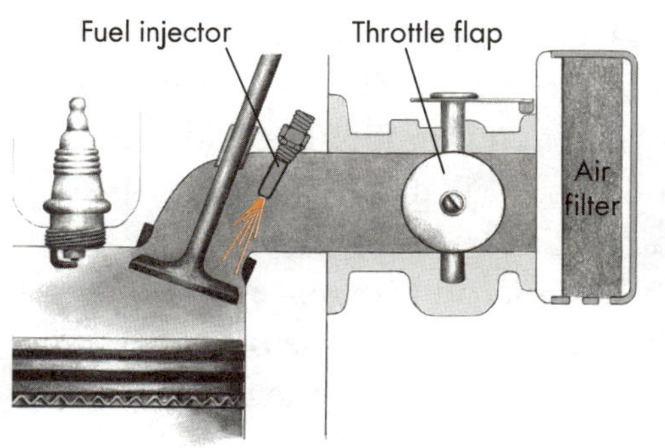


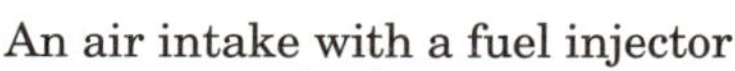
An air intake with a fuel injector

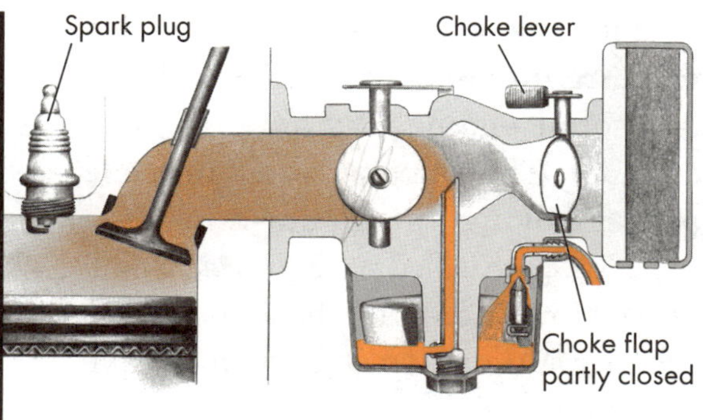

An air intake with a carburetor

engine will run properly.

A ***throttle*** controls the amount of fuel–air mixture entering the engine. This is a valve that regulates the airflow. When the throttle is wide open, the air can rush through freely and the engine runs very fast. When the throttle is partly closed, the air cannot get through as fast and the engine runs more slowly. In this way the throttle controls how fast the engine runs.

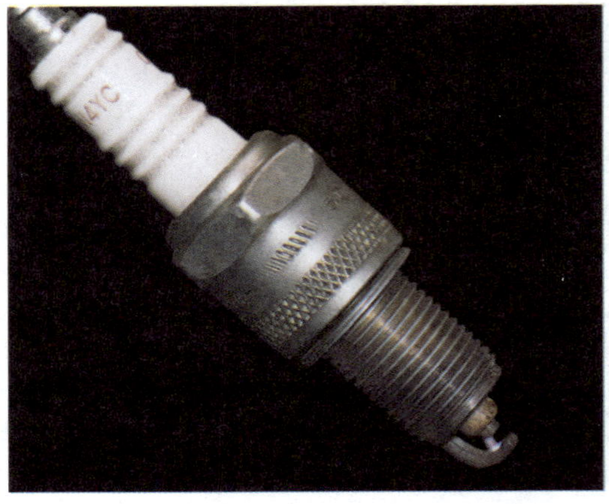

A spark plug produces a tiny spark.

## Study the Lesson

1. Fuel has (potential, kinetic) energy.
2. Fuel must be ——— to change its energy so that it will run a machine.
3. Put the following words in order to show the energy chain of a steam engine.

    fire, steam, fuel, moving piston, heat

4. Unlike the steam engine, a gasoline engine burns the fuel (inside, outside) the engine.
5. What three things must be present before combustion will take place in a gasoline engine?
6. What is the purpose of the spark in a gasoline engine?
7. What two things are mixed by the fuel injector?

**The valves let the fuel–air mixture into and out of the cylinder.** A gasoline engine may have only one cylinder. That means it has just one piston moving up and down inside a tubelike space called the ***cylinder***. Small lawn mower engines have only one cylinder. Most automobile engines have from four to eight cylinders.

Each cylinder has two valves. The ***intake valve*** opens to let the fuel–air mixture into the cylinder. The ***exhaust valve*** lets the burned gases out of the cylinder. The valves open and close at just the right time to keep the engine running.

**The piston harnesses the energy of combustion.** The ***piston*** is the round part of the engine that slides up and down inside the cylinder. The piston must fit tightly, or the expanding gases will escape around its edges and

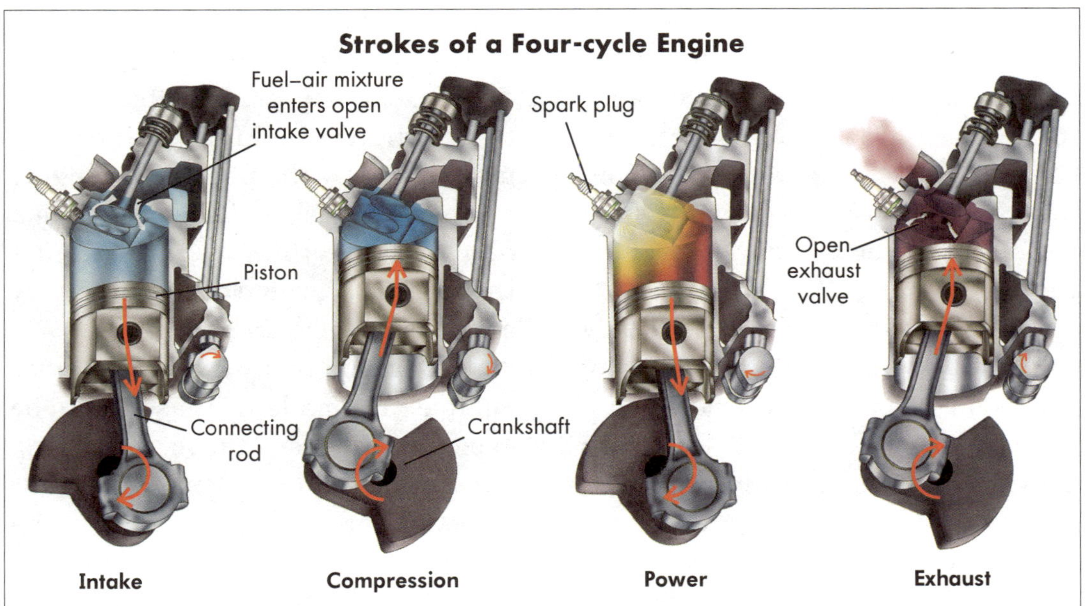


the engine will have very little power.

The piston makes four motions, or strokes, in each cycle. During the first one, called the *intake stroke,* the intake valve opens, the piston moves down, and the fuel–air mixture is drawn into the cylinder. During the second stroke, the piston squeezes the mixture very tightly in the top of the cylinder. This is called the *compression stroke,* since the fuel–air mixture is compressed.

Now an electric spark jumps between two points on a spark plug. The spark sets the gasoline on fire, causing an explosion that drives the piston downward with great force. This is the third stroke, called the *power stroke.* It leaves the cylinder full of burned gases. So the exhaust valve opens, and the piston pushes the burned gases out of the cylinder during the *exhaust stroke.* These gases go through a muffler, which

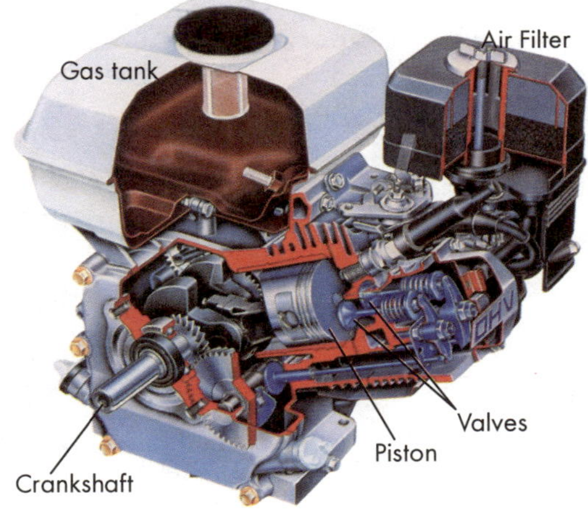


This 4-cycle gasoline engine is a cutaway of a GX-Series Honda engine with overhead valves. Overhead valves help meet strict emission-control laws.

quiets the noise of the explosions.

After the exhaust stroke, the piston moves down for another intake stroke at the beginning of the next cycle: 1-2-3-4, 1-2-3-4, intake-compression-power-exhaust, over and over at high speed. That is how a four-cycle gasoline engine works.

**The crankshaft produces rotary motion.** The up-and-down motion of the piston would not be very useful if it could not be changed to rotary motion. The piston is fastened to a connecting rod, which is joined to a ***crankshaft.*** The crankshaft is turned by the piston moving up and down inside the cylinder. One end of the crankshaft extends from the side of the engine to operate a machine or drive the wheels of a car.

**God made four-cycle gasoline engines possible.** Men often receive the credit for making engines. We marvel at how the parts of an engine can move so fast that they look like a blur, yet everything happens at just the right time to harness fuel energy and run our machines.

God should really get the credit for engines. He made the gasoline to be explosive. He made the metals strong enough to move swiftly without breaking apart. He gave men the ability to design and build engines. The One who made man is greater than the man. Do not forget to praise God for engines that harness the energy of fuel.

## Study the Lesson

8. Choose the correct word for each description.
   a. Regulates the fuel–air mixture to control the speed of the engine.
   b. Is the round space where the piston moves up and down.
   c. Opens to let the fuel–air mixture into the cylinder.
   d. Partly closes off the airflow to make a rich fuel–air mixture.
   e. Is a round part driven downward by expanding gases.
   f. Opens to let the burned gases out of the cylinder.
   g. Changes up-and-down motion to rotary motion.
   h. Uses electricity to make sudden heat.
   i. Carries the force from the piston to the crankshaft.

   choke
   connecting rod
   crankshaft
   cylinder
   exhaust valve
   intake valve
   piston
   spark plug
   throttle

9. Name in order the four strokes of a four-cycle gasoline engine.

10. Name the correct stroke for each description.
    a. The combustion of the gasoline pushes the piston down.
    b. Air and fuel come into the cylinder.
    c. The burned gases are pushed out of the cylinder.
    d. The fuel–air mixture is squeezed into the top of the cylinder.
11. The spark jumps at the beginning of which stroke?
12. Give three ways in which God made the gasoline engine possible.

## Review Exercises

1. The law of thermodynamics states that energy always moves from a ——— level to a ——— level. [22]
2. An animal that feeds on plants and other animals is (carnivorous, herbivorous, omnivorous). [19]
3. A farmer may spread ——— to increase the nutrients in the soil, or he may spread ——— to improve the pH. [18]
4. In the process called ———, plants use ——— and ——— ——— in the presence of sunlight to make sugar. [17]
5. Plants called ——— build up nitrogen compounds in the soil through a process called ——— ———. [15]
6. The closer a planet is to the sun, the (more slowly, more swiftly) it travels and the (shorter, longer) its year is. [7]

## Apply the Lesson

1. Start and run a lawn mower engine. Experiment with the effect of the choke on the running of the engine. Turn the carburetor adjustment screw back and forth until it is running best. Adjust the throttle for different speeds. Adjust the idle (how slow the engine will run). If the engine does not start well, take out the spark plug and check to see if the points are clean. A buildup of carbon can interfere with the spark.

   **Important:** Do this activity only with teacher supervision. Be sure to do it outdoors, for the exhaust is poisonous.
2. Get an old lawn mower engine that no longer runs, and take it apart. Find all the engine parts mentioned in this lesson.

## Lesson 25

# Using Energy for Transportation

"Woe to them that go down to Egypt for help; and stay on horses, and trust in chariots, because they are many; and in horsemen, because they are very strong; but they look not unto the Holy One of Israel, neither seek the LORD!" (Isaiah 31:1).

### Vocabulary

**aileron** (ā′·lə·ron′), a flap used to raise or lower an airplane wing.

**airfoil,** a device shaped to cause lift by reducing air pressure above it.

**bow** (bou), the front end of a ship.

**brakes,** a set of devices that use friction to stop a car.

**bridge,** a raised structure where navigators steer a ship.

**buoyant force,** the upward push of water on a floating object.

**clutch,** a device that disconnects the turning force of an engine from the wheels of a car.

**differential,** a device that lets the two drive wheels of a car turn at different speeds.

**elevator,** a flap that makes an airplane fly higher or lower.

**jet propulsion,** a forward push from gases rushing backward.

**propulsion,** the push that makes a vehicle move.

**rudder,** a blade for steering a ship or an airplane.

**stern,** the back end of a ship.

**transmission,** in a car, a device that has a low gear, a high gear, and reverse.

We are living in an age of travel. People use engines to travel by land, sea, and air. Today many men are trusting in submarines and jet airplanes for their safety instead of in horsemen and chariots. The methods of transportation have changed, but the heart of sinful man is still the same.

That does not mean transportation is wrong. Paul helped to spread the Gospel by traveling on the Mediterranean Sea in sailing ships. Like other products of science, it is the use of the invention and not the invention itself that is either right or wrong.

We must not use transportation to go to wrong places. We must not trust in transportation to keep us safe. We must not become proud of our means of transportation. People of the world will often try to impress others with the power, expense, color, or decorations of their automobiles. The Christian wants to practice humility and good stewardship with his transportation.

**Three things are needed for transportation.** For people or materials to be moved from one place to another, they first need to be supported. Something needs to carry them while they are being transported.

Even then, they will go nowhere unless they are being pushed or propelled in some way. This is called ***propulsion,*** and it is provided by a horse, an engine, or some other source of power.

Finally, there must be a way to guide the motion toward the destination and to stop when the destination is reached. Control is the third important part of transportation.

**Transportation by land.** An automobile is a common vehicle for transportation by land. Most automobiles are propelled by four-cycle gasoline engines, discussed in the last lesson.

Several parts of the automobile help the driver to control the energy of the engine. The rotary motion from the engine crankshaft goes to a ***clutch.*** The clutch has two plates that separate when the driver pushes the clutch pedal. When the plates are separated, the engine runs but does not move the automobile. When the clutch plates are pressed together, the motion of the engine passes on to the transmission.

The ***transmission*** has several gears that change the speed of the automobile. A low gear moves the car slowly. A higher gear is better for

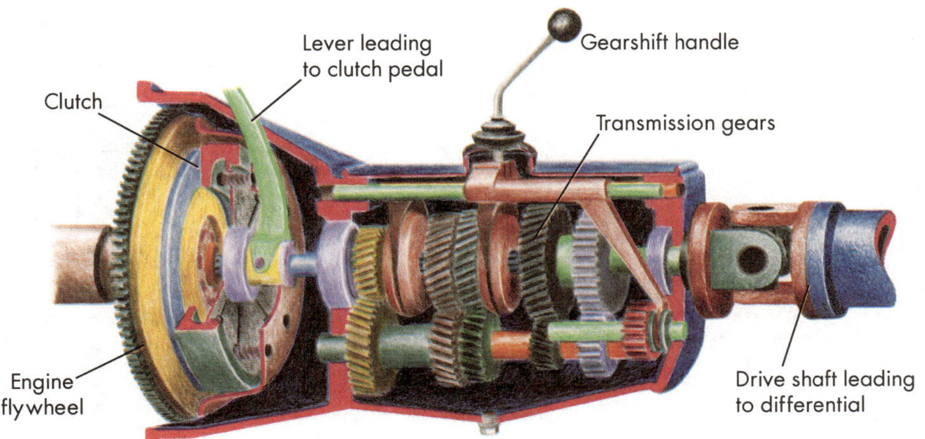

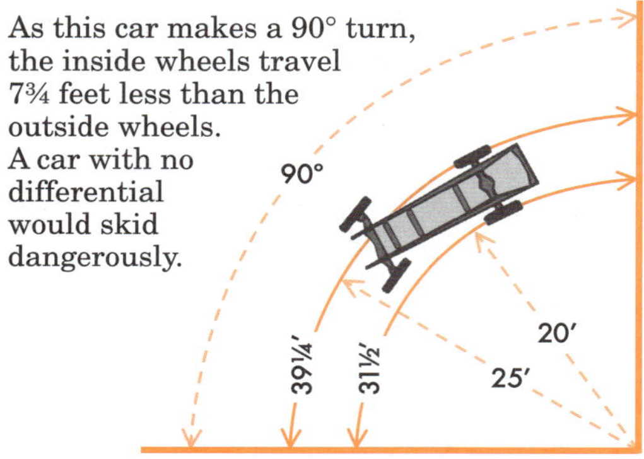


As this car makes a 90° turn, the inside wheels travel 7¾ feet less than the outside wheels. A car with no differential would skid dangerously.

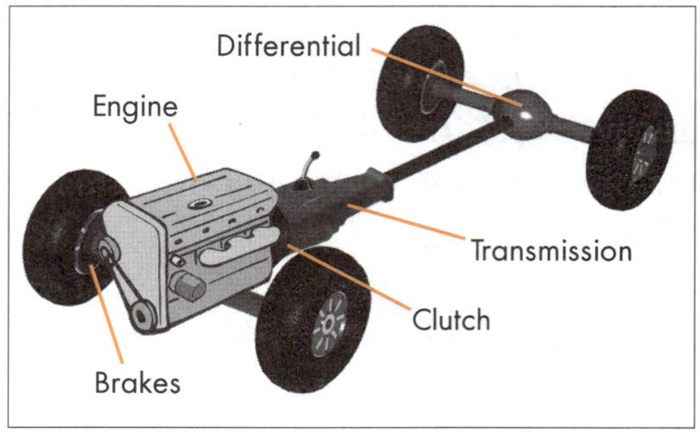


moving swiftly down the road. One set of gears is reverse, which makes the car go backward. Many automobiles have automatic transmissions, which do the work of the clutch and the changing of gears automatically.

A drive shaft goes from the transmission to the ***differential.*** The differential has gears that let the two drive wheels turn at different speeds while going around a curve. For on a curve, the inside wheel must turn slower than the outside wheel.

Today most cars have a front-wheel drive, so the clutch, transmission, and differential are not arranged as shown in the diagram above. However, the same general principles apply to front-wheel-drive cars. A pickup truck is probably the most common vehicle with parts arranged as shown in the diagram.

A steering wheel lets the driver turn the front wheels of the car in the direction he wants to go. The ***brakes*** allow him to stop the car by using friction. In each wheel is a disk that turns with the rest of the wheel. When the driver pushes the brake pedal, the brake pads in each wheel are pushed against the turning disks to slow or stop them. With steering and brakes, a driver can control the motion of the automobile.

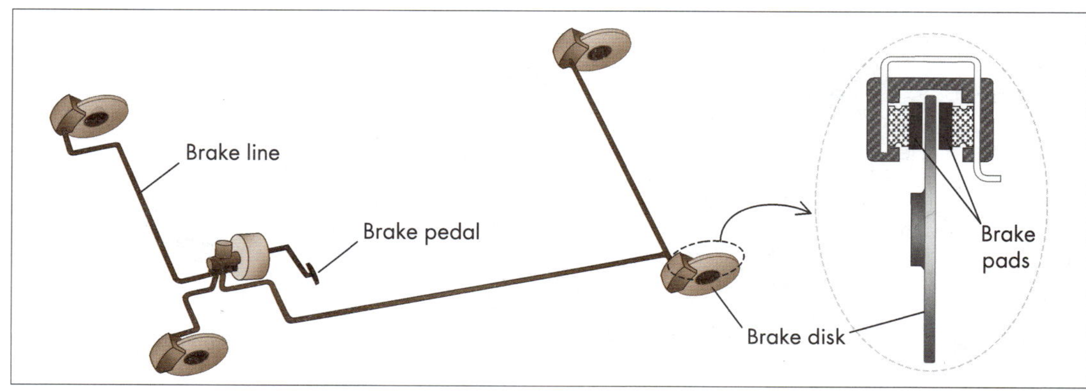

## Study the Lesson

1. Why does the Christian not try to impress others with his automobile?
2. What are three things necessary to provide transportation by land, sea, or air?
3. What part of an automobile provides the energy for propulsion?
4. Match the parts of the drawing and the descriptions with the following words. (You will write each word twice.)

brakes clutch differential transmission

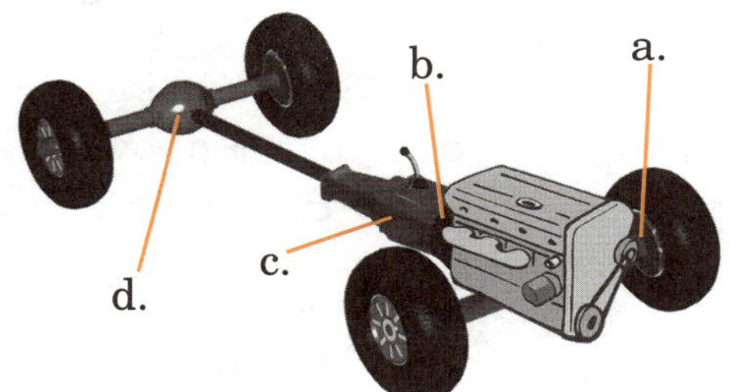


e. Allows one wheel to turn faster than the other.
f. Used to slow or stop the car.
g. Has a low gear, a high gear, and reverse.
h. Has plates that can be separated or pressed together.

5. Which automobile part named above is especially important
   a. when going around a curve?
   b. when starting the engine without moving the car?
   c. when going from 25 to 65 miles per hour?
   d. when bringing the car to a stop?

**Transportation by sea.** Boats and ships are supported by an upward push called ***buoyant force.*** The water pushes up on the bottom of the ship. The long, broad shape of the ship spreads out the weight of its cargo so that the weight takes up more space.

Boats and ships of Bible times depended on wind power to move them along. Most modern ships have large engines that turn propellers at the back of the ship. As the propellers push back on the water, the ship moves forward. Some large ships have propellers that are 25 feet (7.5 m) or more in diameter.

Piloting a ship is more difficult than driving a car. The pilot and other navigators do their work in a raised structure called the ***bridge.*** They steer the ship with a large, flat blade called the ***rudder*** at the back end of the ship. If the rudder is turned to make the ***stern*** (back end) of the ship move right, the ***bow*** (front end) of the ship will move left.

Stopping a big ship is much harder than stopping a car. The ship is so heavy that if the pilot does not come

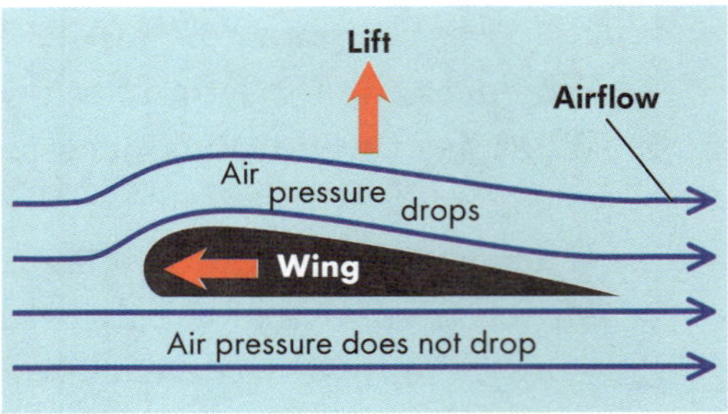


Cross section of an airfoil

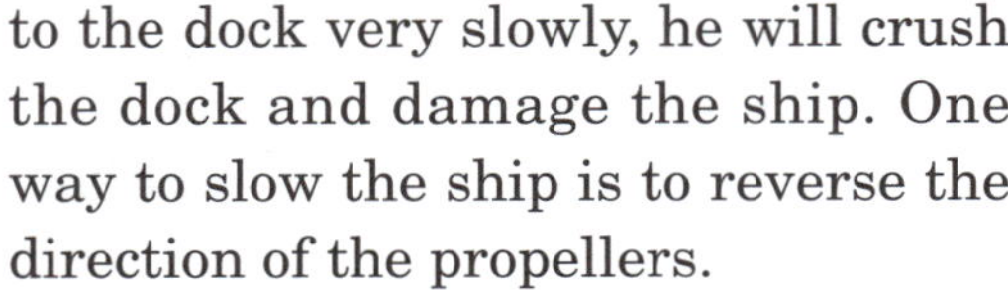

to the dock very slowly, he will crush the dock and damage the ship. One way to slow the ship is to reverse the direction of the propellers.

**Transportation by air.** In the beginning God created birds to "fly above the earth" (Genesis 1:20). For years, people watched the birds and wished they too could fly. But man did not invent the airplane until 1903. Even so, the airplane is a clumsy machine as compared with the body of a bird.

Airplanes are supported by the flow of air around the wings. The wings have a special shape called an ***airfoil.*** The airfoil makes the air go farther and faster above the wing than beneath the wing. This makes less air pressure on top of the wing than under it. The difference in pressure provides the lift that supports the airplane.

Modern airplanes are propelled in two ways. Smaller planes have piston engines fastened to propellers. These propellers are thinner than ship propellers, and they turn much faster. The spinning propellers are like giant fans pushing the air backward. This backward push of air is what pushes the plane forward.

The propeller of a small airplane pushes air backward around the airplane.

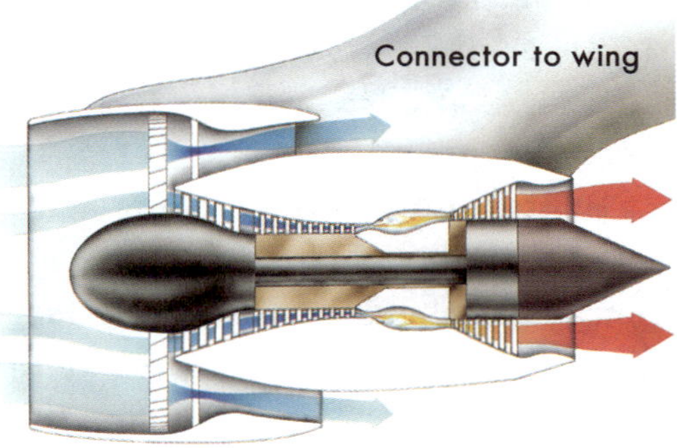


A jet engine for airliners pushes air backward inside the engine.

Most large airplanes are propelled by jet engines. A jet engine also has a propeller, but it is inside the engine housing. The propeller forces air toward the back of the engine, where fuel is added and the mixture is ignited. As the hot, burning gases rush out the back of the engine, the plane is pushed forward. This is called ***jet propulsion.***

A pilot can steer an airplane up and down as well as left and right. To make the plane fly higher or lower, he uses movable flaps called ***elevators*** on the horizontal tailpiece of the plane. Tilting the elevators upward will cause the plane to soar upward.

To turn left or right, the pilot uses the rudder on the vertical tailpiece of the plane. Turning the rudder to the right makes the airplane turn right. As the plane turns, the pilot also uses flaps called ***ailerons*** on the wings to tilt the plane, or it will slide sideways in the air. If he is turning right, the right aileron slopes up to make the right wing go down, and the left aileron slopes down to make the left wing go up. A pilot needs much practice in using the elevators, rudder, and ailerons to steer a plane correctly.

This jet airliner is preparing to land. The flaps and the landing wheels are lowered.

Several things are done to stop an airplane. Large flaps are lowered on the back edge of the wings. The slant of the propellers may be changed so that they push air forward instead of backward. Brakes on the wheels are applied once they start turning on the runway.

At one time, most people who crossed the ocean went by ship. Today most passengers going overseas travel in huge jet airplanes. Ships are used

to transport heavy cargo, such as oil, coal, wheat, and machinery.

**Christians can make excellent use of modern transportation.** Perhaps you know of Christian families who went to other countries to spread the Gospel. Many people visit missionaries to give them help and encouragement. God has opened a great door of opportunity for Christians to use rapid transportation in doing mission work. We should thank God for good ways to travel so that missionaries can take the good news of salvation to other lands.

## Study the Lesson

6. What supports a ship in water?
7. Match the parts of the drawing and the descriptions with the following words, as in exercise 4 above.

bow bridge propeller rudder stern

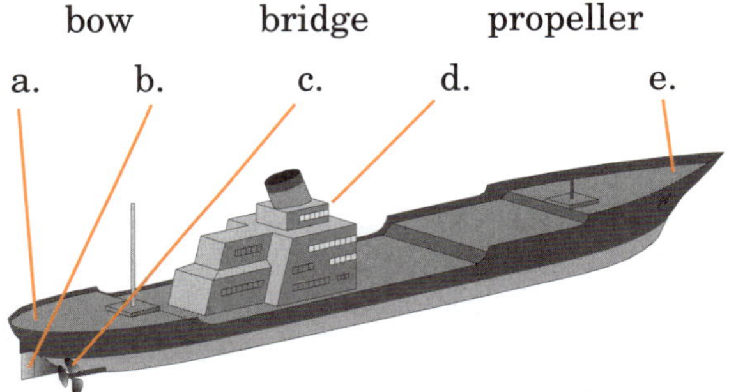


f. Part that steers the ship.
g. Front end of the ship.
h. Back end of the ship.
i. Part that pushes the ship forward.
j. Raised structure where the ship is steered.

8. What is the rudder called in James 3:4?
9. Acts 27:29 uses a vocabulary word of this lesson. Write the word, and explain what it means.
10. The ——— that supports an airplane is caused by the difference between the air pressure above and below the wings.
11. Match the parts of the drawing and the descriptions with the following words.

ailerons elevators propeller rudder

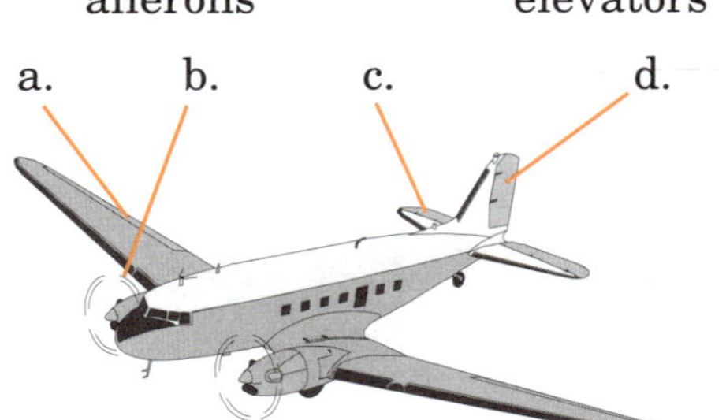


e. Used to make the plane tilt.
f. Used to raise or lower the plane.
g. Used to move the plane forward.
h. Used to turn the plane left or right.

12. What gives the forward push of a jet engine?
13. What special work does modern transportation help Christians to do?

## Review Exercises

1. What three things are needed for a gasoline engine to run? [24]
2. Three sources of free energy are the ———, falling ———, and ———. [23]
3. Carnivorous and herbivorous animals control each other's populations, and this produces a ——— of ———. (Write the whole phrase.) [20]
4. In many plants, sugar is changed to ——— and stored in some part of the plant. [17]
5. Four-fifths of the air is ———, and one-fifth is ———. [13]
6. The gravity of the moon causes the ——— of the ocean. [3]

## Apply the Lesson

1. Ask older persons the advantages of the following automobile features: front-wheel drive, four-wheel drive, disc brakes, emergency brake, power brakes, power steering, automatic transmission, overdrive.
2. Experiment with paper cups floating in water. Add weight to the cup until it is just ready to sink. Weigh the cup and its contents. Then fill the cup level full of water, and weigh the water. (Subtract the weight of the cup from the combined weight of the cup and water.) How do the two weights compare?

   How can a shipbuilder know whether his ship will float before he puts it into the water?
3. Before the age of steam engines, most ships were propelled by wind energy. Find out from an encyclopedia how such ships could make progress against the wind.
4. Observe how an airfoil causes lift. Cut a 2-inch strip of paper 11 inches long. Hold one end with the strip draped over your finger. Bring that end to your mouth, and blow gently over the top of it. What happens to the strip of paper? Blow harder. How high can you lift the paper by blowing?
5. Do research to learn about the pedals and other controls that an airplane pilot uses to steer an airplane.

## Lesson 26

# Unit 5 Review

## A. Vocabulary

Write the letter of the correct word for each meaning.

1. Burning of a material.
2. Push of burning gases that propels some airplanes.
3. Kind of power produced when water turns a generator.
4. Fact that energy cannot be created or destroyed.
5. Upward push of water on a floating object.
6. Ability to make something move or change.
7. Energy in motion.
8. Energy from the sun.
9. Fact that energy moves from a higher level to a lower level.
10. Push that makes any vehicle move.
11. Stored energy.

a. buoyant force
b. combustion
c. energy
d. hydroelectric
e. jet propulsion
f. kinetic energy
g. law of conservation of energy
h. law of thermodynamics
i. potential energy
j. propulsion
k. solar energy

12. Causes combustion in a gasoline engine.
13. Has plates that can be separated or pressed together.
14. Causes lift by reducing air pressure above it.
15. Harnesses the energy in moving air to drive a generator.
16. Has a low gear, a high gear, and reverse.
17. Used to slow or stop a car.
18. Raised structure where navigators steer a ship.
19. Harnesses the energy in moving water to drive a generator.
20. Increases the energy in a quantity of water by raising its height.
21. End of a ship where the propeller is found.

a. airfoil
b. brakes
c. bridge
d. clutch
e. dam
f. spark plug
g. stern
h. transmission
i. water turbine
j. wind turbine

22. Lets the fuel–air mixture into the cylinder.
23. Raises or lowers a wing to tilt the plane.
24. Blade for steering a ship or an airplane.
25. Front end of a ship.
26. Uses sunlight to produce electricity.
27. Used to make an airplane fly higher or lower.
28. Changes the up-and-down motion of a piston to rotary motion.
29. Mixes fuel and air.
30. Controls the speed of a gasoline engine.
31. Allows one drive wheel to turn faster than the other.
32. Round part that slides up and down inside a cylinder.
33. Blocks the airflow to increase the fuel added to the air.

a. aileron
b. bow
c. choke
d. crankshaft
e. differential
f. elevators
g. fuel injector
h. intake valve
i. piston
j. rudder
k. solar cell
l. throttle

## B. Facts

Write the words that belong in the blanks.

1. Water behind a dam and a gallon of gasoline are examples of ——— energy.
2. Wind is not an ideal source of energy because it is not as c——— as energy from moving water.
3. Both wind and moving water are c——— sources of energy, since they can be harnessed without polluting the environment.
4. Fuel oil is a c——— source of energy, since it can be stored in tanks and run through pipes to where it is needed.
5. Electricity is very useful because it is easily c——— into other forms of energy.
6. The law of thermodynamics is strong scientific proof that ——— brought the world into existence.
7. Water wheels with buckets use the ——— of water to harness its energy and run machinery.
8. The one who made all energy is ———.
9. After the exhaust stroke of a four-cycle engine comes the ——— stroke.
10. The spark comes at the beginning of the ——— stroke.

11. The exhaust valve is open during the ——— stroke.
12. If a gasoline engine has fuel and air but will not run, the missing thing may be the ———.
13. An airplane will slide sideways if the pilot uses the rudder without also using the ———.
14. The propulsion for most big airplanes comes from ——— engines.

## C. Concepts

Choose the letter of the best answer in each exercise.

1. Which of the following is a true statement about energy?
   a. Energy must be in the potential form before it can do work.
   b. New energy must be produced daily to supply our needs.
   c. Energy moves from cold areas to be concentrated into hot areas.
   d. Energy moves in only one direction along a chain.
2. The main reason not more wind energy is harnessed today is because
   a. the wind does not blow enough at many places.
   b. wind turbines are expensive and difficult to build.
   c. no good way has been found to change wind energy into electricity.
   d. wind turbines would pollute the environment.
3. Solar cells are often used with storage batteries because
   a. the batteries are needed to strengthen the solar cells.
   b. the storage batteries change the electricity into the form that is needed.
   c. there are times when the solar cells cannot produce electricity.
   d. the storage batteries can easily be replaced when they wear out.
4. Steam engines and gasoline engines are alike because
   a. they both have carburetors.
   b. they both use the combustion of fuel to make heat.
   c. they both heat water to harness the energy.
   d. they both burn fuel inside a cylinder.
5. Steam engines and gasoline engines are different because
   a. the one burns the fuel outside the engine.
   b. the one has a crankshaft.
   c. the one converts up-and-down motion to rotary motion.
   d. the one has a piston that slides inside a cylinder.

6. The law of conservation of energy and the law of thermodynamics agree with all the following things *except*
   a. the Bible.
   b. the study of motion.
   c. the working of modern engines.
   d. the theory of evolution.
7. There are several reasons that God should receive the credit for the gasoline engine. Which of the following is *not* one of those reasons?
   a. He made gasoline to be explosive.
   b. He revealed to man how a gasoline engine can be made.
   c. He gave metals great strength to hold together.
   d. He gave men the ability to invent things.
8. The differential of an automobile is needed when
   a. it is coming to a stop.
   b. its engine is being started.
   c. it is going around a corner.
   d. its wheels are on a slippery place.
9. Buoyant force provides which of the following in transportation by water?
   a. propulsion
   b. control
   c. braking
   d. support
10. An airplane is supported in the air mainly by
    a. the propeller pushing the air downward.
    b. the elevators raising the tail of the plane.
    c. the difference in pressure above and below the wings.
    d. the force of the wind on the bottom side of the wings.
11. The Christian should be thankful for the use of modern transportation to
    a. carry the Gospel to places near and far.
    b. visit interesting places around the world.
    c. show others how God has blessed him with money.
    d. feel safe from enemies that may hurt him.

# Unit 6

# Electricity for Energy and Communication

"I am the LORD that maketh all things; that stretcheth forth the heavens alone; that spreadeth abroad the earth by myself" (Isaiah 44:24).

The use of electricity for everyday jobs began only in the late 1800s. In 1832 Joseph Henry and Michael Faraday showed that electricity could be produced with magnetism. In 1873 the electric motor was invented. Alexander Graham Bell invented the telephone in 1876. Three years later, Thomas Edison invented his electric light bulb. But it took many years before such inventions came into general use.

Today there is hardly a job that does not use electricity in some way. Electricity runs our clocks, cooks our food, starts our cars, drills our holes, and carries our messages thousands of miles. Some men have become very proud of what they can do with electricity. People give the inventors much praise for their work. They direct their praise to the wrong place.

Electricity is not new to God. He created electricity. He created all things. God produces the giant electric lightning. The electric eel, which He created, can produce electric shocks of up to 650 volts. Even the nerves in your body carry messages partly with electricity. No electrical invention depends on anything other than what God provided when He created electricity. To God be the praise for everything you will study in this unit.

## Lesson 27

# Magnetism and Electricity

"Sanctify the LORD of hosts himself; and let him be your fear, and let him be your dread" (Isaiah 8:13).

### Vocabulary

**current,** the flow of electricity.

**electromagnet,** a magnet made by electricity flowing through a coil of wire.

**electron,** one of the tiny particles that make up an electric current.

**induction,** the method of making current flow by moving a wire through a magnetic field.

**magnetic field,** the area of magnetic force around a magnet.

**permanent magnet,** a magnet that keeps its magnetism all the time.

**transformer,** a device that increases or decreases the voltage of electricity.

**volt,** a unit for measuring the pressure of electricity.

God uses many ways to teach men to fear His power. Magnetism and electricity are invisible forces that show themselves in ways as small as attracting a compass needle or as large and powerful as a lightning bolt. Even the strongest men feel weak and the wisest men marvel at God's creation of magnetism and electricity.

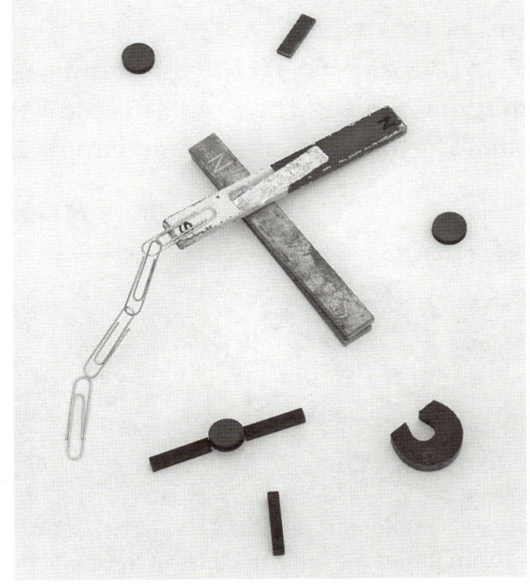

Magnets come in a variety of shapes and sizes.

You have probably used magnets or played with them. Magnets stick to certain kinds of metal. This makes them useful for latching small doors, fastening items to a refrigerator, and holding screws to a screwdriver and for many other purposes. Magnets come in a variety of shapes and sizes, such as flat circles or small cubes. Stronger ones are the bar magnet or the horseshoe magnet, which is a bar bent in a U shape.

**Permanent magnets keep their magnetism.** Using a bar magnet, you can pick up a string of pins. The first pin becomes a magnet strong enough to pick up the second pin and so on down the line until the magnetism in the last pin is too weak to pick up any more. If you pull the first pin away from the bar magnet, all the pins lose their magnetism very quickly. But the bar magnet itself is a ***permanent magnet,*** one that keeps its magnetism all the time.

Each magnet has both a north pole and a south pole. The north pole of a magnet attracts the same point of a compass needle that the North Pole of the earth attracts.

A ***magnetic field*** surrounds a magnet. This is the area affected by the force of the magnet. You can feel this if you bring a magnet close to metal and feel the magnet draw toward the metal. You can think of a magnetic field as invisible lines of magnetic force that leave the north pole, circle around, and enter the south pole. The poles are the strongest points of the magnet because here the lines of force are closer together.

Two magnetic poles of the same kind push away from each other. Two poles of opposite kinds pull toward each other. These push–pull rules are often stated like this: *Like poles repel, and unlike poles attract.*

**Electricity can be used to make an electromagnet.** If electricity flows through a wire, a magnetic field forms around the wire. This field is very weak. If you wind the wire into a coil, the fields add together to make one strong magnetic field. This kind of magnet is called an ***electromagnet*** because it is produced with electricity.

Like a permanent magnet, an

**Magnetic Fields**

Lines of force around a bar magnet

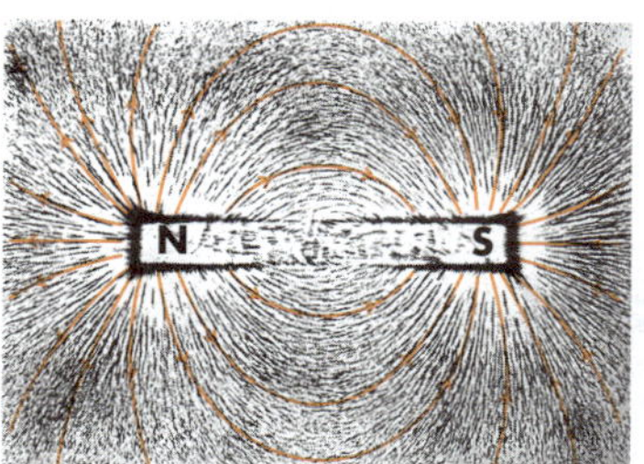


Attracting force of opposite poles

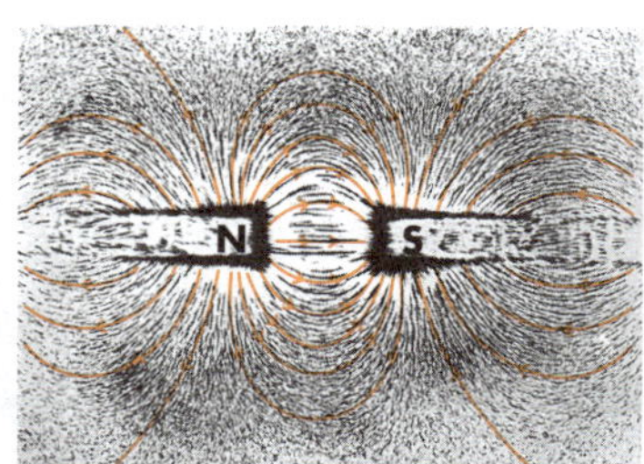


Repelling force of like poles

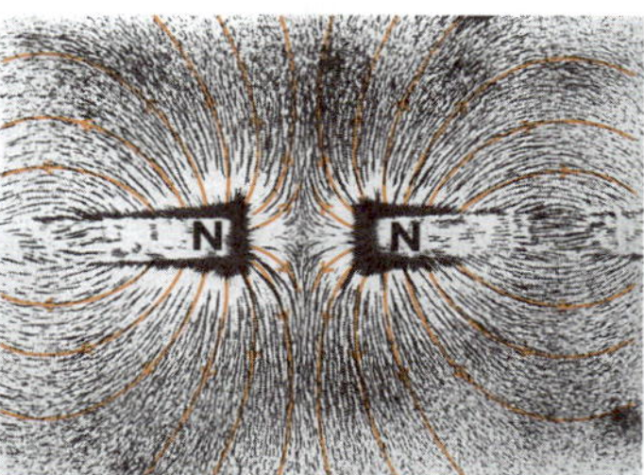


Iron filings can show the lines of force in a magnetic field. These magnets are underneath a sheet of paper sprinkled with iron filings.

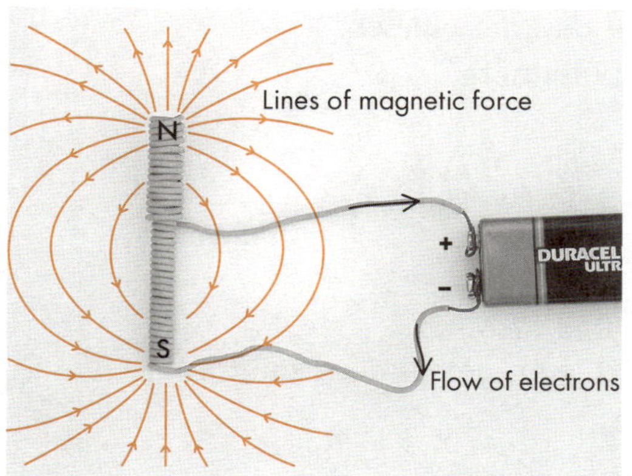


An electromagnet

electromagnet has a north pole and a south pole. Electromagnets follow the same push–pull rules that permanent magnets do: like poles repel, and unlike poles attract.

Electromagnets can be more useful than permanent magnets. They can be turned on and off with the flip of a switch. The north and south poles of an electromagnet can be reversed simply by sending the electricity in the opposite direction through the wire. Also, they can be made stronger or weaker, depending on the number of turns of wire and the strength of the electricity. Electromagnets with one hundred or more turns of wire are used in electric bells.

The wire used for electromagnets is insulated so that the electricity cannot flow directly from one turn of wire to the next. This forces the electricity to go through all the turns of wire in the coil.

This large, round electromagnet is used to load scrap metal onto a railroad car.

## Study the Lesson

1. Write the correct words for these descriptions.
   a. Invisible forces that have become important in modern times. (two answers)
   b. A magnet that keeps its magnetism all the time.
   c. Names for the poles of a magnet. (two answers)
   d. The area of magnetism around a magnet.
   e. A magnet produced with electricity.
2. Why does the north pole of a magnet have that name?
3. Write the correct words to complete this sentence: A magnetic field is made of invisible...

4. What two rules describe the action of magnetic poles?
5. Write *attract* or *repel* for each pair of magnets.

   a. N S | N S

   b. N S | S N

   c. S N | S N

6. Why are electromagnets more useful than permanent magnets? Give at least two reasons.

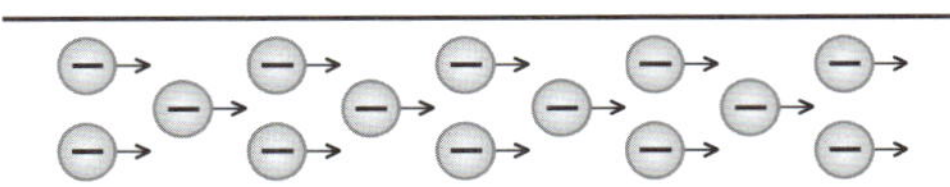

An electric current is electrons flowing in a wire.

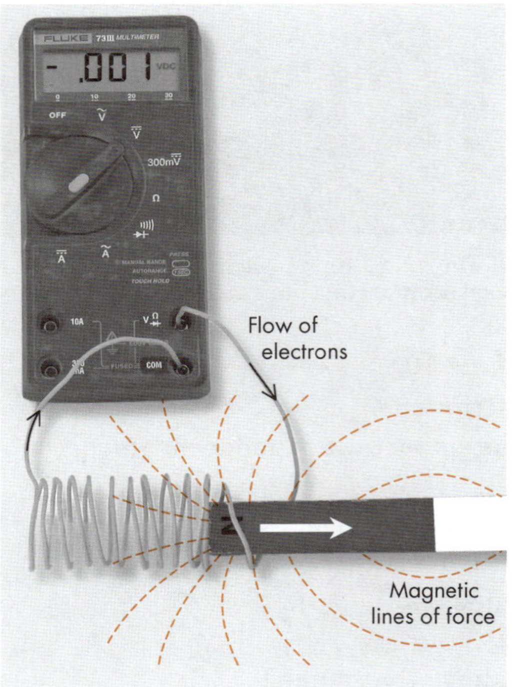


The digital Multimeter shows that one thousandth of a volt is passing through the wire as the magnet moves through the coil.

**A magnet makes an electric current flow through a wire.** Electricity flows through wire in a ***current,*** much as water flows through a hose. The current is made of millions of ***electrons,*** which are tiny particles too small to be seen even with a microscope.

Passing electrons (electric current) through a wire makes a magnetic field around the wire. The opposite is also true: *passing a wire through a magnetic field makes electrons move through the wire.*

You can easily see this by connecting a coil of wire to a millivolt meter with a dial. Slide a bar magnet through the coil. The needle will move, showing that electrons in the wire are moving. The electrons move because the wires are cutting through the lines of magnetic force. This method of producing an electric current is called ***induction*** because the magnetic field induces a current in the wire.

Slide the magnet through the coil, and stop inside the coil. The electrons will stop flowing because the wires are no longer cutting lines of force even though the lines of force still surround the coil. Before induction will produce a current, there must be motion. Either the magnetic field must move through the coil, or the coil must move through the magnetic field.

Notice also that the needle on the meter moves one direction when you push the magnet into the coil and the other direction when you pull it out of the coil. The needle also moves one direction when the coil moves past the north pole of the magnet and the other direction when the coil moves past the south pole. The needle shows which direction the current is flowing through the wire. As you can see, the current can easily stop or change direction.

**Transformers use induction.** An important electrical device is the ***transformer***. It has two separate coils of wire wrapped around a core of steel. When current flows into the first coil, called the primary coil, another current flows out of the other coil, called the secondary coil. But how can current pass from one coil to the other if the two are not connected?

Transformers work with alternating current (AC), which changes direction 120 times each second! This produces a magnetic field that is constantly moving, reversing its north and south poles 120 times per second. The moving lines of magnetic force are cut by the wires in the secondary coil, instead of by a moving bar magnet, and this induces a current in that coil.

A transformer changes the pressure of an electric current, which is

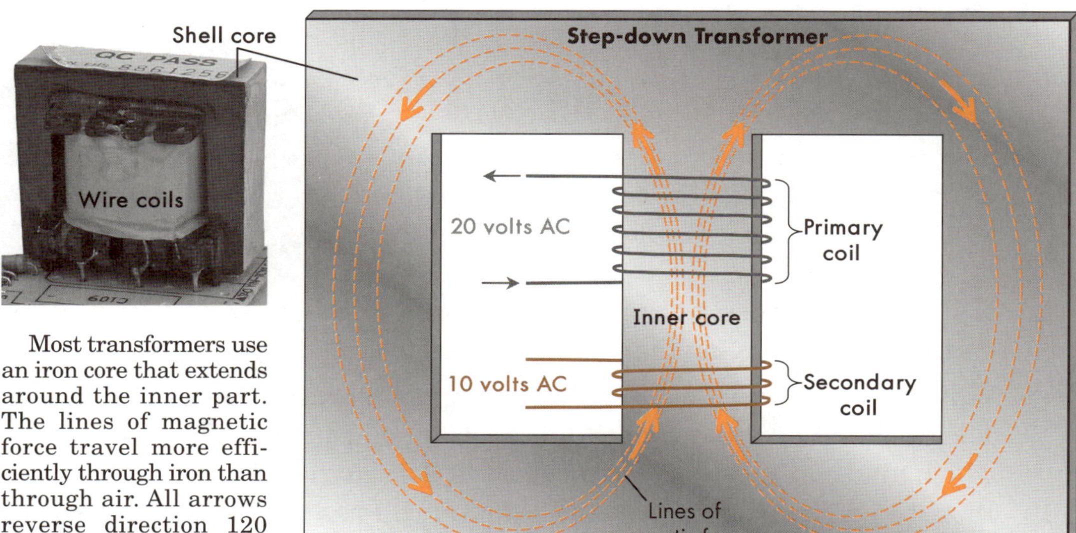


Most transformers use an iron core that extends around the inner part. The lines of magnetic force travel more efficiently through iron than through air. All arrows reverse direction 120 times a second.

measured in ***volts.*** If the secondary coil has fewer turns of wire than the primary coil, the voltage will be lower. This is called a step-down transformer. If the secondary coil has more turns than the primary coil, the voltage will be higher. This is called a step-up transformer.

Transformers come in various sizes. Many small transformers can be plugged into a 120-volt household receptacle to produce 8 to 15 volts. This is safe enough for running electric trains and other toys. Large transformers include those hung on poles outside people's houses, which step down the current from several thousand volts to a safe level of 120 volts.

Let us remember that God created magnetism and electricity. He allowed men to discover these forces in nature, and He gave them wisdom to use these forces to do various tasks.

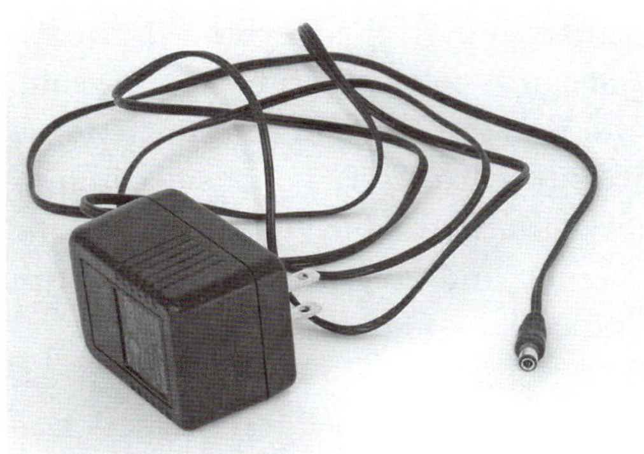

A transformer for a small appliance

A transformer for a house

## Study the Lesson

7. Choose the correct word for each description.

| | |
|---|---|
| a. Tiny particles in a flow of electricity. | current |
| b. Causing electricity to flow by moving a magnet. | electrons |
| c. A flow of electricity. | induction |
| d. Unit for measuring electrical pressure. | transformer |
| e. Device for changing the pressure of electricity. | volt |

8. Why does electricity flow when a bar magnet moves inside a coil of wire?
9. The two kinds of electricity are direct current and alternating current. With which kind can a transformer be used to change the voltage?
10. In a step-down transformer, the primary coil has (more, fewer) turns of wire than the secondary coil.

11. How many volts are used
    a. for regular household electricity? b. for toys such as electric trains?
12. Why should God be praised for the wonders of electricity?

## Review Exercises

1. Name in order the four strokes of a four-cycle gasoline engine. [24]
2. Energy in motion is (kinetic, potential) energy. [22]
3. The study of living things in relation to their surroundings is called ———. [20]
4. The atmosphere protects the earth from most ———, which are speeding rocks from outer space. [13]
5. Dark spots on the sun are called ———, and their number increases and decreases in a cycle of about ——— years. [2]
6. The sun is made mostly of the elements ——— and ———. [2]

## Apply the Lesson

1. Learn about magnetic fields by moving a compass around in the field of a permanent magnet. How far away can you still detect the field? Does the compass always point to a pole of the magnet?

   Lay a magnet under a sheet of paper. Sprinkle some iron filings on the paper. The lines formed by the iron filings will show the direction of the magnetism in the field.
2. Wrap 100 feet of fine insulated wire (#26 or smaller) around a cardboard tube that is a little bigger in diameter than a compass. Scrape off the ends of the wire. Lay the compass level at the center of one end of the coil. Hold the ends of the wire to the terminals of a battery. What happens to the compass needle? What happens if you reverse the wires on the battery? What principle taught in the lesson does this illustrate?

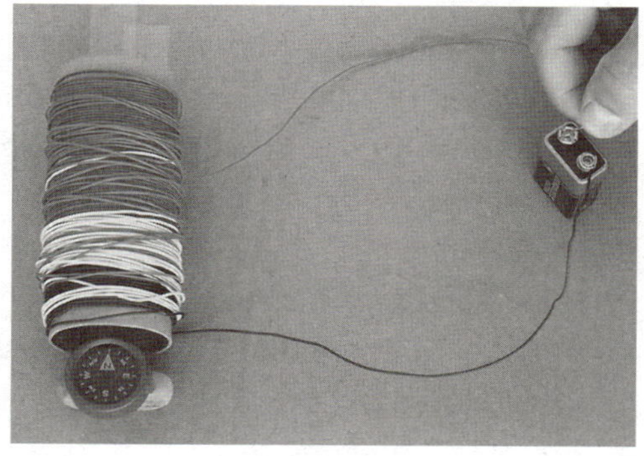

3. Search for transformers. Someone in the class may have a toy transformer that he can bring to school. Doorbells are operated by transformers. If you have an electric bell at your school, find the transformer that operates it. Can you locate the two sets of wires on the transformers you find? Why must transformers have at least four wires?

## Lesson 28

# Electrical Circuits

"He giveth power to the faint; and to them that have no might he increaseth strength" (Isaiah 40:29).

### Vocabulary

**circuit,** a circular path for electricity to follow.

**circuit breaker,** a device that protects a circuit from too much electrical current.

**terminal,** a place for making an electrical connection.

God is the source of all strength and energy, for people as well as machines. If you put an air compressor in your garage, you could run it with a gasoline engine or an electric motor. With a gasoline engine, you would need to keep fuel on hand to run the compressor. With an electric motor, you would need to plug the cord into a receptacle. In either case, the compressor would not run without energy that God created.

Electricity is a very useful form of energy that people use for a large variety of tasks. With electricity, we can light a classroom, ring a bell, drill a hole, or keep cows in a pasture. But electricity does not just automatically come from a receptacle in the wall. In this lesson you will see how electricity is produced and brought to our houses.

**Generating stations produce electricity for us.** A generating station usually has several large generators, which are driven by some kind of power. Hydroelectric stations use waterpower from rivers. Other stations burn coal to produce steam that turns the generators. Still other stations burn fuel oil or use atomic energy. Whatever the source of power, a generating station changes that form of energy into electrical energy.

Generators at these stations produce electricity up to about 20,000 volts. That is quite a bit higher than the 120 volts in your house, but it is not high enough to carry the current efficiently for a very long distance. So, large step-up transformers raise the current to over 500,000 volts so that the electricity can be sent to cities and farms many miles away.

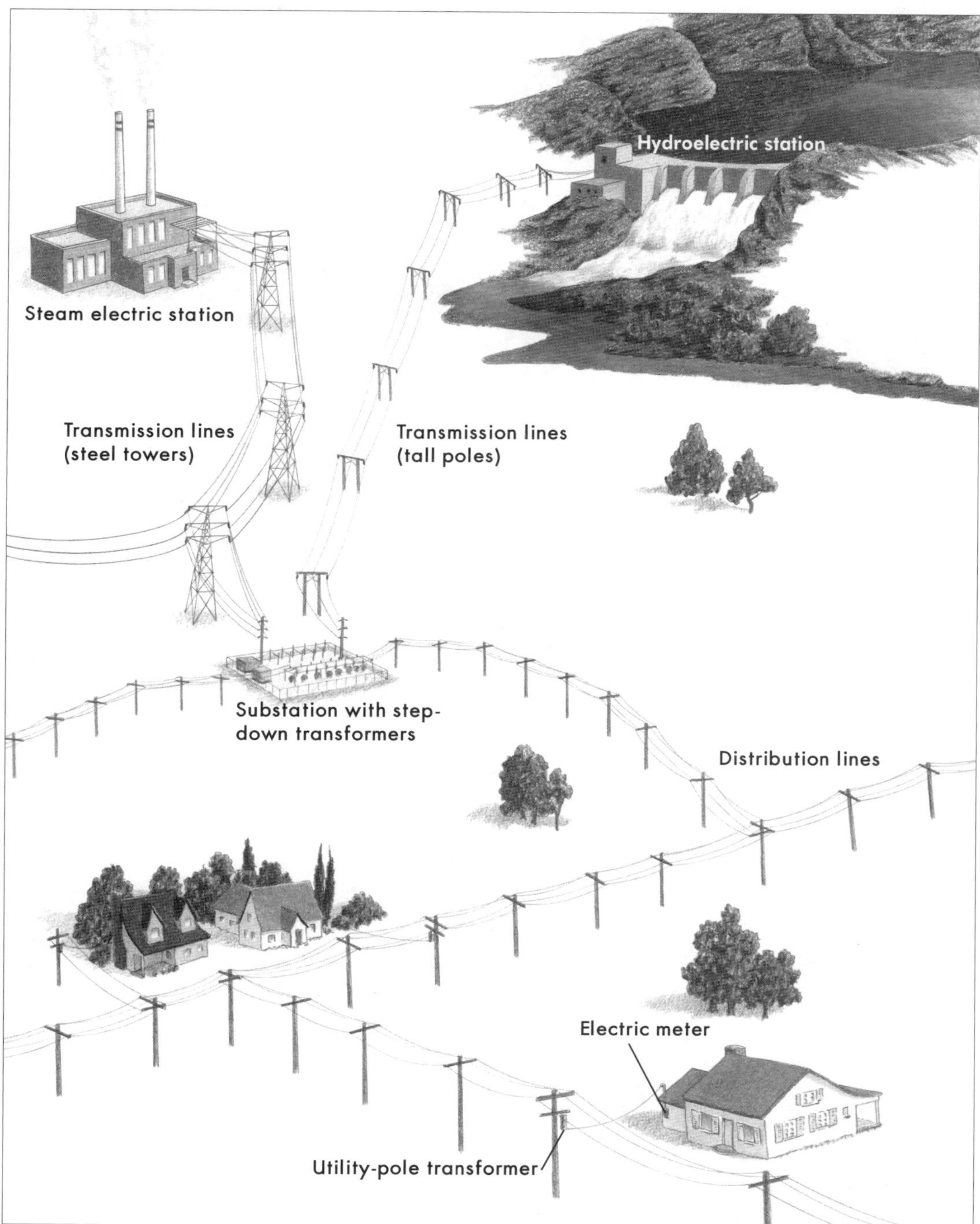


Generated electricity follows a distribution path to serve thousands of homes. But a large industrial factory may use all the electricity that one substation handles.

Steel transmission towers

A local substation

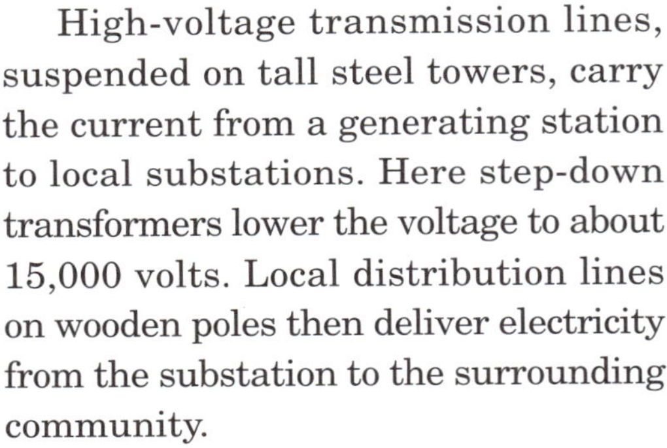

High-voltage transmission lines, suspended on tall steel towers, carry the current from a generating station to local substations. Here step-down transformers lower the voltage to about 15,000 volts. Local distribution lines on wooden poles then deliver electricity from the substation to the surrounding community.

Probably you have seen a canister-shaped distribution transformer close to the top of a pole near your house. This is a step-down transformer that lowers the voltage to the standard 120 volts for household use.

It is amazing to consider the many miles of electric lines along our roads and highways. All those wires are part of a large network of electric lines that link our homes to generating stations possibly hundreds of miles away.

## Study the Lesson

1. Why is electricity a very useful form of energy?
2. Choose the correct term for each description.

   distribution lines — generating station — transmission lines — distribution transformer — substation

   a. Where electricity is produced.
   b. What carries electricity away from its source.
   c. Where high-voltage electricity is changed for a local area.
   d. What carries electricity to people's homes.
   e. What changes electricity for household use.
3. Name three sources of the energy that generating stations change into electricity.

4. Give the voltage of the electricity described in each phrase.
   a. Coming from generators at most generating stations.
   b. In high-voltage transmission lines.
   c. In local distribution lines.
   d. Used in a household.

**Electricity travels in a circuit.** Have you ever seen a row of electric poles carrying just one wire along a road? Probably not. At least two wires are needed to make a ***circuit*** (circular path) for the electric current to follow. Think of it this way. One wire carries the current from the generator to your house, and the other wire carries it back to the generator. This makes a complete circuit.

You can see the importance of two wires in a circuit if you experiment with a small light bulb and a battery instead of a generator. Connect a wire from each battery ***terminal*** (place for making an electrical connection) to each terminal of the bulb. Now electricity has a complete path (circuit) to follow from one battery terminal through the bulb to the other terminal. If one wire runs through a switch, the bulb can easily be turned on and off.

A circuit is closed if it forms a complete path for electricity, and open if it does not. An open circuit may be caused by a switch or some other gap, or by a wire disconnected from a terminal.

All the lights, receptacles, and motors in our houses are wired to form circuits that allow electricity to flow. The wires are usually hidden inside the ceilings and walls, so it is hard to follow the circuits unless they are shown in a diagram.

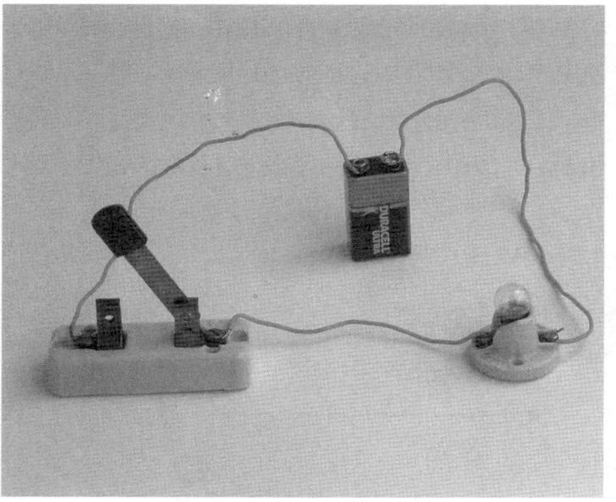

Circuit open—light off

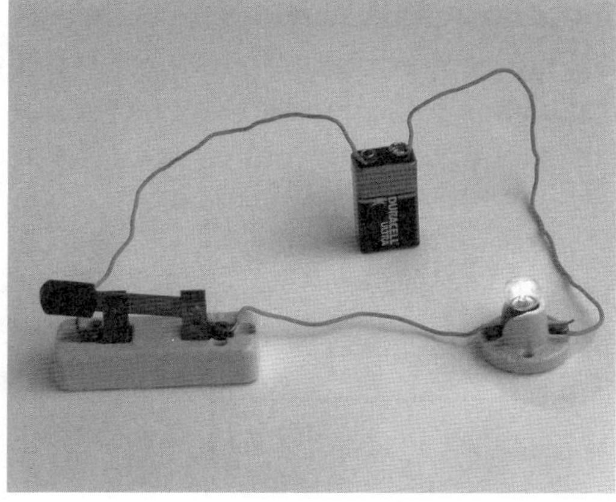

Circuit closed—light on

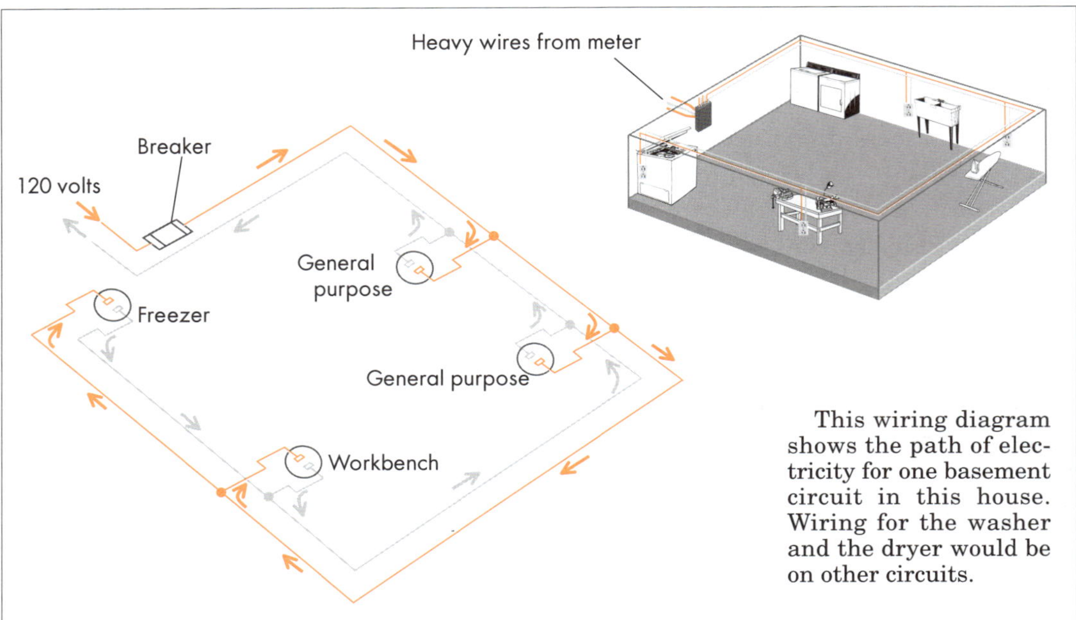


This wiring diagram shows the path of electricity for one basement circuit in this house. Wiring for the washer and the dryer would be on other circuits.

**House circuits begin at a breaker panel.** Heavy wires come from the transformer near the house to the electric meter, which measures how much electricity the house uses. From the meter, wires go to a breaker panel. Here the electricity is divided out to the various circuits in the house.

A breaker panel has ***circuit breakers*** for turning the electricity on or off in the different circuits. Each circuit breaker also protects one circuit. If too much current starts flowing through it, the breaker trips and stops the current. This keeps the wire from getting too hot and starting a fire. Older houses may have a box with fuses instead of breakers. When a fuse blows, however, it cannot be reset and used again like a breaker.

If you examine the breakers in a panel, you will notice that some of

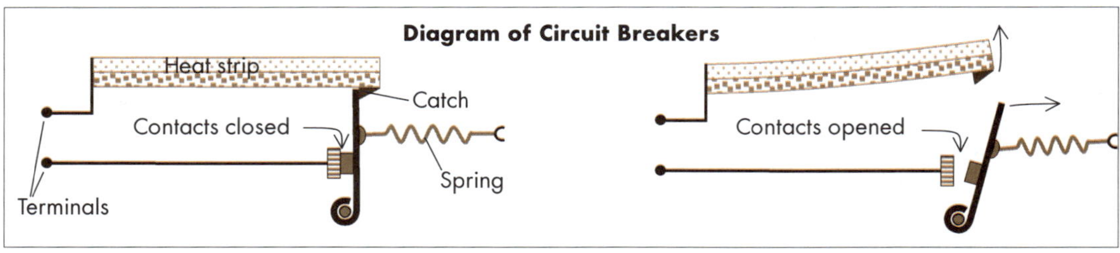


If too much current goes through the heat strip, it becomes hot (and bends) and trips the breaker, opening the contacts.

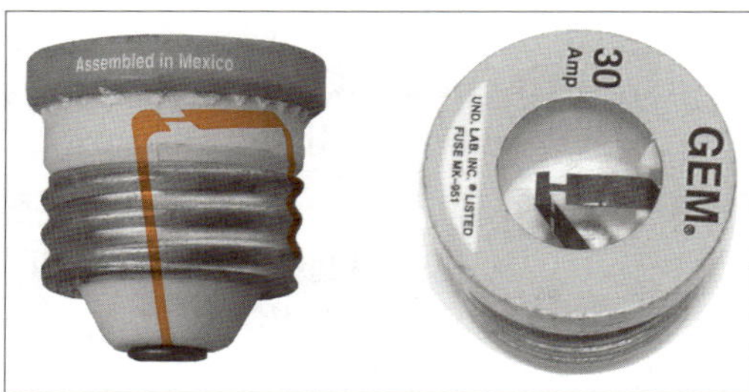


A fuse closes the circuit with a thin metal strip. If too much current flows through the strip, the narrowest section melts away. This blows the fuse and safely breaks the circuit.

them are only half as wide as others. A narrow breaker has a screw for only one wire, and it controls a regular 120-volt circuit, such as for lights and receptacles. A wide breaker has screws for two wires, and it controls a 240-volt circuit, such as for stoves and dryers.

Usually each 120-volt circuit has one black wire called the hot wire and one white wire called the neutral. Think of the black wire as carrying electricity out to the lights and the white wire as bringing it back. The black wire is fastened to the breaker; the white wire is fastened to a bar with all the other neutral wires.

In a 240-volt circuit, both the black and the white wires are hot because both are fastened to the breaker.

A bare wire, called the ground wire, also goes with each circuit. This wire protects you from getting shocked if something goes wrong with an electrical device you are using.

**Switches are used to turn lights on and off.** Usually the switch is connected to the hot wire so that it opens or closes the circuit before the current reaches the light bulb. Follow the wires to see the circuits in the diagrams on page 196.

Sometimes a room has two doors,

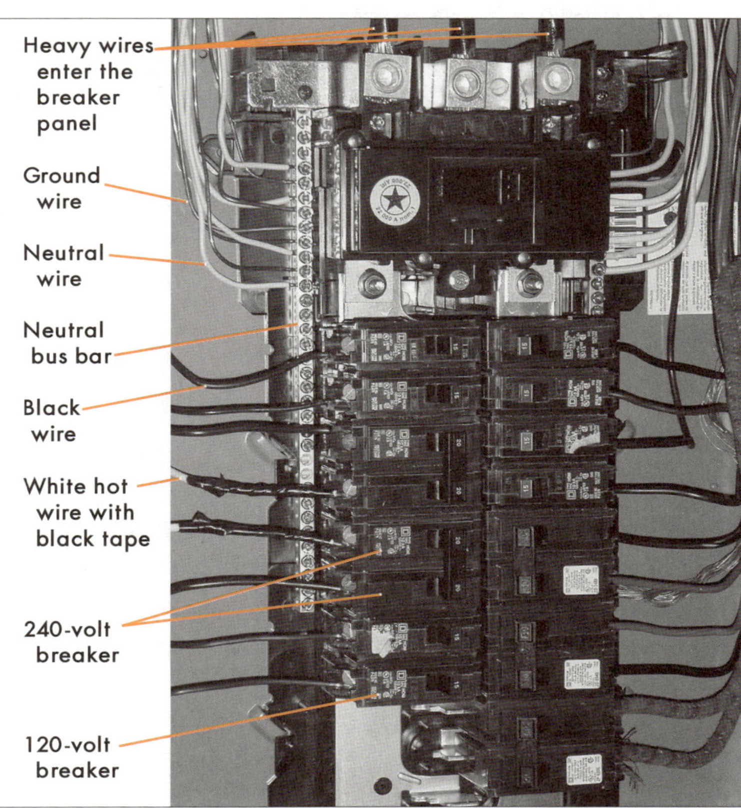

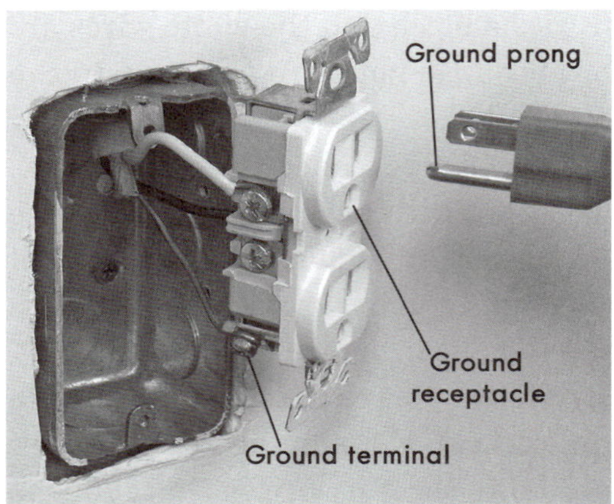


Ground wires are usually bare and ground out stray current from faulty appliances.

and you want to have a switch at each door to turn the same light on and off. In that case, three-way switches are used. A three-way switch has this name because it has three terminals. One is called the common terminal, and the other two are traveler terminals.

A lever inside the switch connects the common terminal to one of the traveler terminals. When you flip the switch to turn on the light, the circuit does not close in the usual way. Rather, the lever flips to the other traveler terminal. But that closes the circuit, and the light goes on. The diagrams below show how a three-way switch is connected to form a circuit.

In the diagrams, flipping switch A closes the circuit and allows current to flow through traveler wire 2. The circuit could also have been closed by flipping switch B so that current would flow through traveler wire 1.

We marvel at God's creation of electricity—such a useful form of energy. It can easily be transmitted many miles, and it can be put to work to do many jobs for us. We should thank God for the privilege to enjoy electricity and for giving men the wisdom to put it to use.

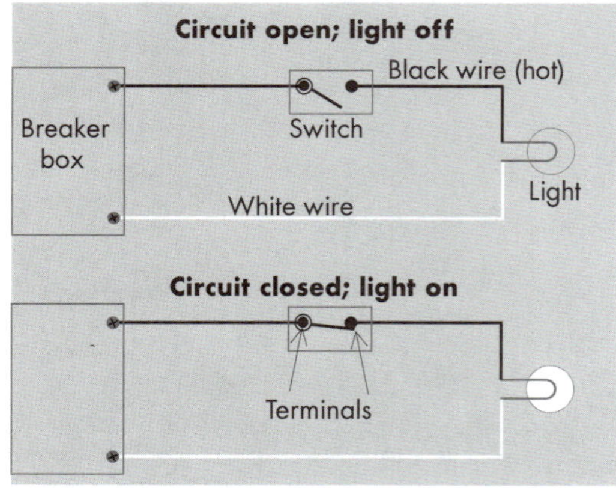


A circuit with a simple two-way switch

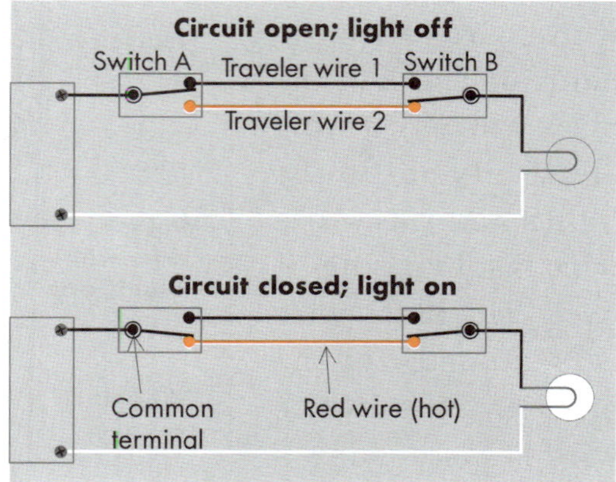


A circuit with three-way switches

## Study the Lesson

5. Write the correct word for each description.
   a. Circular path for electricity.
   b. Place where electricity is divided out to the various circuits in the house.
   c. Device for keeping too much current from flowing through a circuit and for turning electricity on or off in the circuit.
   d. Device that protects a circuit but cannot be reused.
   e. Device for turning on the same light from two places.
6. To turn on an electric light, you (open, close) the circuit. To turn off an electric light, you (open, close) the circuit.
7. Circuit breakers and fuses are important safety devices. Why?
8. Write *black, white,* or *bare.*

   A neutral wire is ———, a hot wire is ———, and a ground wire is ———.
9. When you use an electrical device, why is it good to have a ground wire connected to the device?
10. Write whether each circuit is open or closed.

a. 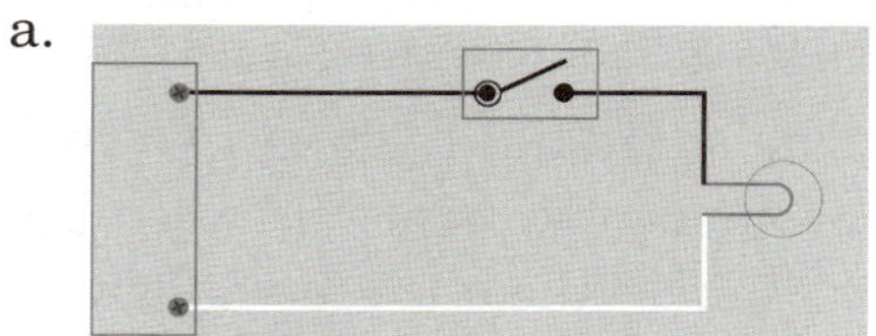

b. 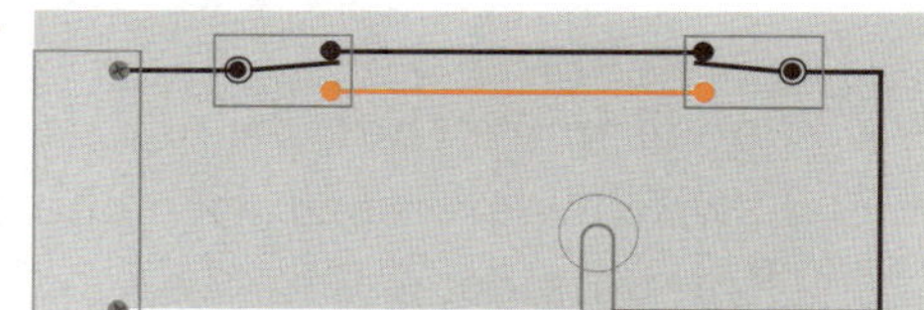

## Review Exercises

1. Write words to complete this sentence: Electricity flows in a wire when the wire passes near a magnet and cuts the invisible... [27]
2. Three sources of free energy are the ———, falling ———, and ———. [23]
3. Stored energy is (kinetic, potential) energy. [22]
4. In the ——— ———, a small animal is eaten by a larger animal, and the larger animal is eaten by a still larger animal. [19]
5. Water is called $H_2O$ because each molecule has two atoms of ——— and one atom of ———. [12]
6. The atmosphere of Venus is mostly ——— ———, and it contains clouds of ——— ———. [7]

## Apply the Lesson

1. Make a simple light circuit. Use a 9-volt battery, a light switch, and a low-volt light socket and bulb (a car trunk light will do). Connect a wire from one terminal of the battery to one terminal of the light socket. From the other terminal of the light, connect a wire to one terminal of the switch. Connect the other switch terminal to the second terminal of the battery.
2. Make a light circuit with three-way switches. Use the picture on the right to wire two three-way switches to a light socket. Fasten two wires to the terminals on a battery.

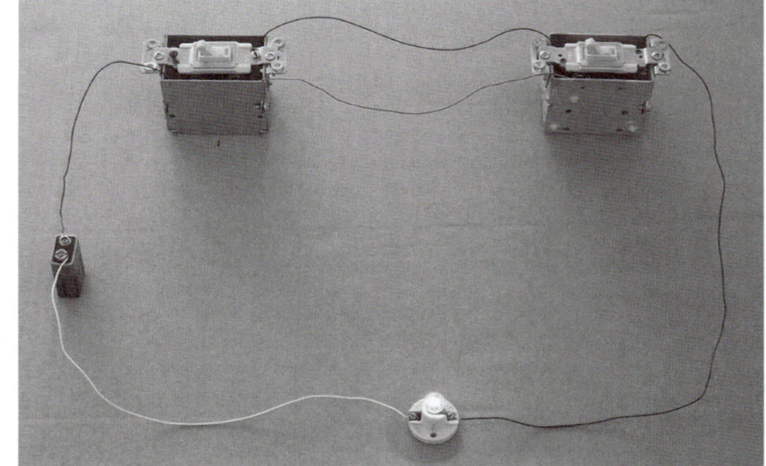

3. Sometimes you need more than two switches for the same light. Then two three-way switches are used with one or more four-way switches between them. On the outside, a four-way switch looks much like a three-way switch. But when you flip a four-way switch, two levers inside move at the same time. The following diagram shows two four-way switches used in a circuit. In switch B, the levers inside are connected to the terminals straight across. In switch C, the levers are connected to opposite terminals. In this position, the levers form an X without touching each other. Follow the path of the electric current. Is the light on or off?

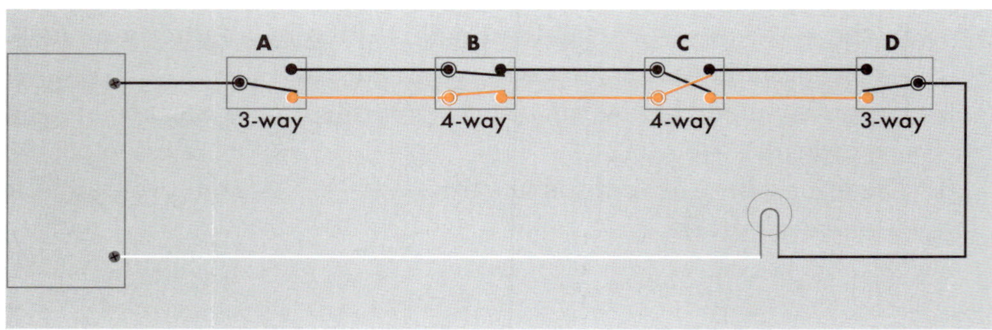

## Lesson 29

# Electricity for Motion, Heat, and Light

"He burneth part thereof in the fire; with part thereof he eateth flesh; he roasteth roast, and is satisfied: yea, he warmeth himself, and saith, Aha, I am warm, I have seen the fire" (Isaiah 44:16).

### Vocabulary

**armature,** the rotating electromagnet inside a motor.

**commutator** (kom′·yə·tā′·tər), a special rotating switch on the armature of a motor.

**field magnets,** stationary magnets inside a motor.

**filament** (fil′·ə·mənt), a thin wire that glows with light when electricity flows through it.

**fluorescent** (flo͝o·res′·ənt), the kind of light given by electricity flowing through vapors.

**heating element,** a wire that makes heat in an appliance.

**incandescent** (in′·kən·des′·ənt), the kind of light given from a filament that glows with heat.

**light-emitting diode** (dī′·ōd′), a small light that uses a tiny amount of electricity.

**Nichrome** (nī′·krōm′), a metal used for heating elements.

**relay,** a switch operated by an electromagnet.

**tungsten** (tung′·stən), a metal with a high melting point, used for light bulb filaments.

We use heat to keep our houses warm and to cook our food. There are other uses for heat, of course, but these have been the two main uses from ancient to modern times. The verse from Isaiah refers to both of these uses. Until recent times, the heat for these purposes came mainly from burning. Today, heat from electricity cooks many people's food and warms their houses.

This verse is in the midst of a discussion about the foolishness of idols. Wood that could have served the good purpose of making heat was used by evil men to make idols. Evil men often take what is intended for good and use it for an evil purpose.

This is also true of electricity. We benefit greatly from electric lights. But lights can be used in a vain way to light up houses and trees at Christmastime. We always want to use electricity for good purposes.

In this lesson you will learn how electricity can be harnessed to produce motion, heat, and light.

**Electromagnets open and close switches.** A ***relay*** is a switch that is opened and closed by electricity. It has an electromagnet close to a movable metal bar. When the coil of the electromagnet is turned on, its magnetism attracts the metal bar and the switch closes.

Some relays pass action from one electrical circuit to another. These relays are used with remote control devices, such as to turn motors on and off. A furnace motor has a relay operated by a thermostat switch in your living room. When you want heat, you turn up the thermostat and it turns on the relay. This causes the furnace to run and heat your house.

An electric bell often operates with a relay. Study the picture below. The current in the bell flows through the switch to the electromagnet. The electromagnet pulls the bar, striking the clapper against the gong. But as this happens, the switch opens and turns off the electromagnet. Then the spring pulls the bar back, the switch closes, and the cycle starts again. The bar moves rapidly back and forth, and the bell keeps ringing as long as the electricity flows.

Switch contacts
Insulation
Movable bar
Spring
Low-volt circuit for electromagnet
Battery
Remote switch
110-volt circuit
Motor

A relay to switch a motor on or off

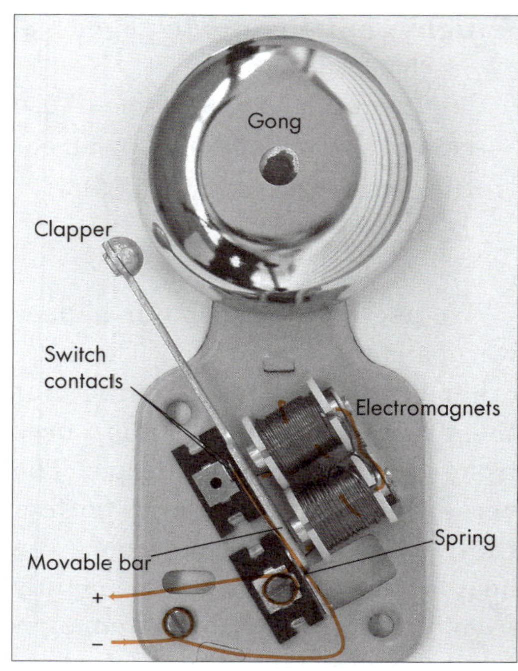


An electric bell

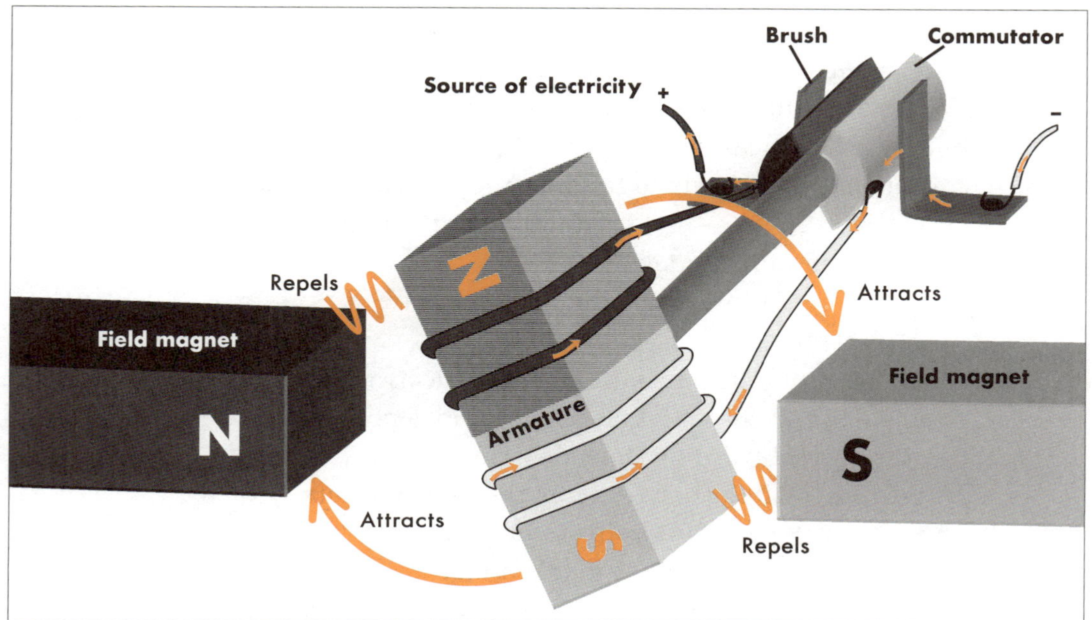


**Electromagnets make motors run.** Small motors turn drills, sewing machines, mixers, and many other useful machines. A simple electric motor has two magnets, called ***field magnets,*** positioned across from each other. One is a north pole, and the other is a south pole.

A movable coil of wire called an ***armature*** can spin freely between the field magnets. An electric current flows into the armature to make it an electromagnet. Now the armature and the field magnets both have magnetic north and south poles. Remember, like poles repel, and unlike poles attract.

The field north pole repels the armature north pole and attracts the armature south pole. These repelling and attracting magnetic fields turn the armature.

As the armature turns, the armature south pole lines up with the field north pole that attracts it. But now a special rotating switch called a ***commutator*** reverses the flow of electricity in the armature. This reverses the north and south poles of the armature, putting the armature north pole beside the field north pole. These like poles repel each other again, so the armature keeps turning.

Motors are made in various ways to do a wide variety of jobs, but they all operate on the basis of the laws of magnetism: like poles repel each other, and unlike poles attract each other.

## Study the Lesson

1. a. According to the lesson, what are two main uses for heat?
   b. What are some other uses for heat from electricity?
2. What force closes the switch of a relay?
3. Write the missing words to tell how an electric bell works.
   a. Electricity in an ——— produces magnetism.
   b. Magnetism pulls a movable ———.
   c. A ——— opens and stops the flow of electricity.
   d. The electromagnet loses its ———.
   e. A ——— pulls the bar back from the electromagnet.
   f. The switch ——— to let electricity flow again.
4. Write the correct word for each description.
   a. A rotating switch that reverses the flow of electricity.
   b. A stationary part that helps to make a motor run.
   c. A movable electromagnet inside a motor.
5. Write the two laws that are operating when any electric motor runs.

**An electric current makes heat.** When an electric current flows through a wire, it heats the wire. How hot the wire becomes depends mostly on how thick the wire is and what kind of metal it is made of.

Wires made of silver, copper, or aluminum produce less heat than other kinds of wires. This is the reason that wires used in household circuits and electric motors are either copper or aluminum. Silver is too expensive, and other kinds of wire make too much heat.

However, appliances such as stoves, toasters, and electric heaters are made to produce heat from electricity. These appliances usually have a ***heating element*** (wire that gets hot), which is made of ***Nichrome.*** Nichrome makes an excellent heating element because when electricity flows through it, it glows red-orange with heat.

Often you can see the heating element in an electric heater or toaster. On an electric stove, the heating element is covered with insulation and placed inside a steel tube. That way

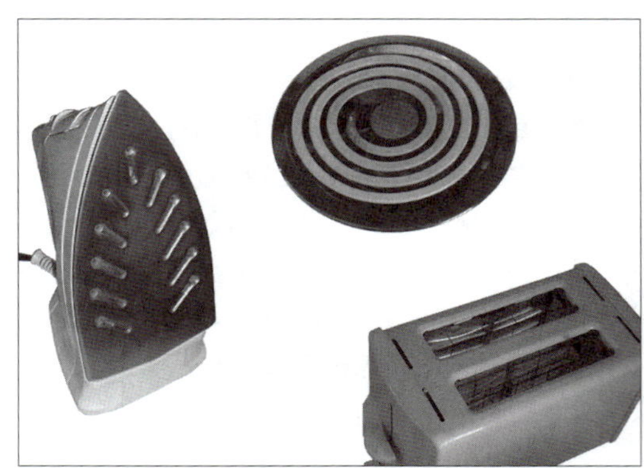

Many appliances contain heating elements.

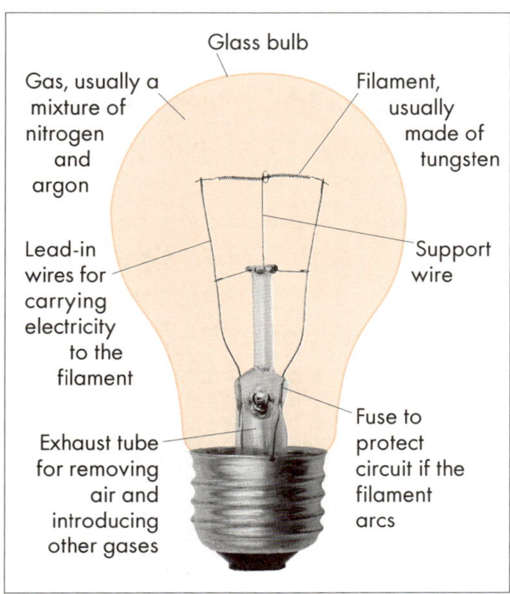


An incandescent lamp

you do not get shocked if you touch the outside of the heating element or place a metal pan on it.

The color of the heating element changes as it gets hotter. It glows dull red first and then bright red. The red changes to orange, then to yellow, and finally almost white.

But before Nichrome gets white hot, it will melt and the wire will break. Or the wire begins to combine with the oxygen in the air. It does not really catch fire, but it is eaten away by the oxygen. Then the old heating element needs to be replaced.

**An electric current can make light.** The simplest kind of electric light is called the ***incandescent*** bulb because it makes light with a thin wire that glows white hot when electricity flows through it. This thin wire, called a ***filament,*** is much like the heating element in a toaster.

The filament is usually made of ***tungsten*** wire wound into a tiny spring shape. Tungsten has a very high melting temperature of 6,170°F (3,410°C). When the light bulb is on, the tungsten gets close to 5,000°F (2,500°C). That is very hot, but not hot enough to melt tungsten. For this reason, tungsten is a good metal for light bulb filaments.

If the hot tungsten filament is exposed to air, it combines with oxygen and soon breaks. To prevent this, the filament is placed inside a glass bulb in which the oxygen is replaced with other gases.

If the tungsten filament does not melt or combine with oxygen, why do light bulbs burn out? While the filament is very hot, some of the tungsten slowly evaporates and puts a dark coating on the inside of the glass bulb.

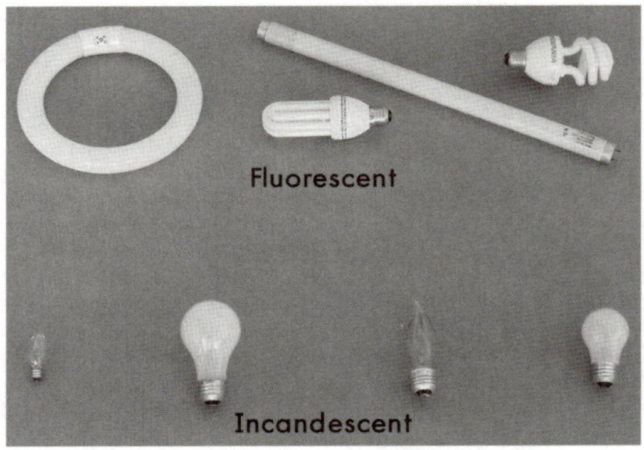


Electric lamps come in many different shapes and sizes. Fluorescent lights cost more apiece but are more economical in the long run.

After a long time, so much tungsten evaporates that the filament becomes very thin and breaks. Then we must replace the light bulb.

**Other electric lights.** A ***fluorescent*** bulb or tube is filled with argon and mercury vapors. It has a filament-like wire at each end that sends electricity through the vapors. This produces ultraviolet light that is invisible to us, but when it strikes the white coating of the tube, the tube glows brightly. Neon lights and sodium-vapor lamps also work on the principle of electricity passing through a gas.

Another special kind of electric light is the ***light-emitting diode,*** or LED. Some calculators have glowing numbers made of LEDs. These small lights use just a tiny amount of electricity.

**Inside a Fluorescent Lamp**

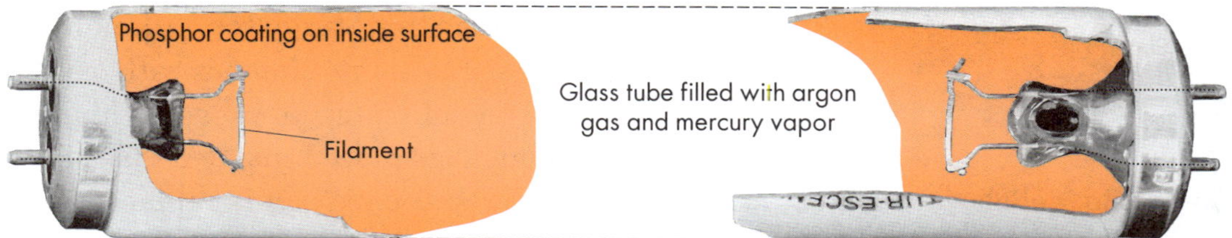


Fluorescent tubes outlast incandescent bulbs and use about one fifth as much electricity.

## Study the Lesson

6. a. What three metals are good for making electrical wire that produces little heat?
   b. Why are only two of these used for wires in houses and electric motors?
7. Why is Nichrome a good metal for heating elements?
8. What two things happen to Nichrome wire if it is heated white hot?
9. Why is tungsten a good metal for the filament of a light bulb?
10. Why is the oxygen removed from a light bulb?
11. Which of these two regular light bulbs will probably burn out first? How can you tell?

a. 

b. 

12. Name the kind of electric light described in each sentence.
    a. A filament glows white hot.
    b. Electricity passing through a vapor makes a special light that strikes a white coating and causes it to glow.
    c. A small amount of electricity produces a tiny light that can be used to make numbers.

## Review Exercises

1. A circuit is ——— if it forms a complete path for electricity, and ——— if it does not. [28]
2. The law of conservation of energy states that energy cannot be ——— or ———. [22]
3. Carnivorous and herbivorous animals control each other's populations, and this produces a ——— of ———. (Write the whole phrase.) [20]
4. Dead plant materials improve the soil by decaying to form ———. [18]
5. In the process called ———, plants use ——— and ——— ——— in the presence of sunlight to make sugar. [17]
6. Between the orbits of Mars and Jupiter are thousands of small bodies called ———. [8]

## Apply the Lesson

1. Make a simple light circuit like the one shown in Lesson 28, except replace the hand switch with a relay. Notice that two separate circuits are used for this arrangement.
2. Examine an electric bell, and find all the following parts: switch contacts, electromagnet, armature (movable bar), spring, clapper, gong. How many volts are used to operate your bell? (This may be stamped on the base.) Connect the bell to a source with the right voltage, and watch the armature work. A bell will run on either alternating or direct current. Why is there sparking in the operation of a bell?
3. Find the heating elements in various appliances, such as toasters, heaters, or stoves.
4. Wrap a burned-out light bulb in cloth, and strike it lightly with a hammer to break the bulb. **Be careful not to cut yourself on pieces of glass.** Examine a piece of filament with a microscope. Study the wires that hold the filament in place. Find the tube through which the oxygen is removed and the special gases are put in.

## Lesson 30

# Electricity for Communication

"And [God] said, Go, and tell this people" (Isaiah 6:9).

### Vocabulary

**amplifier,** a device that strengthens a weak electrical current that carries a sound signal.

**diaphragm** (dī′·ə·fram′), a thin disk that either receives or produces sound vibrations.

**loudspeaker,** a device that changes electricity into sounds.

**microphone,** a mouthpiece for a loudspeaking system.

**receiver,** in a telephone, the device that changes electricity into sounds.

**telegraph,** a device that writes a message from a distance.

**telephone,** a device that carries sound for a distance by using electricity.

**transmitter,** in a telephone, the device that changes sounds into electrical signals.

God has given us the ability to communicate, and we have the responsibility to tell the truth to others. Often we communicate by talking directly. If the ones we are talking to are at a distance, we will shout or go to them. But sometimes the distance is so great that we could not be heard no matter how loudly we shouted.

For many years, letters were almost the only way to communicate with someone far away. A person wrote a message, and someone traveled on foot or horseback to take it to the receiver. With the discovery of electricity came the inventions of the telegraph and telephone. These greatly increased the speed at which a message could be sent.

**The telegraph was the first device for sending messages with electricity.** Samuel F. B. Morse invented the telegraph system used in America. When he learned that electricity can be turned on and off and that it can travel great distances in an instant, he thought that surely electrical signals could be used to send messages.

Morse invented a machine to send messages by using a switch to turn the current on and off. He made another machine to receive the messages that were sent. The electrical signals from

**International Morse Code**

| | | | | | |
|---|---|---|---|---|---|
| A | · – | K | – · – | U | · · – |
| B | – · · · | L | · – · · | V | · · · – |
| C | – · – · | M | – – | W | · – – |
| D | – · · | N | – · | X | – · · – |
| E | · | O | – – – | Y | – · – – |
| F | · · – · | P | · – – · | Z | – – · · |
| G | – – · | Q | – – · – | Period (.) | · – · – · – |
| H | · · · · | R | · – · | Comma (,) | – – · · – – |
| I | · · | S | · · · | Ques. mark (?) | · · – – · · |
| J | · – – – | T | – | Error | · · · · · · · · |

the sender operated a relay that pulled a pencil down against a long strip of moving paper. The pencil wrote a series of short marks (dots) and long marks (dashes).

Morse devised a system of dots and dashes to represent the letters of the alphabet. For example, *how* would be sent as "short-short-short-short" *(H),* "long-long-long" *(O),* "short-long-long" *(W).* His system was later modified somewhat, and today it is known as the international Morse code.

Morse's invention received a fitting name: ***telegraph*** (writing from a distance). His first system was installed between Washington, D.C., and Baltimore, Maryland. On May 24, 1844, the 41-mile line was ready, and Samuel sent the first message: "What hath God wrought!"

Later, the pencil and moving paper of the receiving machine were replaced by a sounder. A person would listen to the clicking sounds and would write down the message as it came in. Telegraph operators became so skilled that they could send and receive messages very rapidly.

Morse's sending and receiving telegraph. The pendulum holds a pencil above a strip of paper.

## Study the Lesson

1. What two facts about electricity made Samuel F. B. Morse realize that it could be used to send messages?
2. The telegraph greatly increased the ——— of sending messages.
3. Why is *telegraph* a good name for the system that Morse invented?
4. Write this sentence with the symbols of the Morse code: *What hath God wrought!* Use slash marks (/) to separate the letters. Disregard the end punctuation.

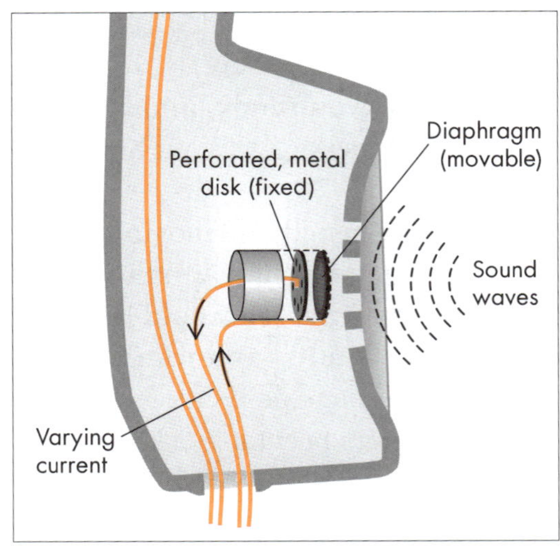


A telephone transmitter

**The telephone sends sounds with electricity.** Sounds are vibrations. Different letter sounds have different vibrations. Alexander Graham Bell invented the ***telephone,*** which changes the vibrations of a person's voice into a varying electric current. At the other end of the line, the receiver changes the varying current back into sound waves.

The sending part of the telephone that you talk into is called the ***transmitter.*** This device is a small cylinder covered by a thin, flexible disk called a ***diaphragm.***

As you speak, the sound of your voice strikes the diaphragm and causes it to vibrate rapidly in and out. When the diaphragm moves closer to a fixed, metal disk, more electricity flows through the circuit. When the diaphragm comes away, less electricity flows through. This causes the current to vary in a way that exactly matches the vibrations of your voice.

The electricity then flows through an ***amplifier,*** a device that makes the varying current strong enough to travel through the telephone lines.

When this varying electric current reaches the ***receiver,*** it goes through a small ***loudspeaker.*** A loudspeaker works on the principles of magnetism: like poles repel and unlike poles attract. The wire is coiled closely

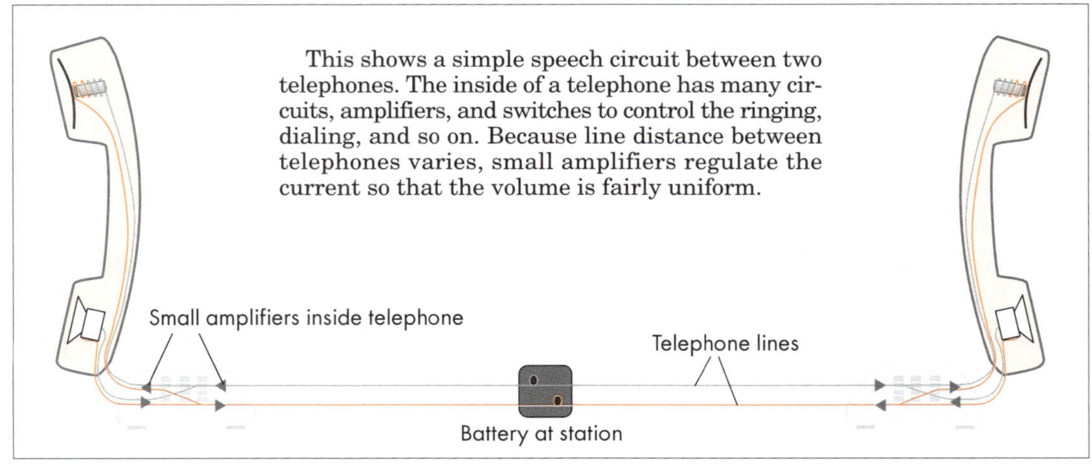


This shows a simple speech circuit between two telephones. The inside of a telephone has many circuits, amplifiers, and switches to control the ringing, dialing, and so on. Because line distance between telephones varies, small amplifiers regulate the current so that the volume is fairly uniform.

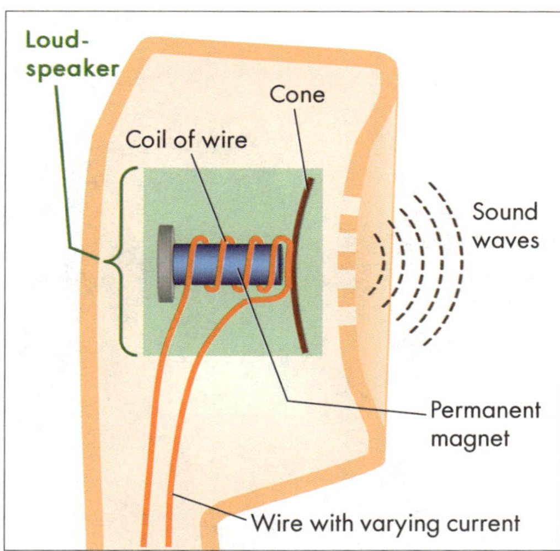


A telephone receiver

around (but does not touch) a permanent magnet. The coil of wire is an electromagnet, and a paper cone is fastened to it.

As the varying current flows through the coil of wire, its magnetic field varies, and the two magnets attract and repel each other. This back-and-forth movement of the wire coil makes the cone vibrate, producing sound waves just like those going into the transmitter.

**Loudspeaking systems make sounds louder.** In large meetinghouses, we often want to make the speaker's voice louder so that everyone can hear well. This is done by using a system that works in much the same way as a telephone.

The speaker talks into the ***microphone,*** which changes sound waves into a small, varying electric current. This small current is strengthened by an amplifier, and then it goes to one or more loudspeakers that change the varying current into sound.

Loudspeaking systems are another way that electricity helps us communicate. The sound of a voice speaking into the microphone comes out of the loudspeaker as a much louder sound.

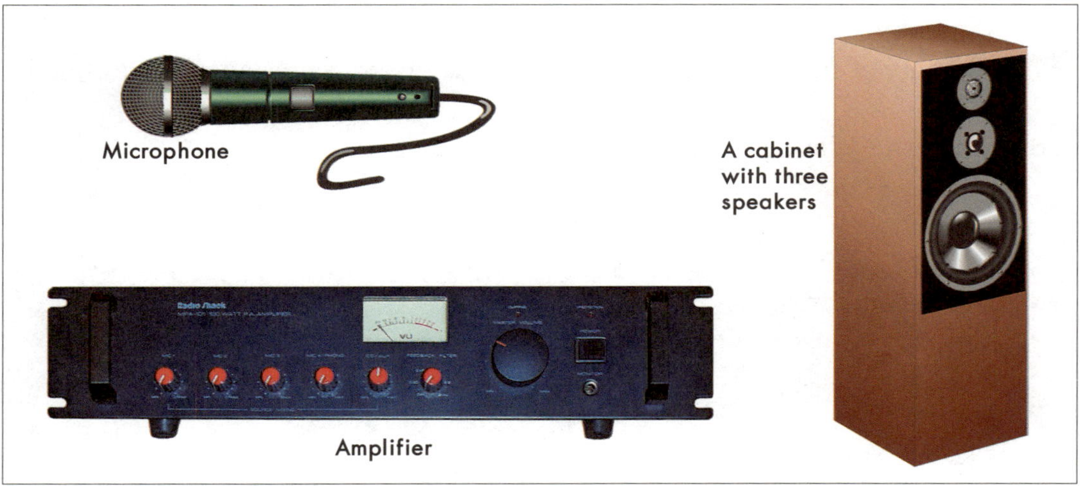


The three main parts of a loudspeaker system

God wants us to communicate good messages to others. The telephone can help us tell others about Jesus. We can use it to invite others to worship services. Loudspeakers can help everyone hear the message of God's Word clearly as a minister preaches. But the telephone can also be used in wrong ways, such as to spread gossip. Loudspeakers are used in places of evil entertainment. So telephones and loudspeakers are not wrong in themselves, but people can use them in wrong ways. When you use electricity to communicate, be careful that you always send good messages.

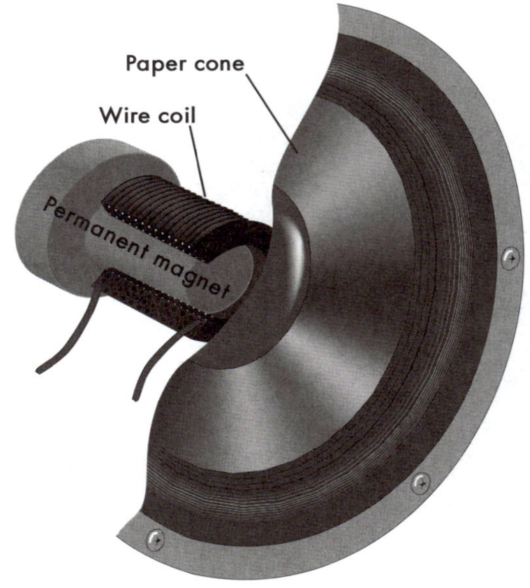

A cutaway view of a large loudspeaker

## Study the Lesson

5. Write vocabulary words to name the following parts of a telephone.
   a. The part that the speaker talks into.
   b. The part that makes sounds like the speaker's voice.
   c. A thin disk that receives sound waves.
6. When the thin disk moves closer to the fixed disk, the flow of electricity (increases, decreases).
7. The part of the loudspeaker that uses electricity to produce vibrations is an ———.
8. Name the following parts of a loudspeaking system.
   a. Has a paper cone that is vibrated by magnetism.
   b. Sends a weak electric current when a person speaks into it.
   c. Changes a weak, varying current into a strong current that varies in the same way.
9. How can we use the telephone in a way that pleases God?

## Review Exercises

1. In an electric motor, a moving electromagnet called the ——— turns as it is attracted or repelled by the ——— ———. [29]
2. A ——— ——— protects a circuit from too much electrical current. [28]
3. Electrical pressure is measured in ———. [27]
4. A farmer may spread ——— to increase the nutrients in the soil, or he may spread ——— to improve the pH. [18]
5. Four of Jupiter's ——— can be seen with a small telescope. [9]
6. The sun produces its energy as particles of ——— unite to form ———. [2]

## Apply the Lesson

1. With a switch and a light bulb or buzzer some distance away (perhaps in another room), send a message by the international Morse code. The international distress signal is SOS. What is the code for this message?
2. Try to find an old telephone receiver (transmitter in one end and receiver in the other). Take the covers off, and examine the transmitter and receiving elements. Connect them in series with a 6-volt or 9-volt battery. You will need to hold the wires to the contacts of the transmitter element or make another way to maintain contact. Wires could be soldered to the contact rings. Fasten long wires to the receiver.

   Have one person talk into the transmitter and another person hold the receiver to his ear. Can the voice be heard clearly at the receiver? Why must direct current (as from a battery) be used? Why would alternating current not work for a telephone? Be sure to disconnect the battery when not in use, or your telephone will run the battery down.
3. Try to find a loudspeaker. Look for the following parts in it: paper cone, wires to the electromagnet, permanent magnet (test it with a piece of iron or a compass), transformer (if any). Using the free ends of the wires connected to the loudspeaker, briefly touch the terminals of a flashlight battery several times. What evidence do you have that the loudspeaker would work?

## Lesson 31

# Unit 6 Review

## A. Vocabulary

Write the letter of the correct word for each description.

| | |
|---|---|
| 1. Path that electricity follows. | a. armature |
| 2. Tiny particles that make up electricity. | b. circuit |
| 3. Changes high voltage to a lower, safer voltage. | c. commutator |
| 4. Rotating electromagnet in a motor. | d. current |
| 5. Rotating switch on an armature. | e. diaphragm |
| 6. Stationary magnet in a motor. | f. electrons |
| 7. Flow of electricity in a circuit. | g. field magnet |
| 8. Part that produces the sound of an electric bell. | h. filament |
| 9. In an electric stove, the part that makes heat. | i. gong |
| 10. Thin disk for receiving sound. | j. heating element |
| 11. Glows white hot in a light bulb. | k. relay |
| 12. Switch operated by an electromagnet. | l. transformer |

| | |
|---|---|
| 13. Area of force around a magnet. | a. amplifier |
| 14. Metal used for filaments in light bulbs. | b. circuit breaker |
| 15. Uses electricity to produce magnetism. | c. electromagnet |
| 16. Metal used for heating elements. | d. fluorescent |
| 17. Unit for measuring electrical pressure. | e. incandescent |
| 18. Small light that uses little electricity. | f. light-emitting diode |
| 19. Changes a weak signal to a strong signal. | g. loudspeaker |
| 20. Mouthpiece for a loudspeaking system. | h. magnetic field |
| 21. Protects a circuit from too much electrical current. | i. microphone |
| 22. Contains a paper cone vibrated by an electromagnet. | j. Nichrome |
| 23. Kind of light from something made so hot that it glows. | k. tungsten |
| 24. Kind of light made by electricity flowing through vapors. | l. volt |

## B. Facts

Write the words that belong in the blanks.

1. If a wire moves through a magnetic field, ——— move through the wire.
2. ——— magnetic poles repel each other, and ——— poles attract each other.
3. A ——— transformer increases the voltage.
4. Electricity is a very useful form of ——— that can be used in many ways.
5. Ordinary household electricity has ——— volts.
6. High-voltage electricity is lowered for a local community at a ———.
7. A circuit must be ——— before electricity will flow through it.
8. In an electric motor, the field south pole attracts the armature ——— pole.
9. Tungsten makes a good filament because it has a high ——— ———.
10. The ——— is removed from a light bulb so that the filament lasts longer.
11. The telegraph system was invented by ——— ———.
12. In a loudspeaker system, sound goes into a ———, the resulting current is strengthened by an ———, and that current goes to one or more loudspeakers.
13. In a loudspeaker, the electricity goes through an ——— that causes the cone to vibrate.
14. It is right to use a telephone or loudspeaker to communicate ——— messages.

## C. Concepts

Choose the letter of the best answer in each exercise.

1. For changing electricity from high voltage to low voltage, a transformer has
   a. a movable coil of wire.
   b. two coils of wire made of different metals.
   c. one coil of wire connected with a second coil of wire.
   d. two coils with a different number of turns of wire on each coil.
2. Which of the following statements about magnets is *not* true?
   a. Each magnet has a north pole and a south pole.
   b. An invisible magnetic field surrounds a magnet.
   c. Unlike poles repel each other, and like poles attract each other.
   d. An electromagnet can be turned on and off.

3. Electricity is induced in a coil of wire if
   a. the coil moves through a magnetic field.
   b. the coil is inside a stationary magnetic field.
   c. the circuit is closed.
   d. the coil of wire is moving back and forth.
4. God should receive the glory for electricity for all the following reasons *except*
   a. God used electricity before man learned how to use it.
   b. God gave men wisdom to know how to use it.
   c. The Bible tells about man's modern use of electricity.
   d. All that electricity can do was made possible by God.
5. A circuit breaker protects
   a. you from getting shocked.
   b. you from turning off the circuit.
   c. a circuit from getting too little current.
   d. the wire in a circuit from getting too hot.
6. A 120-volt circuit has
   a. a narrow breaker, a black hot wire, and a white neutral wire.
   b. a wide breaker, two hot wires, and one neutral wire.
   c. a narrow breaker and two hot wires.
   d. a wide breaker, a black hot wire, and a white neutral wire.
7. Three-way switches allow you
   a. to turn two different lights on and off from one place.
   b. to turn a light on and off without a switch.
   c. to turn the same light on and off from more than one place.
   d. to turn different lights on and off at different times.
8. In which of the following appliances would you expect to find a commutator?
   a. electric relay
   b. electric drill
   c. electric stove
   d. electric bell
9. The main reason an incandescent light is inside a bulb is
   a. to protect the filament from the air.
   b. to protect people from getting burned by the hot filament.
   c. to keep the heat in so that the filament gets hot enough to make light.
   d. to spread out the light that comes from the filament.

10. Nichrome makes a good
    a. telephone wire.
    b. heating element.
    c. light bulb filament.
    d. motor armature.
11. Which of these sentences is *not* true about the working of an electric bell?
    a. Electricity pulls the metal bar with an electromagnet.
    b. The clapper closes the circuit and makes the electricity stop.
    c. The magnetism stops and a spring pulls the bar back.
    d. The switch closes and the electricity flows again.
12. You could expect to find two disks in
    a. a loudspeaker.
    b. a telephone receiver.
    c. an amplifier.
    d. a telephone transmitter.
13. Which of the following is in the right order for the sound of someone's voice to be carried by a telephone system?
    a. fixed disk, diaphragm, wire, cone, electromagnet
    b. cone, electromagnet, wire, fixed disk, diaphragm
    c. wire, diaphragm, fixed disk, cone, electromagnet
    d. diaphragm, fixed disk, wire, electromagnet, cone
14. The telegraph and telephone can both
    a. send a message without wires.
    b. change sound to electrical signals.
    c. be used to send a message rapidly.
    d. make vibrations that sound like your voice.

# Unit 7

## Your Body—Created to Inhabit the Earth

"I have made the earth, and created man upon it" (Isaiah 45:12).

The earth and man were created for each other. In previous units of this science textbook, you have considered how very suitable the earth is as a home for man. The earth has the right range of temperature, the right amount of oxygen, the right gravity, and an abundance of water. These are some ways that God created the earth to be inhabited.

In this unit you will see how God designed the body of man to use the life-sustaining provisions of the earth. The body must be able to find and take in what it needs to live. What is taken in must be used to grow and move. The oxygen, water, and food must be distributed to all parts of the body. The body is well able to do all these things because God created man to be an inhabitant of the earth.

A study of the body can help you say with King David, "I will praise thee; for I am fearfully and wonderfully made: marvellous are thy works; and that my soul knoweth right well" (Psalm 139:14).

# Lesson 32

## Your Sensory System

"We grope for the wall like the blind, and we grope as if we had no eyes" (Isaiah 59:10).

### Vocabulary

**dermis** (dûr′·mis), the second skin layer, containing nerve endings and blood vessels.

**epidermis** (ep′·i·dûr′·mis), the outer skin layer made of tough, dead cells.

**gland,** a body part that produces a substance needed by the body.

**nerve,** a thin cord that carries messages to or from the brain.

**nervous system,** the body system that includes the brain, spinal cord, and nerves, by which the actions of the body are controlled.

**response,** an action performed because of a stimulus.

**sense,** the ability to receive some kind of stimulus.

**sense organ,** a body part, such as an eye or an ear, that receives stimuli and sends messages about them to the brain.

**stimulus** (stim′·yə·ləs), *plural* **stimuli** (stim′·yə·lī′), anything that can cause one to make a response.

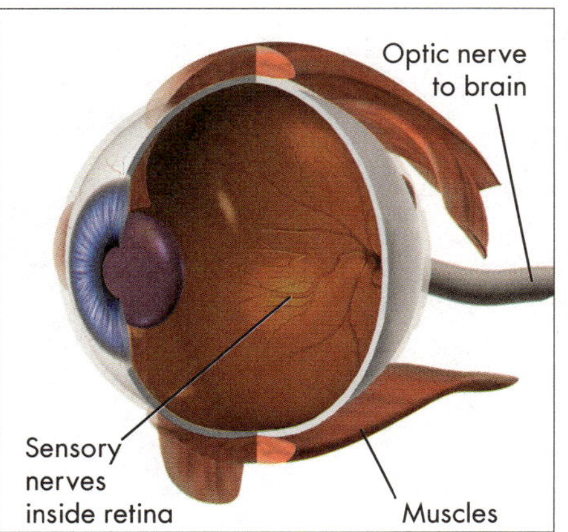


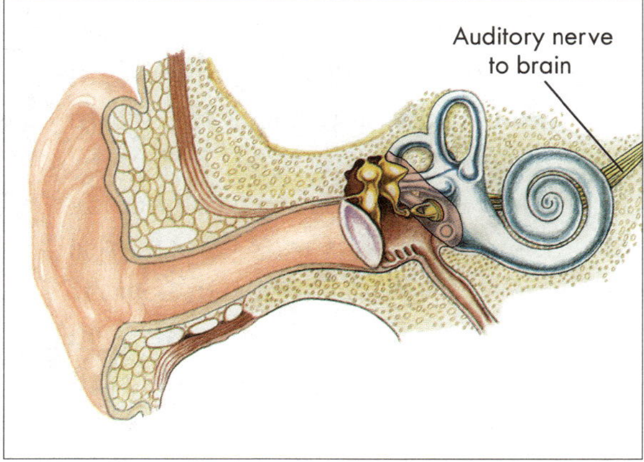


*Left:* A cutaway view of the eye. *Right:* A diagram of the ear. God made the sense of sight and the sense of hearing possible by connecting these organs to the brain. Nerves carry the information from the sense organs to the brain.

A blind person is handicapped because he cannot see the world about him. Blind persons become very good at using their ears. They learn to recognize people by their voices and the sound of their walking.

Some people are deaf. Deaf people can become good at lip reading. They see by the motion of a speaker's lips what words he is saying.

Helen Keller was both blind and deaf. Yet by touch, she could learn about the many things happening around her. She could "hear" what someone was saying by holding her fingers to the speaker's throat and lips. Although Helen Keller did not have the sense of sight or hearing, she was still aware of her environment, the world around her.

**God made the five senses.** All day long, your body sends messages to your brain about what it sees, hears, smells, tastes, and touches. These are called the five ***senses.*** They are the doors through which your brain receives information about the world around you.

All day long, your brain responds to these messages. It tells your legs to move away from the danger it sees. It tells you to open your jacket when you feel too warm. It tells your head to turn toward the person that called your name.

All parts of your body are connected to the brain by a complex network of ***nerves.*** The brain is the headquarters of this network, which is called the ***nervous system.*** A large bundle of nerves, called the spinal cord, extends through your backbone and links all the branches of the nervous system to the brain. Small branches of tiny nerve fibers reach to every bit of skin and every muscle in your body.

Nerves compare in many ways to the electric lines that connect a

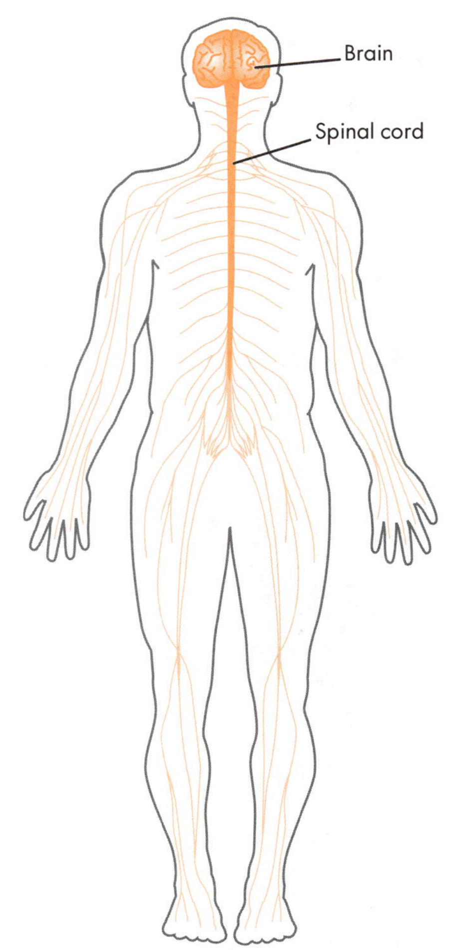


The nervous system

generating station to the communities surrounding it. There are large, heavy transmission lines and lighter distribution lines, all working together to provide circuits to and from the generating station. Nerves carry messages to and from the brain in a similar way.

The body is affected by things such as heat, cold, sound, light, and pain. Each of these is a ***stimulus*** that starts messages on their way to the brain. A ***sense organ,*** such as the eye, the ear, or the skin, receives the messages and sends them by nerves to the brain. The brain then uses other nerves to send messages to the body, telling it to act in certain ways. Such an action is called a ***response.***

Nerves in the ear are very sensitive to the vibrations of sound waves. Taste buds carry messages about the flavors of different foods, and nerves in the nose give information about odors in the air. Nerve endings just under the skin give a sense of touch everywhere on your body.

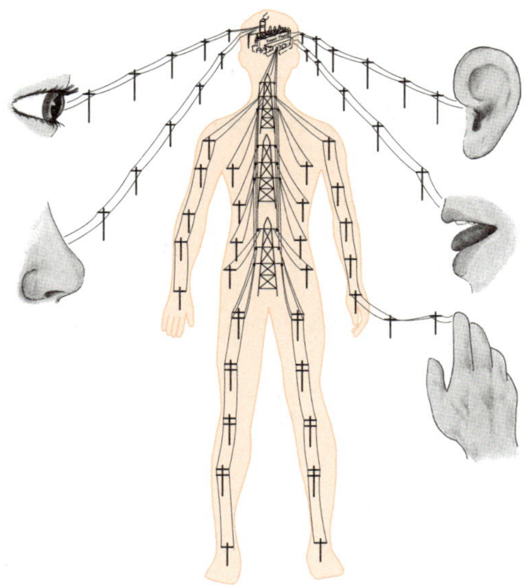

Nerves are somewhat like a system of electrical lines.

Your five senses are gifts from God. You do not have senses for everything. You have no sense of magnetism as some birds do. You cannot hear the high-pitched sounds that help bats to fly in the dark. You do not need senses for these. By seeing, hearing, smelling, tasting, and touching, you receive all the information you need to live on the earth.

**The skin is the largest sense organ of your body.** Nerve endings in your skin give you the sense of touch. You feel pressure if a pencil point pushes against any part of the skin. That means the nerve endings are in every part of your skin.

Nerves send many different messages to your brain. You know how tightly to hold a pencil by touch. Your sense of touch tells you if something is rough or smooth, sharp or dull, hot or cold, hard or soft. If you could not feel pain, some part of your body might be hurt and you would not know it.

Leprosy is a dreaded disease that slowly destroys the sense of touch in the body parts that it affects. A leper can receive a serious burn or other injury without feeling it. Since lepers cannot feel when their eyes become dry, they sometimes go blind because they fail to wet their eyes by blinking. The sense of touch helps to protect you from injury and from becoming blind.

God wisely put a large number of nerve endings in your fingertips so that you can feel even small differences when you rub your fingers across something. Fold a piece of paper, and then open it completely flat again. Now close your eyes, and draw your fingers across the paper. Can you feel where it was folded? The blind use a similar method to read Braille, which is a system of tiny raised dots that stand for letters and words. How wonderful is your sense of touch!

**A Cross Section of Skin**

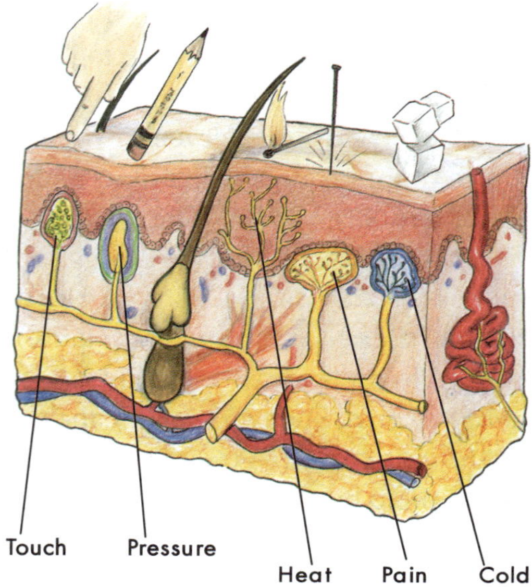


The skin has a variety of nerve endings to sense different types of things.

## Study the Lesson

1. God gave us five ——— so that we can know what is happening in our environment. They are ———, ———, ———, ———, and ———.
2. Choose the vocabulary word that fits each phrase.
   a. A car horn blowing.
   b. Ears to hear the horn.
   c. Ability to hear the horn.
   d. Turning your face toward the car.

   response
   sense
   sense organs
   stimulus
3. As power lines carry electricity to and from a generating station, so ——— carry messages to and from the brain.
4. The largest sense organ of your body is your ———.
5. People with leprosy sometimes go blind because they do not wet their eyes by ———. This happens because they cannot ——— when their eyes are ———.

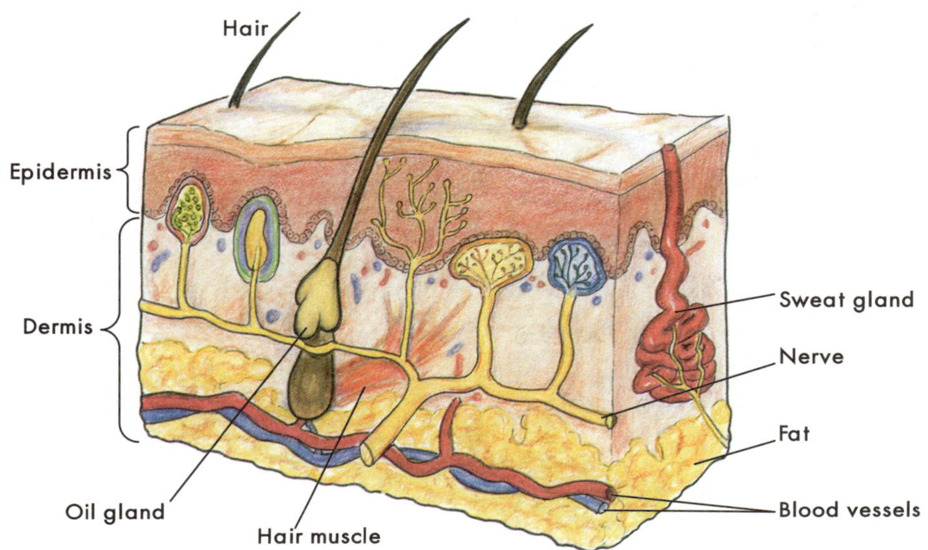


**The skin has two main layers.** The thickest layer of your skin is called the ***dermis.*** It contains tiny blood vessels as well as nerve endings, glands, and fat. (A ***gland*** is a body part that produces a substance needed by the body.) Hair, fingernails, and toenails grow out of the dermis.

Above the dermis is a layer of tough cells called the ***epidermis.*** (The prefix *epi-* means "over" or "upon.") The surface of the epidermis is made of dead cells that are constantly flaking off and being replaced by new cells from below. In this way the entire epidermis is renewed about once every two months. Heavy, repeated rubbing causes extra epidermis cells to grow, resulting in a callus. This is God's way of protecting the areas of your skin that must endure much friction.

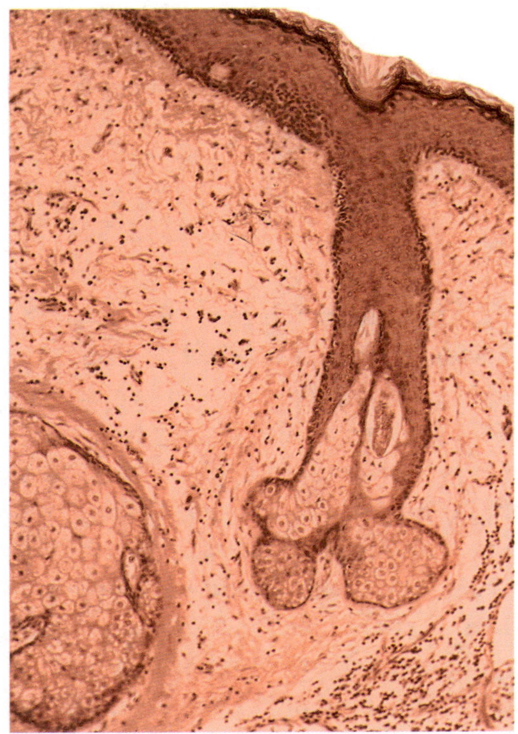

A cross section of the scalp showing an empty hair follicle. The skin surface angles across the upper-right corner.

| Work of the Skin | Part That Does the Work | How It Does the Work |
|---|---|---|
| 1. Protects the body from drying. | Epidermis, oil glands | Epidermis forms tight layer. Oil from oil glands keeps it waterproof. |
| 2. Protects the body from injury. | Dead cells of epidermis | Epidermis forms a tough, protective layer. |
| 3. Gives protection from germs. | Tight layer of epidermis | Dead cells of epidermis keep germs away from living cells. |
| 4. Cools the body. | Outer surface, sweat glands | Heat leaves from the surface. Sweat cools by evaporating. |
| 5. Gives the sense of touch. | Nerve endings | Nerve endings sense pressure, pain, and temperature. |
| 6. Provides padding. | Fat | Fatty areas make soft pads, especially at places like the palm of the hand. |
| 7. Provides insulation. | Fat, hair | Fat slows escape of heat below surface. Hair traps heat in air above. |
| 8. Protects ends of fingers and toes. | Nails | Strong, horny nails give protection from injury. |

Skin does much more for us than provide a sense of touch. The skin acts as a shield to the tender inner parts of the body. It protects the body from dirt, germs, hot sun, and cold winds. The chart above lists several things the skin does for us.

**You must take good care of your skin.** Dirty or sweaty skin gives off an unpleasant odor. We should prevent this by keeping ourselves clean. Regular washing with soap and warm water will also kill germs that can cause sores on the surface of the skin.

If the skin is cut, the body's barrier against germs is broken. That is why you should wash an open wound and apply an antiseptic (a substance that kills germs). Alcohol is a good antiseptic. A bandage helps to keep other germs from entering the wound. God made the skin to heal in a few days, but we can help by washing and bandaging the cut to keep it from becoming infected. God made our skin for some very important reasons, and we should take good care of it.

## Study the Lesson

6. If you get a scratch that does not bleed, you have scratched only the (dermis, epidermis).
7. Thousands of skin cells are rubbed or washed off every day. Why does your skin not wear thin?
8. What is a gland?
9. Name the part in the skin that
   a. gives the sense of touch.
   b. gives off water to cool the body by evaporation.
   c. gives off a substance that keeps the epidermis waterproof.
   d. provides a soft pad.
   e. keeps heat in by trapping air above the skin.
   f. keeps germs from entering the body.
   g. slows the escape of heat before it reaches the surface.
10. What are two helpful results of regularly washing the skin?
11. Why must we be careful to clean an open wound?

## Review Exercises

1. In a telephone, the ——— changes the sound of the speaker's voice into a varying electrical current. [30]
2. In a light bulb, the ——— glows white hot and produces light. [29]
3. What are the two laws of magnetism by which all electric motors operate? [29]
4. The law of conservation of energy states that energy cannot be ——— or ———. [22]
5. An animal that feeds mostly on plants is (carnivorous, herbivorous, omnivorous). [19]
6. Saturn is surrounded by beautiful ——— that look like a disk of gold. [9]

## Apply the Lesson

The more nerve endings in the skin, the more detail you can feel. With a sharp pencil in a compass, open it to one-half inch. Press the compass against a fingertip. Can you feel the two distinct points? Now press it against the back of your neck. How many points do you feel this time? Have another person test you so that you cannot see how far apart the points are. How far apart must the points be to feel each one on the back of your neck? How close together can they be to still feel them both at the tip of your finger? Try different places on your hand and arm.

## Lesson 33

# Your Respiratory System

"He that spread forth the earth, and that which cometh out of it; he that giveth breath unto the people upon it" (Isaiah 42:5).

### Vocabulary

**bronchial tube** (brong′·kē·əl), one of the smaller tubes that carry air to the lungs.

**diaphragm** (dī′·ə·fram′), a sheet of muscle below the lungs, which contracts to bring in air.

**epiglottis** (ep′·i·glot′·is), the flap that closes the top of the trachea in swallowing.

**nasal passages,** the passages in the head where incoming air is warmed and cleaned.

**respiratory system** (res′·pər·ə·tôr′·ē), the body system that includes the lungs, diaphragm, and various air passages, by which oxygen is absorbed and carbon dioxide is released.

**trachea** (trā′·kē·ə), the stiff-walled air passage in the throat.

**vocal cords,** two bands in the throat that vibrate to produce the sound of the voice.

Breathing and life go together. The body cannot live long without breathing. While you are reading this, you are taking about sixteen breaths per minute. When you work or play vigorously, you breathe much faster because then your body must have more oxygen.

**Your body needs oxygen.** The food you eat is fuel for your body as gasoline is fuel for an automobile engine. But an engine cannot run on gasoline alone. It takes in air to help burn the fuel. The burning fuel produces power to run the engine. Carbon dioxide, a result of the burning, leaves the engine through the exhaust pipe.

Your body also uses oxygen to get energy from the fuel in food. You get the oxygen by breathing. Another name for breathing is respiration. The body parts you use in breathing are called the ***respiratory system.*** The lungs are the main organs of the respiratory system. In the lungs, oxygen

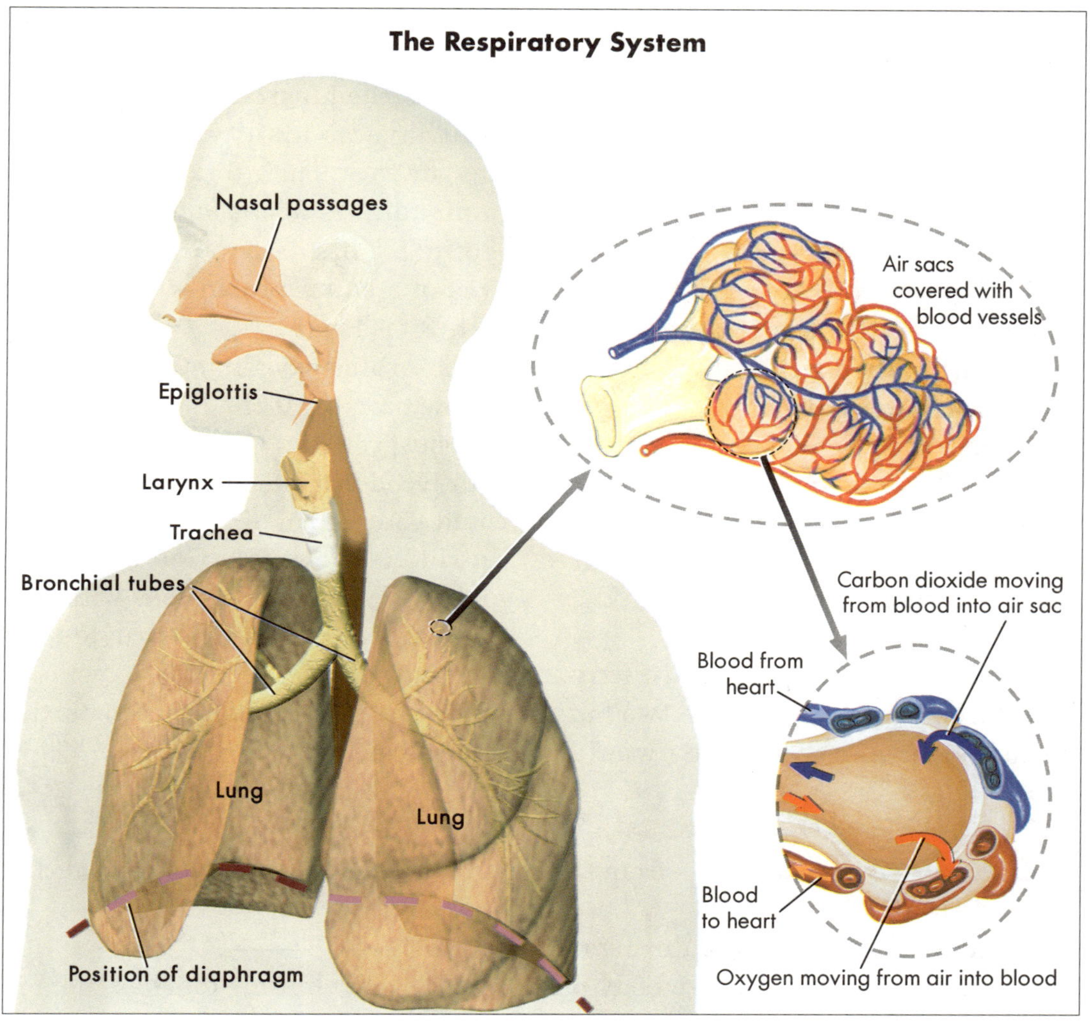


As blood travels around an air sac, it loses carbon dioxide and gains oxygen. The walls of the air sacs and blood vessels are extremely thin so that air can be exchanged easily.

from the air enters the blood.

When the oxygen combines with fuel in your body, carbon dioxide is produced. You do not have an exhaust pipe to release the carbon dioxide, as a gasoline engine does. Rather, the carbon dioxide leaves your body when you breathe out. You inhale the oxygen that your body needs. You exhale waste carbon dioxide. Thank God for a well-designed respiratory system!

**How does air get into the lungs?** Air enters the body through the nose and goes through ***nasal passages*** in the head. Here the air is both warmed and cleaned on the way to the lungs. Small hairs and the moist walls of the nasal passages catch dust. You can see the result of this dust collector if you blow your nose after working in a very dusty area.

In the neck, the air enters a stiff-walled tube called the ***trachea.*** The lower part of the trachea divides into two ***bronchial tubes,*** one going to each lung. The bronchial tubes divide into smaller and smaller tubes that bring air to many tiny air sacs. All these air passages are moist, and they help to warm and clean the air on the way to the lungs.

**Why do the lungs contain tiny sacs?** The lungs are not like two big balloons. If they were, they would have only about 3 square feet (0.3 $m^2$) of surface area to gather oxygen. Instead, the lungs are spongy masses that have as many as 600 million tiny air sacs. Their total surface area in an adult is about 900 square feet (83 $m^2$). That is equal to the floor area of a square room with sides 30 feet (9 m) long!

Absorbing oxygen into the blood is a slow process. If the lungs were two balloons, you could not get oxygen into your blood fast enough to live. Neither could you get rid of the waste carbon dioxide fast enough. God knew this and wisely made your lungs with millions of small sacs that provide the needed surface area for oxygen to enter the blood and for carbon dioxide to come out.

## Study the Lesson

1. Your body needs ——— from the air to combine with the fuel in food that you eat.
2. A waste gas produced during respiration is ——— ———.
3. Put the names of these body parts in the order that air touches them in going to the lungs.

   bronchial tubes, nasal passages, tiny air sacs, nose, trachea
4. All the parts named in exercise 3 are part of your ——— system.
5. What two things do the nasal passages, trachea, and bronchial tubes do to the air on the way to the lungs?
6. The lungs are made of many small sacs to give
   a. much surface area for contact between the air and the blood.
   b. little possibility for the lungs to burst.
   c. more room for air than two large bags would give.
   d. a plentiful supply of sacs in case some become diseased.

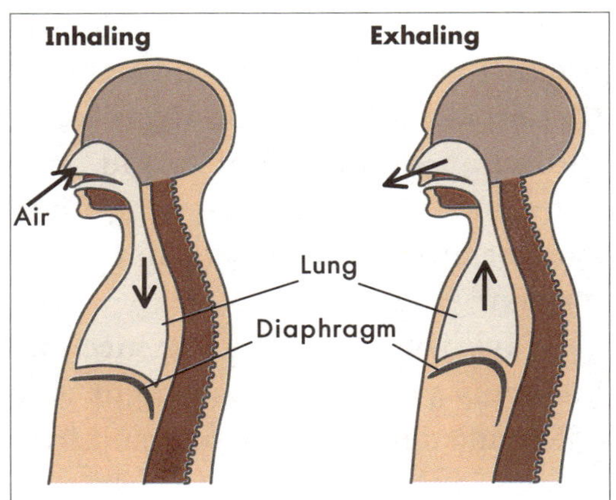


**What causes air to fill the lungs?** Below the lungs is a large sheet of muscle called the ***diaphragm.*** When the diaphragm contracts and pulls downward, the space containing the lungs becomes larger. This produces a slight vacuum, and air pushes down the trachea to fill the lungs.

When the muscles below the diaphragm squeeze the body, the diaphragm moves up and the air is exhaled from the lungs. During shallow breathing as you are probably doing right now, you force the air out simply by relaxing the diaphragm and letting the natural squeeze of the body do the pushing.

As the air leaves the trachea on the way out of the lungs, it passes through the larynx. If you bring together the two ***vocal cords*** in your larynx, the air moving between them will make them vibrate and produce sound. This is your voice, which makes it possible for you to talk and sing.

Your voice is a very special gift from God. Be careful to use this great gift only in ways that please God, who gave it.

**What controls your breathing?** You can decide when to exhale. You do this when you blow up a balloon or blow dust away. You can decide when to inhale. You can even decide to hold your breath for a while. But have you been deciding when to inhale and exhale all the time you were reading this lesson? Do you stop breathing when you go to sleep? If you were to stop breathing, you would stop living.

God knew that sometimes you need to control your breathing, so He gave you the ability to do that. He also knew that most of the time you need to breathe automatically. The part of your brain called the brain stem has a nerve center that controls the rate of breathing. It automatically tells the diaphragm when to contract and when to relax.

If you are sleeping or studying and do not need much oxygen, you breathe slowly. But if the oxygen level in your blood begins to drop, your brain stem automatically makes you start breathing faster. If your body needs a large amount of oxygen, it is very hard to control your breathing. You know how it is when you want to talk after you have run as fast as you can. You are out of breath, and your voice comes in uneven gasps. The control of your breathing is another wise plan for which you should praise God.

**One more wonder.** When you drink water, a small flap called the ***epiglottis*** goes shut just before the water reaches the top of your trachea. The water slides safely past, and the epiglottis opens to let you breathe again. Without the epiglottis, water and food would get into your lungs and make you sick. God did provide coughing to remove things that accidentally get into the trachea. But what a nuisance it would be to eat a meal and need to cough and sputter after every bite! Thank God for your epiglottis.

Have you ever had the hiccups? Suddenly your breath is caught with a jerk and a noise. Hiccups result from spasms in the diaphragm, which cause

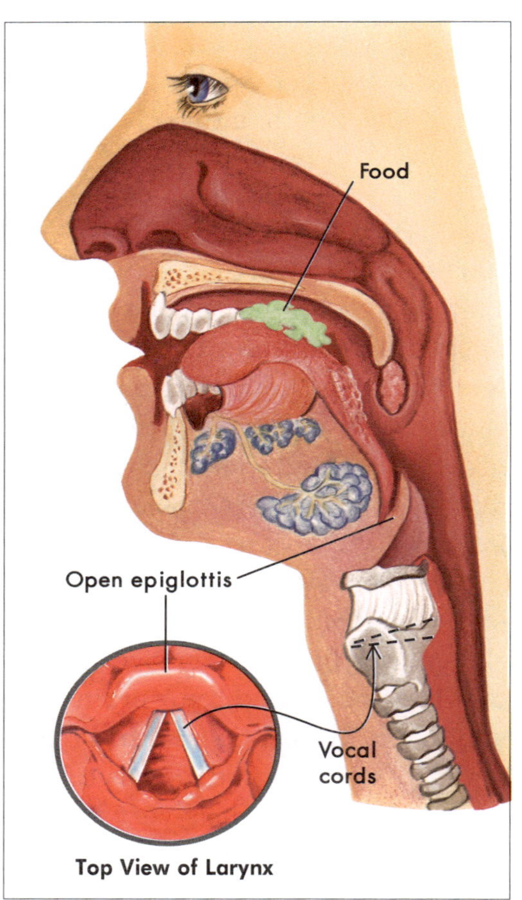

Food being chewed

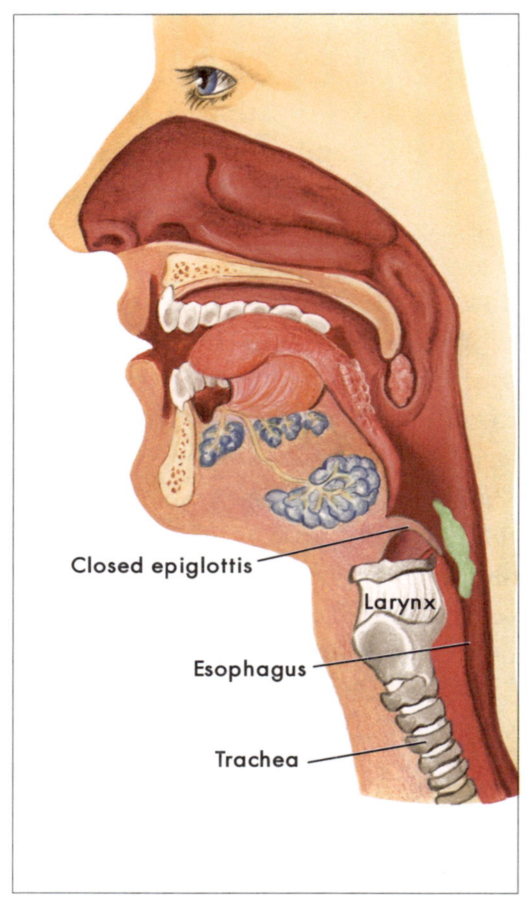


Food being swallowed

you to draw air suddenly into your lungs. When this happens, the epiglottis closes forcibly and you hear the sound of the hiccup.

One good cure for hiccups is to put a paper bag over your mouth and breathe in and out several times. This often stops the hiccups because it increases carbon dioxide in the air you breathe.

## Study the Lesson

7. Which statement best tells what causes air to fill your lungs?
   a. The nose forces air down the trachea.
   b. The lungs expand and push the diaphragm down.
   c. The bronchial tubes swell to make greater volume.
   d. The diaphragm causes the lung space to expand.
8. For normal speaking, you must breathe (in, out) and (bring together, separate) your vocal cords.
9. Write words to complete this sentence: We should be careful to use our voices only in ways that...
10. A nerve center in the brain stem keeps you breathing even when you are ———, and it causes you to breathe ——— when you run.
11. What valuable job does the epiglottis do for you?
12. What is a possible cure for hiccups?

## Review Exercises

1. In a telephone, the ——— changes the varying current into a sound like the speaker's voice. [30]
2. The law of thermodynamics states that energy always moves from a ——— level to a ——— level. [22]
3. An animal that kills and eats other animals is (carnivorous, herbivorous, omnivorous). [19]
4. In many plants, sugar is changed to ——— and stored in some part of the plant. [17]
5. The axis of Uranus is almost (level, vertical) in relation to its orbit. [9]
6. The best displays of aurora borealis, also called ——— ———, occur during times of (many, few) sunspots. [2]

## Apply the Lesson

1. Test your breath for carbon dioxide. Get a clear glass, and fill it halfway with limewater. (Directions for making limewater are given in the teacher's guide.) Use a straw to blow your breath into the limewater for one minute. What change do you see in it? This is the chemical test for carbon dioxide.
2. How much air can your lungs hold? Fill a gallon jug completely with water. While holding the water in with your hand, turn it upside down so that the opening is in a tub of water. Insert the end of a two-foot piece of tubing into the mouth of the jug. Take as big a breath as you can, and blow it out as completely as you can through the tubing. Remove the tubing, cover the mouth of the jug with your hand, and set it upright. Pour the leftover water into a measuring cup, and subtract that amount from one gallon. The result is your lung capacity.
3. Observe the automatic change in your rate of breathing. Count the number of breaths you make in one minute while sitting quietly after studying. Then run as fast as you can to the edge of the schoolyard and back, and count the breaths per minute. How long does it take for your breathing to return to its quiet rate?
4. Learn to perform the abdominal thrust to help a person who is choking on food lodged in the trachea. Stand behind the person with your arms around his waist. Place your fist against the person's stomach just below the ribs. Hold your fist with your other hand, and give three hard thrusts upward and inward. Your hands and arms should be just at the bottom of the ribs and should slip up under them as you pull back. If the maneuver is successful, it will dislodge whatever is in his throat, and he will be able to breathe again.

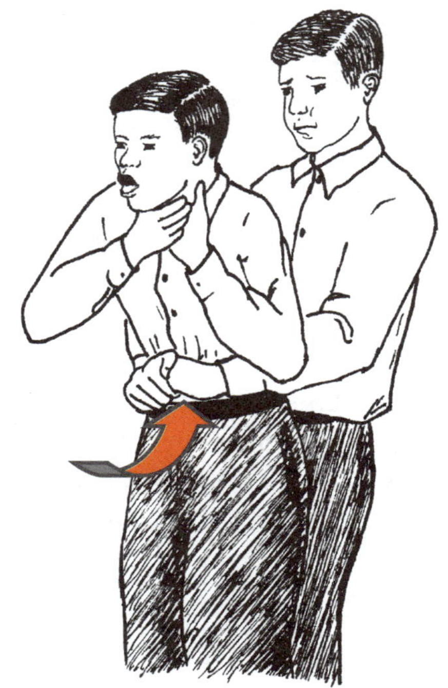

## Lesson 34

# Your Digestive System

"An hungry man dreameth, and, behold, he eateth; but he awaketh, and his soul is empty" (Isaiah 29:8).

### Vocabulary

**absorption,** the receiving of dissolved materials into the blood.

**digestive system,** the body system that includes the stomach and intestines, by which food is changed into a material that dissolves.

**enzyme** (en′·zīm), a chemical that causes digestion.

**esophagus** (i·sof′·ə·gəs), a tube with muscles to move food to the stomach.

**fiber,** the material in food that will not digest.

**gastric juice,** the liquid added in the stomach to digest food.

**large intestine,** the tube where undigested food is stored to be passed out of the body.

**saliva** (sə·lī′·və), the watery fluid in the mouth that starts the digestion of food.

**small intestine,** the tube where enzymes are added to food and where dissolved food is absorbed through villi.

**villi** (vil′·ī), small fingerlike parts in the small intestine, which absorb food.

God gave your body an appetite for food so that you will eat what your body needs. Hunger is very real, and just dreaming about food or looking at pictures of food does not satisfy the body.

How terrible it would be if you were hungry and there were no food in your environment! But the earth is well supplied with a great variety of foods. God told Noah, "Every moving thing that liveth shall be meat for you; even as the green herb have I given you all things" (Genesis 9:3). Fruits, grains, vegetables, fish, cattle, poultry, milk, and eggs provide many different foods with good flavors and all the materials our bodies need to be healthy. The study of food is very interesting, and it shows God's love and wisdom in providing for our physical needs.

**Food must be dissolved.** The food you eat enters the bloodstream after

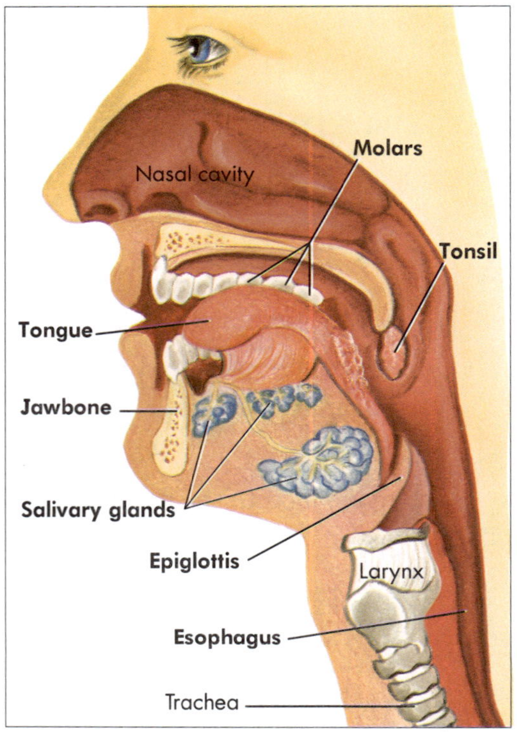

The upper digestive system

digestion. Blood carries the food to all parts of your body. However, your blood does not carry potatoes, corn, and meat in their normal state. These foods must first be dissolved. How long do you think it would take to dissolve a piece of bread? It would rot before it dissolved. Sugar is about the only food you eat that dissolves without the help of digestion.

Digestion is the process of dissolving food so that it can be taken into the bloodstream. The part of your body that digests food is called the ***digestive system.*** Digestion is the breaking of food into small pieces and dissolving it with chemicals.

Digestion begins in the mouth, where the teeth grind food into small pieces. The tongue pushes the food between the teeth, and the teeth break and crush it. This crushing is done mainly by the molars, which are several flat teeth toward the back of the jaw. The better the food is ground, the better the chemicals can do their work of digestion.

The first chemical your body adds to food is ***saliva.*** Glands in the upper and lower jaws produce saliva. It is mostly water, which softens the food and helps it to slide easily down the throat.

Saliva also contains an enzyme that starts the digestive process. An ***enzyme*** is a chemical that causes digestion. The enzyme in saliva changes starch into sugar that can be taken into the bloodstream. Starch is the food material in bread, cereal, crackers, potatoes, and cakes. Digestion begins in the mouth when food is chewed and mixed with saliva.

**Chewed food travels to the stomach.** Digestion is not completed in the mouth. Many foods are not affected by the enzyme in saliva. After chewing, you swallow the food and it goes down a tube called the ***esophagus.*** The esophagus has muscles in its walls. The muscles tighten behind the food to push it down. At the bottom of the esophagus, the food enters the stomach.

The stomach does three things for your body. (1) It stores food so that you can eat an entire meal in a short time. (2) It adds enzymes called ***gastric juices*** that dissolve many kinds of food. The gastric juices are much stronger than saliva. (3) The walls of the stomach have muscles that squeeze the food back and forth to mix it well with the gastric juices. The work of the stomach goes on long after you leave the table.

## Study the Lesson

1. Before the food you eat can do your body any good, it must be ———.
2. The process of changing food so that it can be absorbed by the body is called ———.
3. What is one kind of food that the body can use without digestion?
4. What do molars do to the food to help with digestion?
5. Name the chemicals described.
   a. Any chemical that helps to digest food.
   b. A watery solution added to food in the mouth to begin digesting starch.
   c. A strong digestive liquid added to food in the stomach.
6. What are three things that the stomach does for you?

**Partly dissolved food enters the intestines.** From the stomach, the food goes a little at a time into the ***small intestine.*** This tube is called small because it is only about one inch in diameter. But it is about 20 feet long! The walls of the small intestine have muscles like those in the esophagus, which move the food forward by squeezing.

In the first part of the intestine, other strong enzymes are added to digest the carbohydrates, proteins, and fats. Fats are the hardest to digest. That is why you should avoid eating many fatty foods, especially when you have stomach or intestinal problems.

Enzymes in saliva, gastric juices, and intestinal juices dissolve most of the food and prepare it to enter the bloodstream. Already in the stomach, some of the dissolved food goes into the blood. But most of the dissolved food enters the bloodstream in the small intestine.

**Dissolved food is absorbed.** Food enters the bloodstream as the blood flows through very small blood vessels. These blood vessels cannot have openings in them, or the blood would leak out. Then how does the food get into the bloodstream?

Dissolved food enters the blood by a process called ***absorption.*** Very slowly, dissolved food soaks into the blood through the walls of the tiny blood vessels. Absorption is so slow that a large area is needed for the body to get enough food and water. This is the same problem that God solved in the lungs by making them with millions of tiny air sacs.

In the small intestine, God made millions of ***villi*** to absorb food. The villi stick out like tiny fingers from the walls of the intestines. Tiny blood vessels in the villi bring the blood close to the dissolved food. Slowly the food and water are absorbed into the blood. The millions of tiny villi give a much greater surface area than if the intestinal walls were smooth.

**Undissolved food is stored.** God did not give you enzymes to digest everything in the food you eat. Fruits and vegetables have tough cell walls that your body cannot digest. Sometimes this indigestible material is called ***fiber.*** The lack of an enzyme to digest fiber is not a mistake on God's part. Your intestines need fiber to help keep them healthy. If you eat plenty of fruits and vegetables, your digestive system will get all the fiber it needs.

After the undigested material leaves the small intestine, it enters the ***large intestine.*** This intestine has a larger diameter than the small intestine. Here more water is removed from the food, and what is left is stored to be passed out of the body.

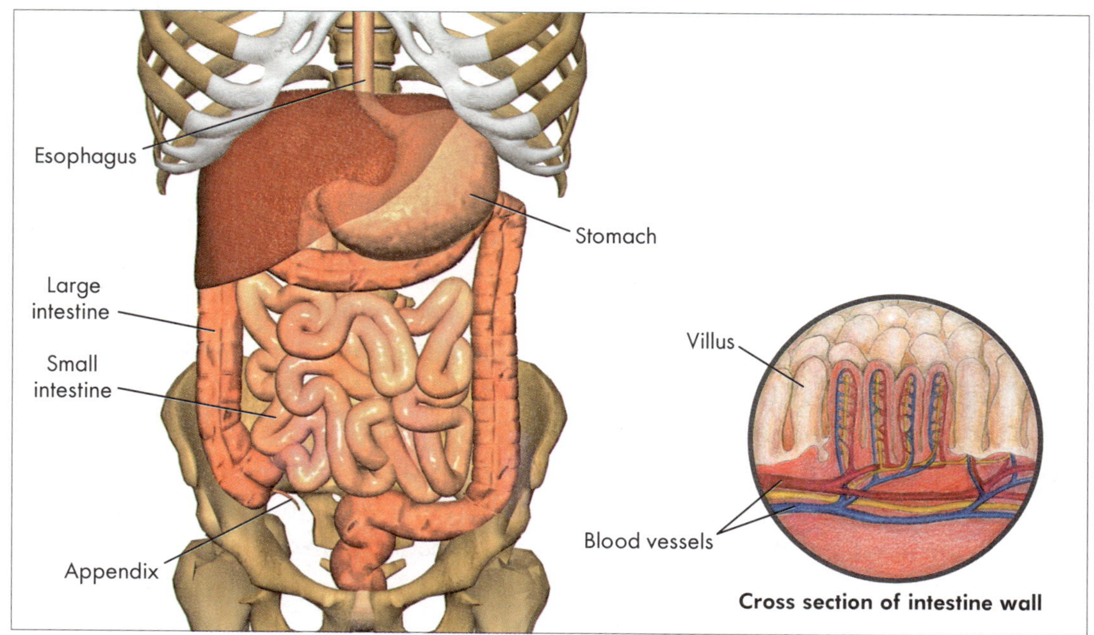


The lower digestive system. The large intestine is sometimes called an upside-down horseshoe that fits over the small intestine.

**Be a good steward of your digestive system.** A healthy digestive system is a gift from God. Take time to eat, and chew your food thoroughly so the enzymes can digest the food easily. Eat a variety of foods, including fruits and vegetables with plenty of fiber for the health of the large intestine. Avoid unkind words and actions at mealtime. Nervous tension makes it hard for the digestive system to work properly. Do not overeat, and do not load your system with hard-to-digest fatty foods. The Bible condemns the glutton. He not only is wasteful but also abuses his own body.

This magnified section of small intestine clearly shows the fingerlike shape of villi.

God intends that we enjoy the food we eat. One of His witnesses to man is "fruitful seasons, filling our hearts with food and gladness" (Acts 14:17). But God did not give us an appetite just to have the pleasure of eating. He made nourishing food, and He gave us a digestive system to help our bodies use the food we eat. The next time you thank God for your food, think about the wonders of the food and of your body that uses it to stay alive.

## Study the Lesson

7. Name the part of the digestive system that each description refers to.
   a. A long, narrow tube where most of the food is absorbed into the blood.
   b. A tube with muscles that push the food toward the stomach.
   c. A wider tube that stores undigested food after it leaves the small intestine.
   d. A bag-shaped organ between the esophagus and the small intestine.
8. The purpose of the villi is
   a. to move the food through the small intestine.
   b. to make a large surface area for absorbing food.
   c. to give off a digestive enzyme in the small intestine.
   d. to slow down the flow of food through the small intestine.
9. Tough, indigestible material in food is sometimes called ———.
10. What two things does the large intestine do with undigested food?

11. Write the missing words to make good health rules.
    a. Eat slowly, and ——— your food thoroughly.
    b. Eat plenty of foods that give the large intestine enough ———.
    c. Avoid ——— words and actions at mealtime.
    d. Avoid eating too much, as a ——— does.
    e. Do not load your system with ——— ———, which are hard to digest.
12. Find *glutton* in a Bible concordance. Write the reference of a verse in Proverbs that condemns the glutton.

## Review Exercises

1. In an electric motor, a moving electromagnet called the ——— turns as it is attracted or repelled by the ——— ———. [29]
2. Name in order the four strokes of a four-cycle gasoline engine. [24]
3. An animal that feeds on plants and other animals is (carnivorous, herbivorous, omnivorous). [19]
4. In the oxygen cycle, people and animals breathe out ——— ———, which plants use, and plants give off ———, which people and animals breathe. [15]
5. The location of Neptune was predicted by the use of ———. [9]
6. Mercury is ——— on one side and ——— on the other because it rotates very slowly. [7]

## Apply the Lesson

1. You can taste the evidence of an enzyme at work. Take a bite from a saltine cracker, and chew it thoroughly. Notice how it begins to taste sweet after a while. This happens because the enzyme in your saliva is changing the starch into sugar.
2. You can also see the evidence of an enzyme at work. Collect about 1/3 test tube of saliva. Several students can spit into different test tubes and then pour their saliva together. Prepare some starch by adding ½ teaspoon of cornstarch to ½ cup (120 ml) of water. Boil this mixture for 5 minutes, and let it cool to body temperature.

   The enzyme in saliva will work only on cooked starch. Put ½ inch of the boiled starch into each of two test tubes. Add ¼ inch of saliva to only one of the test tubes, and shake them both. Set the test tubes in warm water for 15 minutes, and then test each mixture with Fehling's (fā′·lingz) solution. If it turns red or yellow, it contains sugar. Which test tube has sugar? Which does not have sugar? What is the reason for the difference?

## Lesson 35

# Your Circulatory System

"But now, O LORD, thou art our father; we are the clay, and thou our potter; and we all are the work of thy hand" (Isaiah 64:8).

### Vocabulary

**artery,** a blood vessel that carries blood away from the heart.

**auricle** (ôr′·i·kəl), a receiving chamber of the heart.

**capillary** (kap′·ə·lar′·ē), a tiny blood vessel with walls one cell thick.

**circulatory system** (sûr′·kyə·lə·tôr′·ē), the body system that includes the heart and blood vessels, by which blood is circulated through the body.

**plasma** (plaz′·mə), the yellowish water solution of the blood.

**pulse,** the change of blood pressure that shows the heartbeat.

**red corpuscle** (kôr′·pə·səl), a red blood cell, which carries oxygen to the body cells and carries waste carbon dioxide away.

**vein,** a blood vessel that carries blood back to the heart.

**ventricle** (ven′·tri·kəl), a pumping chamber of the heart.

**white corpuscle** (kôr′·pə·səl), a white blood cell, which fights germs.

This year you have learned about wonders in the heavens. You have seen wonders in the way God made the earth. In this unit you have been studying wonders in your own body. Everything is the work of God's hand, and it is a wonderful work indeed!

Your body is made of millions of cells. Every cell must have food and oxygen to live. What carries food from the small intestine to each cell? What carries oxygen from the lungs to each cell? And what carries the waste materials away from each cell? God gave you a ***circulatory system*** to do these things so that you can live. The circulatory system circulates blood through all parts of the body.

**"The blood is the life"** (Deuteronomy 12:23). God created the blood as a wonderful liquid to carry food and oxygen to every living cell in the body. You have seen the red blood flowing out of a cut or scratch. Blood is a mixture of water and cells that makes an ideal carrier for the materials needed to keep your cells alive. If you weigh about 80 pounds, your body has about two and one-half quarts of this precious liquid. Adults have about five quarts of blood.

A little over half of the blood is a yellowish water solution called ***plasma.*** Dissolved food enters the bloodstream from the villi of the small intestine. Plasma distributes the food, along with salt and other minerals, to cells throughout the body. One of the minerals is calcium, which is needed for your blood to clot when you are bleeding. Plasma also carries waste materials from the cells to the kidneys, where the wastes are removed.

Slightly less than half of your blood is made of red corpuscles that float freely in the plasma. The ***red corpuscles*** are disk-shaped cells that carry oxygen from the lungs to the cells of your body. They then carry the waste carbon dioxide back to be given off in the lungs. To do their job, red corpuscles contain a protein called hemoglobin (hē′·mə·glō′·bin). This red iron compound is what gives blood its red color. An average adult has about 25 trillion red corpuscles. Sometimes a person looks pale because he does not have enough red corpuscles. Why do you think doctors tell such persons to eat foods rich in iron?

***White corpuscles*** are another kind of cells in your blood. They are larger than red corpuscles, but your blood has only about one white corpuscle for every 700 red corpuscles. The white corpuscles do the very important job of fighting germs. As you learned, the skin is very good at keeping germs out of the body. But some germs do get in through injuries to your skin, the air you breathe, and the food you eat. The white corpuscles kill most of these germs before they make you sick. If you do get sick, the white corpuscles fight the germs so that you can get well. God created the white corpuscles as His way of healing many diseases.

The red corpuscles can be likened to tank trucks hauling oxygen to the cells and taking carbon dioxide away. But the white corpuscles can be likened to fire trucks running here and there to get rid of things that

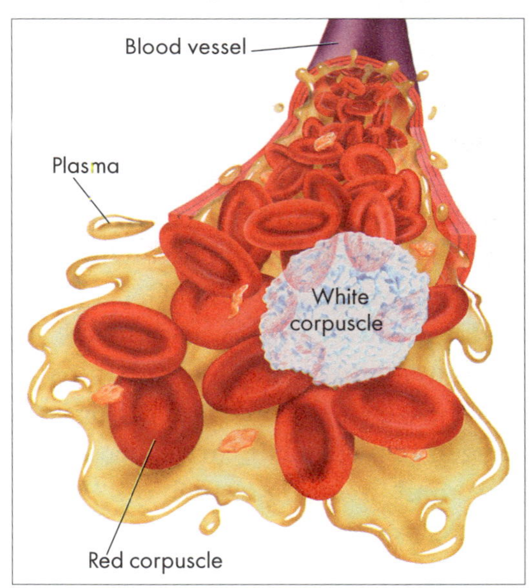

would harm the body. The blood both supports life and protects life. "The blood is the life." Without it, we would die.

**The heart circulates the blood.** The heart is the pump of the circulatory system, and the blood vessels are the pipes that carry blood to all parts of your body. Let us look first at the heart.

Your heart is a muscle about the size of your fist, with four hollow chambers inside. When the heart muscle contracts, it squeezes blood out. When the muscle relaxes, blood flows into the heart. The heart usually beats more than 60 times a minute to pump the blood. This makes the blood vessels swell, or ***pulse.*** When a doctor holds your wrist to check your pulse, he is finding the rate of your heartbeat by counting the number of swellings he feels per minute.

To make the blood flow in the right direction, the heart has one-way valves. These valves open to let the blood flow out when the heart contracts, but they close tightly to keep the blood from flowing backward. Two valves let blood flow into the heart, and two valves let it flow out.

The lower two chambers of the heart that do the pumping are called ***ventricles.*** Above the ventricles are receiving chambers called ***auricles.***

The heart is actually two pumps in one. There are two auricles and two ventricles. The right ventricle pumps blood to the lungs. The blood that comes back from the lungs goes to the left auricle and then into the left ventricle. The left ventricle pumps the blood out to all the other parts of the body. The blood that comes back from the body goes to the right auricle and then to the right ventricle to start its circulation over again. With two ventricles and two auricles, you have a four-chambered heart.

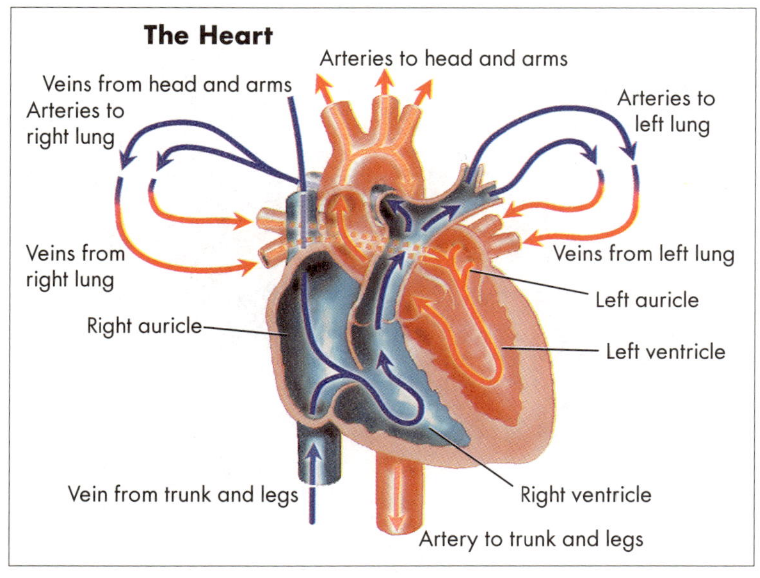

## Study the Lesson

1. Why are the heart, blood, and blood vessels called the circulatory system?
2. Name the parts of the blood that do the following things for the life of your cells.
   a. Carrying food and minerals from the small intestine to each cell.
   b. Carrying oxygen from the lungs to each cell.
   c. Carrying carbon dioxide from each cell to the lungs.
   d. Carrying dissolved wastes from each cell to the kidneys.
3. Name the part of the blood that each phrase describes.
   a. Disk-shaped cells containing hemoglobin.
   b. Yellowish water solution.
   c. Cells that fight germs.
   d. Makes up over half of the blood.
   e. Contain an iron compound.
4. What is meant by the statement, "The blood is the life"?
5. What does a doctor find when he checks your pulse?
6. Because the heart is a ———, it can contract to pump the blood.
7. The heart has ——— to keep the blood flowing in the right direction.
8. Name the four chambers of the heart.

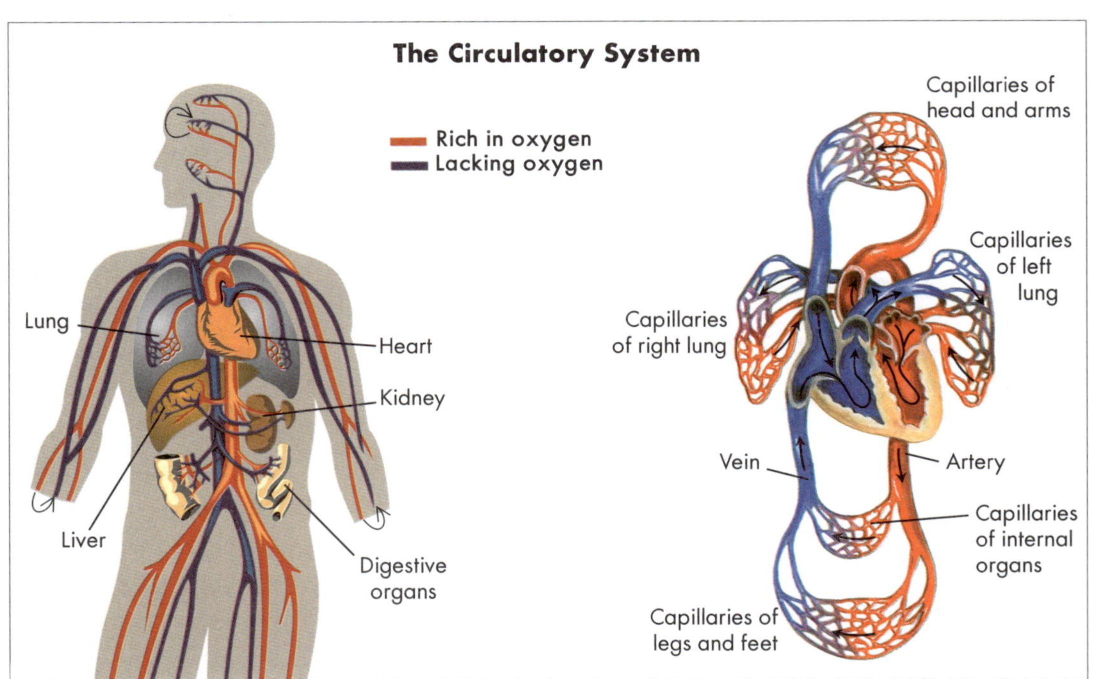

**Blood vessels carry the blood.** Blood leaving the ventricles of the heart is under pressure. Doctors use an instrument that squeezes the arm to measure the blood pressure. The blood vessels carrying blood away from the heart are called ***arteries,*** and they have tough walls to withstand the pressure. (You feel the changing pressure in an artery when you check your pulse.) One set of arteries carries blood to the lungs, and one set carries blood to other parts of the body.

The blood vessels carrying blood back to the heart are called ***veins.*** Since this blood has lost most of its pressure, the veins have thinner walls than the arteries. Some of the veins have one-way valves that let the blood flow only toward the heart.

How does the blood get from the arteries to the veins? The arteries and veins connected to the heart have a big diameter. They branch into smaller and smaller vessels leading to all parts of the body. Finally the vessels join a network of very tiny tubes called ***capillaries.*** The capillaries are so small that blood cells go through them one by one. The walls of the capillaries are only one cell thick. Food, oxygen, and wastes leave and enter the blood through the thin walls.

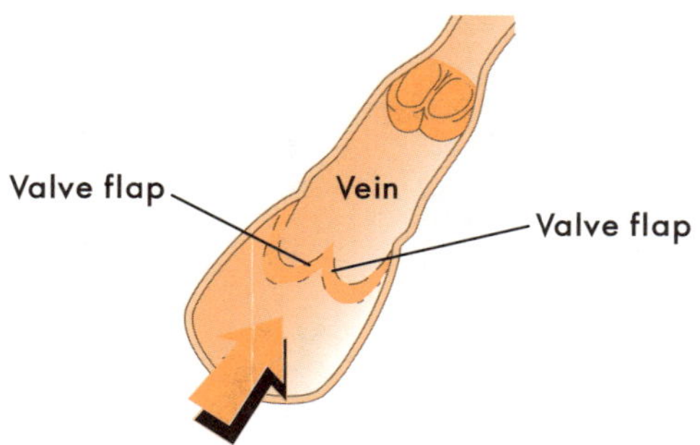


The valve in a vein consists of two flaps to let the blood through one way. If the vein swells so much that the flaps do not touch each other, blood can leak backward. This results in poor circulation and varicose veins.

The capillaries come close to every living cell in the body. There is no part of the dermis where you would not bleed from capillaries being cut. The tiny sacs of the lungs are surrounded with capillaries. The villi of the small intestine have a network of capillaries close to the surface. The capillaries bring life-giving blood to the living cells in the body.

**The circuit of the blood.** In one complete circuit, the blood goes through a double loop of blood vessels. First, the blood goes to the lungs and comes back to the heart. Next, it goes out to the body, passing through smaller and smaller arteries until it reaches the capillaries. Then it enters the veins and comes back to the heart.

Around and around the blood travels, bringing food and oxygen to the cells and carrying waste materials away. The circulatory system is like a trucking company. The blood is like the trucks, and the arteries and veins are like the interstate highways. The capillaries are like the country roads and streets.

Unlike the trucking company, you do not pay for the service of your circulatory system—or of the other body systems. God gave you these systems because you need them to live. Your body belongs to God, and you are a steward of it. A steward takes care of what belongs to someone else. So you must take good care of your body and use it only in ways that please God.

God created all the systems that work together to make your body the wonder that it is. You can say with David, "I will praise thee; for I am fearfully and wonderfully made: marvellous are thy works" (Psalm 139:14).

## Study the Lesson

9. Name the part of the circulatory system that each description refers to.
   a. A pumping chamber of the heart.
   b. A blood vessel that carries blood away from the heart.
   c. A network of tiny blood vessels that bring blood to every cell.
   d. A blood vessel that carries blood back to the heart.
   e. A receiving chamber of the heart.
10. Which blood vessels have
    a. strong, heavy walls?
    b. thin walls and one-way valves?
    c. walls that are one cell thick?
11. Which diagram shows the blood circulation correctly?

a. 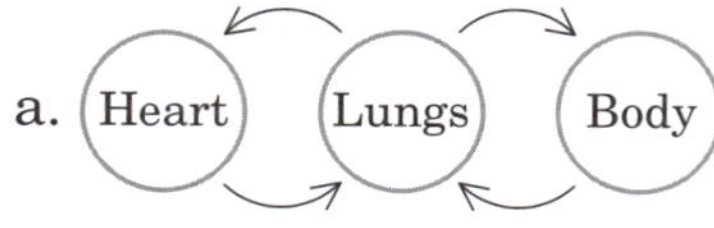


c. 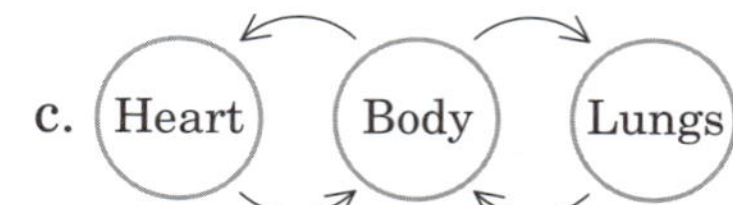


b. 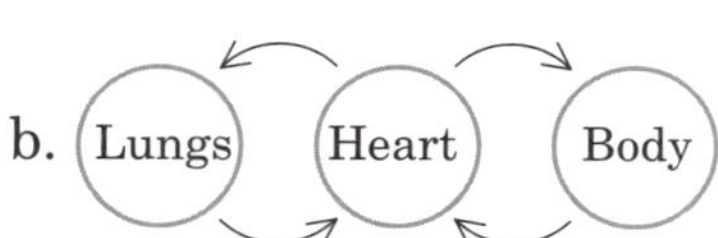


d. 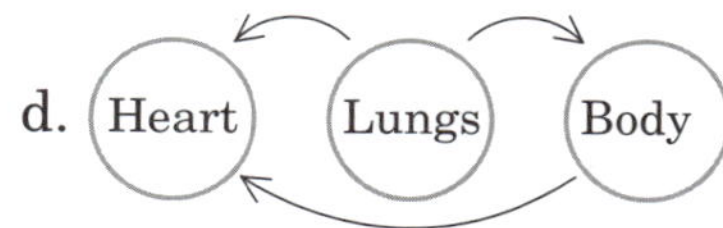


12. How does the blood from the arteries get to the veins?
13. The work of the circulatory system is most like the work of
    a. a telephone company.
    b. an electric company.
    c. a manufacturing company.
    d. a trucking company.
14. How did all the wonders of the body come to be the way they are?
15. You are a ——— of your body, since it really belongs to God.

## Review Exercises

1. What are the two laws of magnetism by which all electric motors operate? [29]
2. What three things are needed for a gasoline engine to run? [24]
3. Carnivorous and herbivorous animals control each other's populations, and this produces a ——— of ———. (Write the whole phrase.) [20]
4. Plants called ——— build up nitrogen compounds in the soil through a process called ——— ———. [15]
5. Sometimes the superior planets appear to move backward in relation to the stars. This is called ——— motion. [9]
6. Venus rotates ——— on its axis, which cannot be explained by evolution. [7]

## Apply the Lesson

1. Look at blood through a microscope. Prick the end of your finger with a pin that has been sterilized with alcohol. Touch a clean microscope slide against the blood that comes from the pinprick. Cover the spot of blood with a cover glass. Place the slide under a microscope, and focus it on the blood. This will let you see the red corpuscles. What shape do they have? What color? Are any of them clumped together? Can you count the ones you see?
2. Check your own pulse. The arteries are deeper than the veins. The veins are what you see on the back of your hand. You will need to press deeply to feel the pulse of the arteries. With your left hand turned down, use the fingers of your right hand to feel the pulse on the underside of the left wrist. Count the number of pulses in one minute. What does this tell you? Also try to check your pulse by feeling the side of your neck, just below the angle of your jawbone.

## Lesson 36

# Unit 7 Review

## A. Vocabulary

Write the letter of the correct word for each meaning. You will not use all the letters.

1. Ability to receive some kind of stimulus.
2. Receiving of dissolved materials into the blood.
3. System that changes food into a material that dissolves.
4. Change of blood pressure that shows the heartbeat.
5. System that takes in oxygen and gives off carbon dioxide.
6. Chemical that causes digestion.
7. Action performed because of a stimulus.
8. System that carries food and oxygen and removes wastes.
9. Anything that can cause one to make a response.
10. Body part that receives stimuli.
11. System that includes the brain and a network of thin cords.

a. absorption
b. circulatory system
c. digestive system
d. enzyme
e. nerve
f. nervous system
g. pulse
h. respiratory system
i. response
j. sense
k. sense organ
l. stimulus

12. Skin layer with nerve endings and blood vessels.
13. Area in the head that warms and cleans air.
14. Tube with muscles to move food to the stomach.
15. Organ that adds enzymes and removes food through villi.
16. Blood vessel that carries blood back to the heart.
17. Tiny blood vessel with walls one cell thick.
18. Stiff-walled air passage in the throat.
19. One of the smaller passages that carry air to the lungs.
20. Material in food that will not digest.
21. Blood vessel that carries blood away from the heart.
22. Outer skin layer made of tough, dead cells.

a. artery
b. bronchial tube
c. capillary
d. dermis
e. epidermis
f. esophagus
g. fiber
h. large intestine
i. nasal passages
j. small intestine
k. trachea
l. vein

23. Blood cell that carries oxygen.
24. Sheet of muscle for bringing air into the lungs.
25. Watery fluid that starts digestion in the mouth.
26. Pumping chamber of the heart.
27. Source of sound for speaking.
28. Small fingerlike parts that absorb food.
29. Flap that closes the top of the trachea in swallowing.
30. Blood cell that fights germs.
31. Receiving chamber of the heart.
32. Liquid added in the stomach to digest food.
33. Yellowish water solution of the blood.

a. auricle
b. diaphragm
c. epiglottis
d. gastric juice
e. gland
f. plasma
g. red corpuscle
h. saliva
i. ventricle
j. villi
k. vocal cords
l. white corpuscle

## B. Facts

Write the words that belong in the blanks.

1. A person who has ——— loses the sense of touch in the affected areas.
2. The ——— is renewed about once every two months because the surface cells are constantly flaking off and being replaced.
3. Washing the skin helps to get rid of germs and to avoid an unpleasant body ———.
4. The air coming out of the lungs has more ——— ——— than the air going in.
5. The nasal passages both ——— and ——— the air before it goes into the lungs.
6. You should use your voice to sing or say things that please ———.
7. In the mouth, the food is broken and crushed by the ———.
8. Digestion begins in the mouth when an enzyme in ——— turns starch into sugar.
9. To help keep the large intestine healthy, you should eat food that has plenty of ———.
10. You should not eat much food rich in ——— because it is hard to digest.
11. Avoid ——— talk at mealtime so that the digestive system can do its job.
12. You have a heart with ——— (how many?) chambers.
13. The ——— ——— have a material containing iron that can carry much oxygen and carbon dioxide.
14. You should take good care of your body because God made you a ——— of it.

## C. Concepts

Choose the letter of the best answer in each exercise.

1. Which of these is a stimulus?
   a. The calling of your name by your mother.
   b. Raising your hand to answer a question.
   c. The ability to see in a poorly lighted room.
   d. One of the nerve endings in your skin.
2. Which of these is in the right order?
   a. sense organ, stimulus, brain, nerve
   b. stimulus, nerve, brain, sense organ
   c. stimulus, sense organ, nerve, brain
   d. sense organ, stimulus, brain, sense organ
3. The skin is a heat insulator because it has
   a. capillaries.
   b. sweat glands.
   c. nerve endings.
   d. fat.
4. Which statement is correct?
   a. The skin helps you get oxygen from your environment.
   b. The respiratory system gives something to and takes something from the blood.
   c. The digestive system carries materials to all parts of the body.
   d. The circulatory system prepares food for use by your cells.
5. Which of these is in the right order?
   a. nasal passages, tiny air sacs, trachea, bronchial tubes
   b. trachea, bronchial tubes, nasal passages, tiny air sacs
   c. trachea, tiny air sacs, nasal passages, bronchial tubes
   d. nasal passages, trachea, bronchial tubes, tiny air sacs
6. The lungs have many tiny sacs instead of one large sack because
   a. the tiny sacs help the lungs endure more pressure.
   b. the tiny sacs are easier to keep clean.
   c. the tiny sacs provide more surface area.
   d. the tiny sacs allow the lungs to hold more air.
7. The rate of breathing is automatically controlled by
   a. the brain stem.
   b. the diaphragm.
   c. the heart.
   d. the lungs.

8. Which of these does the stomach *not* do for the body?
   a. Adds enzymes to digest food.
   b. Stores food from a meal.
   c. Mixes food with enzymes.
   d. Stores food for passing out of body.
9. Which of these is in the right order?
   a. esophagus, small intestine, stomach, large intestine
   b. esophagus, stomach, small intestine, large intestine
   c. stomach, large intestine, esophagus, small intestine
   d. stomach, esophagus, large intestine, small intestine
10. When the pulse is checked, changes of pressure are felt in
    a. an artery.
    b. the capillaries.
    c. the heart.
    d. a vein.
11. Which of these does *not* have a network of capillaries?
    a. villi
    b. epidermis
    c. brain
    d. epiglottis
12. Which of these is in the right order?
    a. veins, arteries, heart, capillaries
    b. capillaries, heart, veins, arteries
    c. heart, veins, capillaries, arteries
    d. arteries, capillaries, veins, heart
13. The way the body is made is the result of
    a. many changes happening by chance.
    b. the planning of the one who lives in the body.
    c. the discoveries of science.
    d. the design of the One who owns the body.

## Lesson 37

# Final Review

Most of the exercises in this lesson come from the Review Exercises in this book. They will help you to prepare for the final test.

## Unit 1

1. The sun is a steady star and not a ——— star like Mira. [1]
2. How many earth diameters would it take to equal the diameter of the sun? [1]
3. Water must be in the ——— state for life to exist. [1]
4. The sun is about ——— miles away from the earth. [1]
5. The sun is made mostly of the elements ——— and ———. [2]
6. Heat and light travel through empty space by ———. [2]
7. Dark spots on the sun are called ———, and their number increases and decreases in a cycle of about ——— years. [2]
8. The sun produces its energy as particles of ——— unite to form ———. [2]
9. The best displays of aurora borealis, also called ——— ———, occur during times of (many, few) sunspots. [2]
10. The moon goes through one cycle of its ———, or different shapes, in ——— days. [3]
11. The gravity of the moon causes the ——— of the ocean. [3]
12. The moon is unsuitable for life because it has no ——— or ——— and because its temperature is both too ——— and too ———. [3]
13. A lunar eclipse occurs when the shadow of the ——— falls on the ———. [4]
14. A solar eclipse occurs when the shadow of the ——— falls on the ———. [4]
15. A solar eclipse is total when the size of the moon appears (equal to, smaller than) the size of the sun. [4]
16. A solar eclipse is annular when the size of the moon appears (equal to, smaller than) the size of the sun. [4]

## Unit 2

17. The orbits of the planets, and especially those of the comets, are in the shape of (a circle, an egg, an ellipse). [6]
18. The planets located inside the earth's orbit are called ——— planets. [7]
19. The closer a planet is to the sun, the (more slowly, more swiftly) it travels and the (shorter, longer) its year is. [7]

20. Mercury is hot on one side and cold on the other because it rotates very (slowly, swiftly). [7]
21. The atmosphere of Venus is mostly ——— ———, and it contains clouds of ——— ———. [7]
22. Venus rotates ——— on its axis, which cannot be explained by evolution. [7]
23. The axis of Mars is ———, which causes it to have ——— as the earth does. [8]
24. Between the orbits of Mars and Jupiter are thousands of small bodies called ———. [8]
25. Sometimes the superior planets appear to move backward in relation to the stars. This is called ——— motion. [9]
26. Four of Jupiter's ——— can be seen with a small telescope. [9]
27. Saturn is surrounded by beautiful ——— that look like a disk of gold. [9]
28. The axis of Uranus is almost (level, vertical) in relation to its orbit. [9]
29. The location of Neptune was predicted by the use of ———. [9]

## Unit 3

30. The earth's axis is tilted ——— degrees, and this causes the ——— of the earth. [11]
31. To be at a place that has sunshine at midnight, you would need to go north of the ——— ——— or south of the ——— ———. [11]
32. Water is called $H_2O$ because each molecule has two atoms of ——— and one atom of ———. [12]
33. Water moves upward through soil by a process called ——— ———. [12]
34. Four-fifths of the air is ———, and one-fifth is ———. [13]
35. The atmosphere protects the earth from most ———, which are speeding rocks from outer space. [13]
36. Almost what fraction of the earth is covered with water? [14]
37. The oceans help to make the surrounding land (warmer, colder) in winter and (warmer, cooler) in summer. [14]
38. A ——— is a movement of ocean water from one place to another. [14]
39. In the water cycle, water falls from clouds as ———, streams and rivers carry it to the ———, and then it ——— to form clouds again. [15]
40. In the oxygen cycle, people and animals breathe out ——— ———, which plants use, and plants give off ———, which people and animals breathe. [15]
41. Plants called ——— build up nitrogen compounds in the soil through a process called ——— ———. [15]

## Unit 4

42. In the process called ———, plants use ——— and ——— ——— in the presence of sunlight to make sugar. [17]
43. In many plants, sugar is changed to ——— and stored in some part of the plant. [17]
44. Dead plant materials improve the soil by decaying to form ———. [18]
45. A farmer may spread ——— to increase the nutrients in the soil, or he may spread ——— to improve the pH. [18]
46. An animal that feeds mostly on plants is (carnivorous, herbivorous, omnivorous). [19]
47. An animal that kills and eats other animals is (carnivorous, herbivorous, omnivorous). [19]
48. An animal that feeds on plants and other animals is (carnivorous, herbivorous, omnivorous). [19]
49. In the ——— ———, a small animal is eaten by a larger animal, and the larger animal is eaten by a still larger animal. [19]
50. Carnivorous and herbivorous animals control each other's populations, and this produces a ——— of ———. (Write the whole phrase.) [20]
51. The study of living things in relation to their surroundings is called ———. [20]

## Unit 5

52. The law of conservation of energy states that energy cannot be ——— or ———. [22]
53. The law of thermodynamics states that energy always moves from a ——— level to a ——— level. [22]
54. Energy in motion is (kinetic, potential) energy. [22]
55. Stored energy is (kinetic, potential) energy. [22]
56. Three sources of free energy are the ———, falling ———, and ———. [23]
57. What three things are needed for a gasoline engine to run? [24]
58. Name in order the four strokes of a four-cycle gasoline engine. [24]
59. Three things needed for any transportation are ———, ———, and ———. [25]

## Unit 6

60. Write words to complete this sentence: Electricity flows in a wire when the wire passes near a magnet and cuts the invisible... [27]
61. Electrical pressure is measured in ———. [27]

62. A circuit is ——— if it forms a complete path for electricity, and ——— if it does not. [28]
63. A ——— ——— protects a circuit from too much electrical current. [28]
64. In an electric motor, a moving electromagnet called the ——— turns as it is attracted or repelled by the ——— ———. [29]
65. What are the two laws of magnetism by which all electric motors operate? [29]
66. In a light bulb, the ——— glows white hot and produces light. [29]
67. In a telephone, the ——— changes the sound of the speaker's voice into a varying electrical current. [30]
68. In a telephone, the ——— changes the varying current into a sound like the speaker's voice. [30]

## Unit 7

69. For greater surface area, the lungs have millions of small ———, and the small intestine has millions of ———. [33, 34]
70. Blood cells called ——— ——— carry oxygen, and blood cells called ——— ——— fight germs. [35]
71. Name the four important body systems that you studied in Unit 7. [32–35]

# Glossary

This glossary lists the vocabulary words with their definitions, as used in this book. The numbers in brackets give the pages in the text.

**absorption,** the receiving of dissolved materials into the blood. [231]

**aileron** (ā′·lə·ron′), a flap used to raise or lower an airplane wing. [170]

**airfoil,** a device shaped to cause lift by reducing air pressure above it. [170]

**amplifier,** a device that strengthens a weak electrical current that carries a sound signal. [206]

**Antarctic Circle,** the boundary around the southern "land of the midnight sun." [79]

**aquifer** (ak′·wə·fər), a layer of broken rock or soil containing water. [87]

**Arctic Circle,** the boundary around the northern "land of the midnight sun." [79]

**arid** (ar′·id), the kind of climate that is so dry that few plants can grow. [79]

**armature,** the rotating electromagnet inside a motor. [199]

**artery,** a blood vessel that carries blood away from the heart. [237]

**asteroid** (as′·tə·roid′), one of the planet-like rocks between Mars and Jupiter. [59]

**atom,** the smallest possible particle of an element. [87]

**auricle** (ôr′·i·kəl), a receiving chamber of the heart. [237]

**aurora australis** (ə·rôr′·ə ô·strā′·lis), lights in the southern sky produced when the solar wind causes gases in the upper atmosphere to glow; also called *southern lights.* [18]

**aurora borealis** (ə·rôr′·ə bôr′·ē·al′·is), lights in the northern sky produced when the solar wind causes gases in the upper atmosphere to glow; also called *northern lights.* [18]

**bow** (bou), the front end of a ship. [170]

**brakes,** a set of devices that use friction to stop a car. [170]

**bridge,** a raised structure where navigators steer a ship. [170]

**bronchial tube** (brong′·kē·əl), one of the smaller tubes that carry air to the lungs. [224]

**buoyant force,** the upward push of water on a floating object. [170]

**capillary** (kap′·ə·lar′·ē), a tiny blood vessel with walls one cell thick. [237]

**capillary action** (kap′·ə·lar′·ē), the upward movement of water by making surfaces wet. [87]

**carbohydrate** (kär′·bō·hī′·drāt′), a sugar or starch, with two hydrogen atoms for each oxygen atom. [117]

**carnivorous** (kär·niv′·ər·əs), a kind of animal that kills other animals for food. [130]

**chlorophyll** (klôr′·ə·fil), the green material in plants that makes food when light shines on it. [117]

**chloroplast** (klôr′·ə·plast′), a small plate containing chlorophyll in a plant cell. [117]

**choke,** the device on an engine that blocks the airflow to increase fuel added to air. [163]

**circuit,** a circular path for electricity to follow. [190]

**circuit breaker,** a device that protects a circuit from too much electrical current. [190]

**circulatory system** (sûr′·kyə·lə·tôr′·ē), the body system that includes the heart and blood vessels, by which blood is circulated through the body. [237]

**climate,** the general weather of an area in a year. [79]

**clutch,** a device that disconnects the turning force of an engine from the wheels of a car. [170]

**combustion,** the burning of a material. [163]

**comet,** a small heavenly body traveling in a very oblong orbit, which forms a tail as it nears the sun. [46]

**commutator** (kom′·yə·tā′·tər), a special rotating switch on the armature of a motor. [199]

**compound,** a material made of more than one element. [87]

**conjunction,** the lining up of planets that makes them appear close together. [66]

**crankshaft,** a shaft that changes the up-and-down motion of pistons to rotary motion. [163]

**crater,** a bowl-shaped hole on the surface of the moon. [25]

**cultivation,** the action of breaking up the soil. [123]

**current,** a large stream of slowly moving ocean water. [101]

**current,** the flow of electricity. [183]

**cylinder,** in a gasoline engine, a round space with a piston moving up and down inside. [163]

**dam,** a barrier in a river that concentrates the energy in water by collecting it and raising its height. [156]

**dermis** (dûr′·mis), the second skin layer, containing nerve endings and blood vessels. [217]

**diaphragm** (dī′·ə·fram′), a thin disk that either receives or produces sound vibrations. [206]

**diaphragm** (dī′·ə·fram′), a sheet of muscle below the lungs, which contracts to bring in air. [224]

**differential,** a device that lets the two drive wheels of a car turn at different speeds. [170]

**digestive system,** the body system that includes the stomach and intestines, by which food is changed into a material that dissolves. [231]

**ecology** (i·kol′·ə·jē), the study of living things in relation to their surroundings. [136]

**electromagnet,** a magnet made by electricity flowing through a coil of wire. [183]

**electron,** one of the tiny particles that make up an electric current. [183]

**elevator,** a flap that makes an airplane fly higher or lower. [170]

**ellipse** (i·lips′), the oblong, circular shape of the orbits of planets. [46]

**energy,** the ability to make something move or change. [149]

**environment,** all the things and conditions around a living thing. [136]

**enzyme** (en′·zīm), a chemical that causes digestion. [231]

**epidermis** (ep′·i·dûr′·mis), the outer skin layer made of tough, dead cells. [217]

**epiglottis** (ep′·i·glot′·is), the flap that closes the top of the trachea in swallowing. [224]

**esophagus** (i·sof′·ə·gəs), a tube with muscles to move food to the stomach. [231]

**exhaust valve,** a valve that lets burned gases out of a cylinder of a gasoline engine. [163]

**fertile** (fûr′·təl), rich in the nutrients needed by plants. [123]

**fiber,** the material in food that will not digest. [231]

**field magnets,** stationary magnets inside a motor. [199]

**filament** (fil′·ə·mənt), a thin wire that glows with light when electricity flows through it. [199]

**fluorescent** (flo͝o·res′·ənt), the kind of light given by electricity flowing through vapors. [199]

**food chain,** the passing of food from one living thing to another. [130]

**fresh water,** water that is not salty like the ocean. [87]

**fuel injector,** a device that mixes fuel with air for a gasoline engine. [163]

**gastric juice,** the liquid added in the stomach to digest food. [231]

**gland,** a body part that produces a substance needed by the body. [217]

**gravity,** the pull between heavenly bodies. [46]

**growing season,** the time between the last frost in spring and the first frost in fall. [79]

**heating element,** a wire that makes heat in an appliance. [199]

**helium** (hē′·lē·əm), a very light gas; an element first discovered on the sun. [18]

**herbivorous** (hûr·biv′·ər·əs), a kind of animal that eats plants for food. [130]

**host,** the source of a parasite's food. [136]

**humus** (hyōō′·məs), decayed plant and animal material in the soil. [123]

**hydroelectric,** the kind of power produced when water turns a generator. [156]

**hydroponics** (hī′·drə·pon′·iks), a method of growing plants without soil. [123]

**incandescent** (in′·kən·des′·ənt), the kind of light given from a filament that glows with heat. [199]

**induction,** the method of making current flow by moving a wire through a magnetic field. [183]

**inertia,** the force that keeps a moving object traveling in a straight path. [46]

**inferior planet,** one of the planets (Mercury and Venus) that orbit the sun inside the earth's orbit. [52]

**infrared** (in′·frə·red′), the kind of rays that produce heat. [95]

**intake valve,** a valve that lets the fuel–air mixture into a cylinder of a gasoline engine. [163]

**jet propulsion,** a forward push from gases rushing backward. [170]

**kinetic energy,** energy in motion. [149]

**large intestine,** the tube where undigested food is stored to be passed out of the body. [231]

**law of conservation of energy,** the fact that energy cannot be created or destroyed. [149]

**law of thermodynamics,** the fact that energy moves from a higher level to a lower level. [149]

**legume** (leg′·yōōm′), a plant that puts nitrogen compounds into the soil. [107]

**lichen** (lī′·kən), a scaly growth on rocks, consisting of a fungus and algae. [136]

**light-emitting diode** (dī′·ōd′), a small light that uses a tiny amount of electricity. [199]

**loudspeaker,** a device that changes electricity into sounds. [206]

**lunar** (lōō′·nər), of the moon. [31]

**lunar eclipse** (i·klips′), the darkening of the moon by the shadow of the earth. [31]

**magnetic field,** the area of magnetic force around a magnet. [183]

**magnetosphere** (mag·nē′·tō·sfir′), the magnetic region above the atmosphere that protects the earth from the solar wind. [95]

**mesosphere** (mez′·ə·sfir′), the layer of the atmosphere where rocks from space become meteors and burn up. [95]

**meteor,** a streak of light caused by a speeding rock from space as it enters the earth's atmosphere. [59]

**meteorite,** a rock from space that strikes the earth's surface. [59]

**microphone,** a mouthpiece for a loudspeaking system. [206]

**molecule,** the smallest possible particle still having the properties of a substance. [87]

**nasal passages,** the passages in the head where incoming air is warmed and cleaned. [224]

**nerve,** a thin cord that carries messages to or from the brain. [217]

**nervous system,** the body system that includes the brain, spinal cord, and nerves, by which the actions of the body are controlled. [217]

**Nichrome** (nī′·krōm′), a metal used for heating elements. [199]

**nitrate** (nī′·trāt′), a compound with nitrogen in a form that plants can use. [107]

**nitrogen fixation,** the process of putting nitrogen from the air into compounds that plants can use. [107]

**nutrient,** one of the soil chemicals that plants need to grow. [123]

**oasis** (ō·ā′·sis), a place in a desert with enough water for plants. [87]

**omnivorous** (om·niv′·ər·əs), a kind of creature that eats plants and animals. [130]

**opposition,** the position of a superior planet when it is in the direction opposite from the sun. [59]

**orbit,** the circular path of a planet or satellite. [46]

**ozone** (ō′·zōn′), a gas in the atmosphere that filters out ultraviolet light. [95]

**parasite,** a living thing that lives in or on another living thing. [136]

**percolation** (pûr′·kə·lā′·shən), the downward movement of water through the soil. [123]

**permanent magnet,** a magnet that keeps its magnetism all the time. [183]

**pH,** a measure of how acid or base a soil is. [123]

**phase,** one of the different shapes in the monthly cycle of the moon. [25]

**photosynthesis** (fō′·tō·sin′·thi·sis), the process of making food by putting water and carbon dioxide together with the power of light. [117]

**piston,** a round part that slides up and down inside a cylinder of a gasoline engine. [163]

**planet,** one of the heavenly bodies that orbit the sun. [46]

**plasma** (plaz′·mə), the yellowish water solution of the blood. [237]

**polar,** the kind of climate so cold that plants cannot grow. [79]

**population,** the number of living things of one kind. [136]

**potential energy,** stored energy. [149]

**predator,** an animal that kills other animals for its food. [130]

**prey,** an animal that a predator seeks for its food. [130]

**propulsion,** the push that makes a vehicle move. [170]

**protein,** a compound containing nitrogen and other important elements that are used by the body for growth and repair. [107]

**pulse,** the change of blood pressure that shows the heartbeat. [237]

**radiation,** the transfer of light and heat energy directly through space. [18]

**ray,** one of the lines extending out from a crater. [25]

**receiver,** in a telephone, the device that changes electricity into sounds. [206]

**red corpuscle** (kôr′·pə·səl), a red blood cell, which carries oxygen to the body cells and carries waste carbon dioxide away. [237]

**relay,** a switch operated by an electromagnet. [199]

**renewable,** able to be used over and over. [107]

**respiratory system** (res′·pər·ə·tôr′·ē), the body system that includes the lungs, diaphragm, and various air passages, by which oxygen is absorbed and carbon dioxide is released. [224]

**response,** an action performed because of a stimulus. [217]

**retrograde** (ret′·rə·grād′), in a backward direction. [66]

**rudder,** a blade for steering a ship or an airplane. [170]

**saliva** (sə·lī′·və), the watery fluid in the mouth that starts the digestion of food. [231]

**satellite,** a heavenly body in orbit around a planet. [25]

**scavenger** (skav′·ən·jər), an animal that seeks dead animals for food. [130]

**sea,** one of the smooth, dark areas on the surface of the moon. [25]

**semiarid** (sem′·ē·ar′·id), the kind of climate with 10 to 20 inches of rain each year. [79]

**sense,** the ability to receive some kind of stimulus. [217]

**sense organ,** a body part, such as an eye or an ear, that receives stimuli and sends messages about them to the brain. [217]

**small intestine,** the tube where enzymes are added to food and where dissolved food is absorbed through villi. [231]

**soil,** a mixture of finely ground rocks and humus, in which the roots of plants can grow. [123]

**solar** (sō′·lər), of the sun. [13]

**solar cell,** a device that uses sunlight to produce electricity. [156]

**solar eclipse,** any darkening of the sun by the moon. A solar eclipse is *partial* if only part of the sun is covered. It is *annular* if all of the sun is covered except a thin ring around the edge. It is *total* if the sun is completely covered. [31]

**solar energy,** the energy from the sun. [156]

**solar flare,** a bright spot on the sun caused by a storm. [18]

**solar system,** the sun and all the heavenly bodies in orbit around it. [13]

**solar wind,** a stream of fast-moving particles from the sun. [18]

**solvent,** a liquid that dissolves other materials. [87]

**spark plug,** a device that makes a spark to cause combustion in a gasoline engine. [163]

**stern,** the back end of a ship. [170]

**stimulus** (stim′·yə·ləs), *plural* **stimuli** (stim′·yə·lī′), anything that can cause one to make a response. [217]

**stratosphere** (strat′·ə·sfir′), the layer of the atmosphere that filters out ultraviolet rays. [95]

**subarctic,** the kind of climate that is dry and cold, but not as cold as the polar climate. [79]

**sunspot,** a dark, round spot on the sun caused by a storm. [18]

**superior planet,** one of the six planets that orbit the sun outside the earth's orbit. [52]

**symbiosis** (sim′·bē·ō′·sis), the living together of two different things for certain benefits. [136]

**telegraph,** a device that writes a message from a distance. [206]

**telephone,** a device that carries sound for a distance by using electricity. [206]

**temperate,** the kind of climate that is neither very hot nor very cold and usually has four seasons. [79]

**terminal,** a place for making an electrical connection. [190]

**throttle,** a device that controls the speed of a gasoline engine. [163]

**tide,** the rise or fall of the ocean surface because of the gravity of the moon. [25]

**trachea** (trā′·kē·ə), the stiff-walled air passage in the throat. [224]

**transformer,** a device that increases or decreases the voltage of electricity. [183]

**transit,** the passing of a planet across the face of the sun. [52]

**transmission,** in a car, a device that has a low gear, a high gear, and reverse. [170]

**transmitter,** in a telephone, the device that changes sounds into electrical signals. [206]

**tropical,** the kind of climate that is hot and wet. [79]

**tropic of Cancer,** the northernmost latitude of sunlight from straight overhead. [79]

**tropic of Capricorn,** the southernmost latitude of sunlight from straight overhead. [79]

**troposphere** (trō′·pə·sfir′), the lowest layer of the atmosphere, where weather occurs. [95]

**tungsten** (tung′·stən), a metal with a high melting point, used for light bulb filaments. [199]

**ultraviolet,** the kind of invisible, cancer-causing rays from the sun. [95]

**variable star,** a star that changes in brightness. [13]

**vein,** a blood vessel that carries blood back to the heart. [237]

**ventricle** (ven′·tri·kəl), a pumping chamber of the heart. [237]

**villi** (vil′·ī), small fingerlike parts in the small intestine, which absorb food. [231]

**vocal cords,** two bands in the throat that vibrate to produce the sound of the voice. [224]

**volt,** a unit for measuring the pressure of electricity. [183]

**water table,** the underground level to which the soil is soaked with water. [107]

**water turbine,** a device for harnessing energy in moving water to drive a generator. [156]

**weather,** the condition of the atmosphere at a certain time. [79]

**wetland,** a place where the underground water level is near the surface. [87]

**white corpuscle** (kôr′·pə·səl), a white blood cell, which fights germs. [237]

**wind turbine,** a device for harnessing energy in moving air to drive a generator. [156]

# Index

# Illustration Credits

Aaron Martin: 22 (left), 124 (all top), 125, 127, 160 (bottom left), 166, 185 (right).
Adobe: 152 (fire).
Cartesia: 80, 81.*
Christy Collins: 137 (bottom).
Comstock.com: 18, 28 (bottom), 67 (top).
Comstock/Corel/Nova: 26.
Corbis: 235.
Corel Corporation: 9, 12 (right), 16 (top photo), 88 (both left), 93, 101, 102, 103, 109 (top), 120 (bottom right), 121,* 131, 132, 137 (top), 139, 140, 141 (left), 152 (falls, trap, container), 153 (right), 157, 158, 164, 174 (both left), 175 (top), 221 (bottom).
Corel/Hemera/Samuel Hoover: 172 (top right), 173.
Corel/Samuel Hoover: 27 (top), 31, 37, 56, 66, 92 (top drawings), 96 (drawings).
Digital Vision: front cover, 98 (right), 148, 152 (tree), 182.
Dynamic Graphics, Inc.: 32 (top left), 92 (photo), 117 (right), 141 (right), 154.
Flat Earth Collection: 153 (left).
Joel L. Reinford: 27 (bottom).
John Mark Shenk: 163, 165, 171.
Lee C. Coombs: 71 (bottom right).
Lester Miller: 109 (bottom), 134 (birds), 217 (right).
Lester Showalter: 15, 21, 22 (right).
Lester Showalter/Samuel Hoover: 184.
LifeART, © 2005 Lippincott Williams & Wilkins: 218,* 217 (left),* 225 (person),* 234 (not inset).*
Lisa Weaver: 107, 111, 219, 220, 221 (top), 234 (inset).
Map Resources: 85, 105.
Marian Baltozer: 230.
Mary Jane Miller: 92 (bottom), 98 (left), 120 (bottom left), 133, 225 (insets), 228 (not inset), 232, 240 (right).
Merlin Heatwole: 227.
NASA: 71 (bottom left).
NASA; courtesy of Space Images: 28 (top right).
NASA/Turbo Photo: 16 (bottom), 28 (top right).
Nova Development Corporation: 12 (left), 29, 54, 55 (left), 67 (bottom), 70 (bottom), 176,* 209 (microphone and speakers),* 228 (inset), 239, 240 (left), 241.
Nova/Samuel Hoover: 53 (top), 208 (bottom), 210.
Peter Balholm: 149, 167 (top), 174 (bottom right), 175 (bottom), 191, 238.
PhotoDisc by Getty Images: 19 (bottom), 23, 28 (left), 32 (middle left and top right), 50, 55 (right), 59, 63 (left), 70 (top), 71 (top), 78, 96 (earth photo), 156, 160 (top), 192 (left).
Samuel Hoover: 13, 14, 20, 33, 47, 49, 51, 52, 53 (bottom), 61, 62, 69, 83, 88 (right), 89, 100, 106, 108, 110, 112, 120 (top), 126, 128, 152 (battery), 160 (bottom right), 172 (top left and bottom), 174 (top right), 183, 185 (top), 186, 187, 188, 189, 192 (right), 193, 194, 195, 196, 197, 198, 200, 201, 202, 203, 204, 208 (top), 209 (receiver and amplifier), 216.
Samuel Hoover; courtesy of East Kentucky Science Center: 63 (right)
Samuel Hoover/Dale Yoder: 84.
Smithsonian Institution, Neg. #14,593B: 207.
Steven Mast: 32 (bottom).
Stockbyte: 116, 124 (bottom).
Swedish Solar Telescope, Royal Swedish Academy of Sciences; courtesy of Space Images: 19 (top).

*The royalty-free drawing is modified from its original to better serve this science course.